CHRISTIAN ORI...

Christian Origins: Theology, Rhetoric and Community is an exploration of the historical course and nature of early Christian theology, which concentrates on setting it within particular traditions or sets of traditions.

In the three sections of this volume, Reading Origen, Reading the Fourth Century, and Christian Origins and the Western Tradition, the contributors reconsider classic themes and texts in the light of the existing traditions of interpretation. They offer critiques of early Christian ideas and texts and reconsider the structure and origins of standard modern readings. The contributors employ a variety of methodological approaches to analyse the interplay between ancient philosophical traditions and the development of Christian thought and to redefine the parameters between the previously accepted divisions in the traditions of Christian theology and thought.

Christian Origins: Theology, Rhetoric and Community provides a ground-breaking study of many of the key areas of current research in early Christian theology and highlights new areas of investigation.

Lewis Ayres is Lecturer in Christian Doctrine at Trinity College, Dublin. He is the editor of *The Trinity: Classical and Contemporary Readings* (Oxford 1998), *The Passionate Intellect: Essays on the Transformation of Classical Traditions* (New Brunswick, NJ 1995) and author of the forthcoming *Augustine's Trinitarian Theology*.

Gareth Jones is Lecturer in Systematic Theology at the University of Birmingham. He has been critically acclaimed as one of the front rank of contemporary theologians in the UK and has written widely on systematic and modern theology. He is the author of *Critical Theology: Questions of Truth and Mind* (Polity Press 1995).

CHRISTIAN ORIGINS

Theology, Rhetoric and Community

*Edited by Lewis Ayres and
Gareth Jones*

London and New York

First published 1998
by Routledge
11 New Fetter Lane, London EC4P 4EE

Simultaneously published in the USA and Canada
by Routledge
29 West 35th Street, New York, NY 10001

Typeset in Garamond by Routledge

Printed and bound in Great Britain by Creative Print and Design
(Wales), Ebbw Vale

British Library Cataloguing in Publication Data
A catalogue record for this book is available from the British Library

Library of Congress Cataloguing in Publication Data
Christian origins : theology, rhetoric, and community / edited by
Lewis Ayres and Gareth Jones.
Includes bibliographical references and index.
1. Philosophy and religion–History of doctrines–Early church,
ca.30–600. 2. Theology–History–Early church, ca. 30–600. 3.
Religious thought–To 600. 4. Christianity–Philosophy. 5. Church
history–Primitive and early church, ca. 30–600.
I. Ayres, Lewis. II. Jones, Gareth (S. Gareth J.)
BR100.C526   1998
                                230'.09'015–dc   97–26997
                                                              CIP

ISBN 0–415–10750–4 (hbk)
ISBN 0–415–10751–2 (pbk)

CONTENTS

CONTENTS

CONTRIBUTORS

Lewis Ayres is Lecturer in Christian Doctrine at Trinity College, Dublin.

Michel René Barnes is Assistant Professor of Patristics at Marquette University, Wisconsin.

David Dawson is Associate Professor of Religion and Comparative Literature, and MacCrate Professor in Social Responsibility, Haverford College, Pennsylvania.

Mark Edwards is University Lecturer in Patristics, Oxford University.

Susanna Elm is Associate Professor of History, University of California at Berkeley.

Wayne Hankey is Carnegie Professor of Classics, Dalhousie University and King's College, Halifax, Nova Scotia.

John Milbank is a Fellow of Peterhouse, Cambridge, and Reader in Divinity, University of Cambridge.

Catherine Pickstock is a Research Fellow at Emmanuel College, Cambridge.

Daniel H. Williams is Assistant Professor of Patristics at Loyola University, Chicago.

ABBREVIATIONS

1

INTRODUCTION

A project in the study of Christian origins

Lewis Ayres

I

This volume is intended as the first of a series. Each volume will be focused around a particular theme and will usually consist of specially commissioned chapters. Before I introduce this first collection itself, the parameters and purpose of the wider project need some explanation. Two initial statements about those parameters should be made. First, the series as a whole will be concerned to encourage research in the field of Christian origins which has theological concerns in view. Second, the time period included within the series will often be broader than might at first be imagined. While most volumes and contributions to volumes will focus around that period normally taken to be constitutive of 'patristics' (ca. 100–ca. 600), in some cases contributions or whole collections will cover material as far as the changes in Christian thought which occurred during the eleventh to the early fourteenth centuries. The remainder of this section of the introduction offers a more detailed account of and justification for these two statements. The second section of the introduction concerns the contents of this particular volume.

By 'having theological concerns in view' I mean contributing towards the better understanding of the historical course and nature of Christian thought and theology as a particular tradition or set of traditions stretching from the first century to the present day. Two things are noteworthy about this definition: firstly, the phrase 'thought and theology', which describes the focus of the project as a whole. Secondly, this phrase attempts to distinguish schools of scholarship by reference to their 'concerns' or overall 'ends', rather than by prescribing a particular set of methods or techniques as normative. Positively this attempt is intended to indicate that a wide variety of methods and approaches may find a place within the overall scope of this project, as long as they contribute to its goals. Of course, many aspects of scholarship on the antique world may contribute in *ad hoc* ways to the study of Christian thought although not being themselves directly concerned with that thought. For this reason the series will include material from a wide variety of 'schools' of early Christian study, but only when particular pieces are directly relevant to other pieces in the same volume or to the overall theme of a collection.

My concern that the series has a clear overall sense of purpose, while still being able to encompass a variety of methodological approaches, stems from awareness of the plurality of approaches in modern early Christian studies. This plurality consists not simply in the existence of many different methods, but, most importantly, in both the existence of a number of sometimes incommensurable governing assumptions, and in a plurality of ends for which study is undertaken. Unfortunately, there has been little serious consideration of how this pluralism affects the nature of the various sub-fields that constitute early Christian studies, how those sub-fields interact, and how they may understand their own aims and purposes against this wider background.

This plurality of approaches and plurality of competing assumptions about the period has a number of consequences for all the sub-fields incorporated in the area, of which two require mention here. First, the very diversity of the field will exert pressures on particular individuals within it, pushing exponents of less popular styles of investigation into isolation or – a scenario repeated in many other disciplines in the humanities in the past century – simply to adopt the methods and assumptions of the larger groups. In the light of this possibility, clarity about the existence, purpose and self-perception of the different styles of current early Christian studies is essential. Most obviously, accusations that a certain school or method will be 'inevitably distorting' whereas another will not, is philosophically very difficult to sustain in such a simple form. Different approaches need to give much more sophisticated accounts of their integrity and of their hermeneutic principles, and one might hope that the attempt to do so would make the diversity and connections or common concerns between different schools of interpretation more clearly apparent.

Thus I suggest that the diversity of current approaches to early Christian studies demands primarily some clarity about ends, and then an attempt to work towards clarity about the consonance of particular methods with particular governing assumptions. The very bare outline of the overall project that I offer here is intended as a contribution towards thinking through the structure and purpose of one possible style of research in Christian origins within the current range of options.

The title 'Christian Origins' may itself be read as reflecting one other aspect of the project. Volumes in the series will often include pieces considering or reconsidering the significance of aspects of early Christian thought for later Christian thought, and will also attempt to look at ways in which early Christianity has been and is now seen as giving rise to later Christian thought. In some cases this will involve looking at and reconsidering lines of influence between early and medieval Christian thought: in others it will involve modern theologians writing on the significance and use of early Christian authors, and on the influence of those authors on modern thought.

The project will also contribute to the increasing adoption by theologians and scholars of early Christianity of newer approaches to the relationship between theology and philosophy and to theology's historical context. These two themes are closely related. This century's debates about the relationship of theology and philosophy in early Christianity have often been rather sterile. In many cases this is because inherited debates about the 'helleniza-tion' of Christianity have predisposed many 'liberal' (as well as 'orthodox') theologians to see either a necessary opposition between 'Gospel' and 'hellenism', or a necessary admittance of Christianity's *transformation* by 'Greek' thought. Of course, many other themes have also contributed towards the often sterile nature of these debates; this is simply the most well known. Over the last fifteen or twenty years some scholars have begun to take very different views of the development of Christian thought. Many have been more willing to consider interactions between antique philosoph-ical traditions and Christian thinkers without immediate transposition of any such interaction into the terms of the Gospel/hellenism debate. There is also a greater openness to seeing the interaction between Christian and non-Christian as a complex multi-layered set of interactions between discourses which all have 'philosophical', 'spiritual' and 'ritual' aspects. Yet others have begun to see how so much previous debate has been shaped by late nineteenth- and early twentieth-century thought about the integrity of 'revelation' – 'revelation' being largely considered as a form of knowledge – and by purely historical-critical criteria for the 'adequate' interpretation of scripture.

Critique of these themes themselves has begun to enable both a new subtlety in appreciation of the structures of early Christian thought and a new subtlety in understanding ways in which the 'scriptural' and the 'conceptual' in early Christianity interact. One key consequence of these approaches is the increasing realization that many of the professional distinc-tions between scholars of 'New Testament', 'patristics', 'Church history' and 'systematics' (to name only those which are of most immediate concern here) are increasingly problematic. These divisions best serve those who continue to uphold the attitudes to different 'periods' of the Christian tradition that played such a large part in the formation of theological *curricula* in the nine-teenth century. For a variety of reasons, philosophical and theological, these may now be seen as a hindrance rather than a help in the study of the Christian tradition. This project hopes to encourage and develop approaches which follow these broad lines of thought.

Having explored the meaning and context of 'having theological concerns in view', I want now to turn to the period covered by the project. As stated above, the period that will sometimes be encompassed within the 'Christian

Origins' series is broader than that normally considered as comprising simply the early Christian or patristic period. The project will centre around the standard accepted period for patristic study (ca. 100–ca. 600), but will also cover aspects of the period up to and around the series of shifts in the Western Church known as the 'Gregorian reform' and in some cases on as far as the death of Aquinas, and, in the East, aspects of the period up to the Palamite controversy and the strong late medieval influence of Latin styles of theology on Byzantine thought. There are a number of reasons for extending the period to be covered so widely.

First, the ending of patristic study around 600 is, from a number of viewpoints, rather arbitrary. A variety of theological arguments may of course be made for the significance of the period of the 'first seven Councils' (or, in some cases, the first four only), or for the significance and authority of a vaguely defined 'early' period. However theologically significant or useful these arguments may be, once they are used to describe boundaries between subject areas, they often have the result of placing the period immediately following in a shadow which hides continuities and the slowness of the transformations in theological style and content which do occur. It is also fairly easy to give examples of how some of the choices with which many modern scholars continue to operate serve very particular concerns to which we may now no longer wish to subscribe. For example, many nineteenth-century Western accounts of Christian thought offer points at which one might distinguish 'patristic' from 'medieval'; but these are highly arbitrary and often motivated primarily by attempts to argue for Aquinas or early Scholasticism as the high point of a period which surpasses the patristic (and often begins with Augustine, who may then receive the accolade 'early medieval'). For Orthodox authors without this concern, such a division has never made any sense – although some *have* accepted nineteenth-century Western views of the nature of a Greek/Latin division. Of course, some significant changes occurred in both East and West during the fifth, sixth and seventh centuries, but it is hard to make out an easy case asserting that they are more significant for the history of Christian thought than those which occurred during the fourth-century controversies, or between the third and fourth centuries. There are very few substantial reasons (other than reinforcing some of the ideological perspectives of particular 'professional' distinctions) for treating Christian origins as either purely an extension of New Testament study or as a period cut off from what came before or after.

These negative arguments may be reinforced by a number of positive arguments for extending the period covered by 'Christian Origins'. In many cases trajectories of thought which begin to be articulated in the post-Chalcedonian period follow directly through into later centuries; and similarly many themes of theological debate continue in similar terms and styles of literature long past the period where patristic study is normally taken to end. An example may easily be provided. The pseudo-Dionysian corpus is 'patristic', and represents a key stage in early Christian engagement with late antique non-Christian thought (at whatever immediate remove). Once one accepts this premise then the central influence of that corpus on the Christian thought of the centuries which followed (when it had re-emerged in the West) provides one vital example of how it may seem more important to examine the continuities and developments across these periods rather than to accept an arbitrary delineation of where 'patristic' ends and 'medieval' begins. I am not trying to argue here that the only reason for studying some 'medieval' texts alongside 'patristic' texts is that the medieval texts are a continuation of previous lines of thought. This one example is only intended to indicate that the acceptance of an easy and appropriate break between these periods may be easily argued against and that positive arguments for a more fluid approach may easily be made.

The two *termini ad quem* that I do offer for the project are intended to be flexible. One key aspect of the rationale for their choice is this: a number of factors in the West between the period of the 'Gregorian reform' and the death of Aquinas (here a fairly symbolic figure) do seem to lead to a shift in the structure and style of theology that allows us to speak with increasing accuracy about the growth of theologies that are becoming 'modern', and that in many ways are distinct from the theologies previous to that period. One might identify three such factors: the fourteenth-century shifts in accounts of the relationship between the theological analysis of creation independent of reference to the presence of the triune God, often broadly focused around the work of Scotus; the changes in Church structure which came as the 'Gregorian reform' had an impact on the Church at large; and the shifts in modes and styles of theological learning and writing with the rise and changes in cathedral 'school' and 'university' structure. Taken together these three aspects of the period indicate that here we begin to see the move towards the theological developments of the later medieval period and the Reformation. Of course there were many continuities across this period too, but nevertheless the period of these shifts seems the appropriate ending point for contributions to this project.

The last paragraph does not offer a full justification for the choice of the broad *termini* of this project, but rather indicates one key set of reasons. The usefulness of these *termini*, and the grounds on which one can argue their case more strongly, will, I hope, become apparent through the life of the series. However, even here, it should be said that the positive reasons outlined above are ones drawn entirely from the Latin world (my initial negative reasons apply to all). Similar arguments need also to be aired in the field of Greek Christianity and Byzantine studies. As mentioned above, the broad *terminus* for contributions from the Byzantine world is the Palamite controversies. At more length I would make the arguments first that those controversies begin to effect a shift in Byzantine thought, and second that around that period it is possible to see an increasing influence of later medieval Latin theological styles on Byzantine thought. As in the case of the Latin world these *termini* are intentionally broad; it is proposed that their usefulness be tested in future work.

As stated above, books in the project will always take as their point of departure themes beginning in the 'patristic' period, as it is usually understood. It will simply be that, in some cases, those themes are best or most helpfully considered over a wider time period. It is hoped that a number of gaps in current scholarship may be filled through the assumption of these *termini*, and that the project will contribute towards the reconsideration of the periodization that has been taken for granted for much of the twentieth century.

II

Each of the volumes in the series will be focused around a particular theme and the vast majority of the chapters for each volume will be individually commissioned. We will, of course, welcome submissions and suggestions for volumes, but in general our aim is not to produce simply another journal-like product or another *jahrbuch*, but a series of focused collections with a clear overall purpose and agenda. This first volume is divided into three sections, each of which shows ways in which whole future volumes may be organized. Each of these sections also includes chapters which are not simply illustrative of possibilities for the wider project but make important contributions to their respective fields.

The first section offers a series of chapters re-reading one theme or set of themes in one key early Christian author; in this case David Dawson and Mark Edwards write on Origen. Both of these chapters concern areas of discussion related to allegory and the common accusation that Origen's approach represents an archetypal pollution of Christianity by 'Platonism'.

The second section of the volume offers a series of chapters looking at the fourth century from the sorts of perspective that we hope to include within the project. Michel Barnes and Daniel Williams both look at the fourth century as a whole. Barnes offers a new synthetic account of the fourth century as trinitarian 'canon' in the light of recent reconsideration of that century's controversies. Williams reconsiders the traditional claim by many 'Free Church' theologians that post-Constantinian Christianity broke traditional links between local communities and their creeds. The questioning of this aspect of Free Church accounts of the fourth century raises wider questions. John Milbank's chapter offers an example of a systematic theologian engaging critically with a key patristic figure, Gregory of Nyssa. Milbank concentrates on the importance of *apatheia* for Gregory and argues that the theme has been largely misunderstood in recent theology. Susanna Elm's chapter considers the conflict between Theophilus of Alexandria and John

Chrysostom, exploring the lack of reference to doctrinal issues in the standard accounts of the controversy, both modern and patristic. Elm's chapter offers an excellent example of the importance of reconsidering the traditional ways in which key controversies or figures have come to be represented.

The third set of chapters concentrates on exploring themes in connection with their significance for the later history of Christian thought. Wayne Hankey's chapter reconsiders many recent interpretations of Aquinas's work, but does so through the exploration of what the influence of pseudo-Dionysius on Aquinas means for such reconsideration. This chapter provides an excellent example of the continuities between the period normally considered as 'patristic' and the wider period encompassed by this project. Catherine Pickstock's chapter looks at Augustine's *De musica*, placing the account given there within the wider context of the Western tradition's accounts of music. This consideration is used as the key to understanding aspects of the Augustinian account of creation, participation and transcendence.

Many people have been involved in planning this first volume and the idea as a whole. Most importantly Richard Stoneman, Senior Editor at Routledge, has shown remarkable patience and persistence over the course of the last few years. I am extremely grateful for his encouragement of the project. All of the contributors, especially those who submitted their chapters some time ago, are also to be thanked for their great patience and trust. The Arts and Social Sciences Benefactions Fund of Trinity College Dublin provided me with a most generous grant for research, some of which connected directly with this project, and I very gratefully acknowledge their help. Michel Barnes and Steve Fowl have both been of great help in formulating the introduction.

Dr Gareth Jones of the University of Birmingham has co-edited this volume; from the next volume Professor Michel Barnes, Assistant Professor of Patristics in the Department of Theology at Marquette University, will be co-editor for the series.

Part I

READING ORIGEN

2

CHRIST OR PLATO?

Origen on revelation and anthropology

Mark Edwards

The term Platonist is occasionally conferred on Christian Fathers as a compliment by those who still believe that pagan learning has the first claim on the attention of the West. In modern theologians, however, it is usually pejorative, and most of all when (as in the case of Origen) it forms the hybrid 'Christian Platonist'. While the Lutheran urges that any commerce with philosophy repeals the writ of grace for a gospel based on human striving, his liberal opponent now maintains that it was Plato, not his Maker, who pronounced the joys of heaven incompatible with the business of the earth.[1] On both sides the cry goes up for a biblical theology which owes nothing to the secular tradition of the churches, or (in spite of the whole New Testament) to the Greeks.

I shall argue here that Origen's theology is as biblical as any, but this is not to imply that a defence of him requires us to belittle his indebtedness to Plato. Origen builds his creed upon the Trinity, the incarnation and the resurrection, the second and third of which were as absurd to the ancient pagan as to the modern liberal. It was in his exposition of the first that he made his lasting contribution to ecclesiastical doctrine by affirming the eternal generation of the Son and the Holy Spirit. He thus presented himself and the Christian faith with an enigma: if it is in the eternal *nature* of God to be a Trinity and not merely (as others taught) in his *economy*, how can this eternal nature manifest itself in the experience of his temporal creation? Origen gives a Christian solution to this problem, but his knowledge of Platonism made him the earliest theologian to perceive that an understanding of the Godhead is the basis of exegesis, since both imply a theory of the relation between eternity and time.

I

Plato holds that the present world can offer us no true and stable objects of cognition, since nothing that we see or touch is perfect and unchanging in its kind. The kind is known as an intellectual concept or idea, and the

11

particular phenomena are recognized by comparison with this. But for the idea, the phenomenon could not be so much as spoken of, but some degree of difference from the idea is entailed by its very presence in the world. Invulnerable to doubt and time, exempt from all the vagaries of opinion, the idea is self-identical, and, being truly what it is, is truly said to 'be'. Our senses, on the other hand, introduce us to a realm of generation or 'becoming', which is related to the true one as the shadow or *eidolon* to the body; nevertheless, it is only the phenomena that guide us to the ideas, by their very combination of determinable qualities with unqualified and contingent imperfections, and the phenomenon may therefore be commended as a similitude or icon of the real.

While the sensible object is not fully self-identical, it must have some share in being; its logical dependence on the idea means that the latter must be present in some measure if the sensible particular is to be anything at all. Since the imperfections in the particular are a threat to its identity, it aspires to the condition of the idea.[2] Such at least is the understanding of the later Platonists, confirmed by the teleology of Aristotle and Plato's own account of love or eros, which, being desire for union with the object, confers upon the lover the possession of that object, since he has a claim by nature on the fullness that supplies his own defect.[3] Love, participation and similitude – *ephesis*, *methexis* and *homoiotes* – are the three Platonic notions of the relation between particulars and ideas. All three are expressed together in the axiom that the lover strives to be one with the beloved, for this union is the most complete similitude, the fullest participation and the final goal of love.

Desire is for the beautiful, and the Beautiful is, if not the whole, an aspect of the Good.[4] This is the end of action, as desire is its beginning; moreover, it is the source of the ideas, since it is only by partaking of the Good that they acquire their own perfection. Since nothing can subsist except in so far as it aspires to this perfection, the Good is the ultimate origin and measure of all existents; it is thus the immediate parent of the ideas, which are thus the purest objects of cognition and are said to depend upon it, both to be and to be cognoscible, as earthly things depend upon the sun.[5]

Since the ideas can neither come to be nor pass away, they exist by logical necessity and there cannot be any evil either in them or in their unconstrained effects. As the phenomenal world derives from these alone, it too is good, in so far as it participates in being. But how can the immutable and perfect take any part in generation, and why should the result of this be a blemished world of change and contradiction? The *Timaeus* gives an answer which appears to be little more than a poetic repetition of the question: a demiurge, resolving to communicate the beauty of the intellectual paradigm to everything, imposed it upon the nature which is most devoid of stable and determinable properties, creating the best of possible universes as an everlasting image of the Good.[6] The paradigm is the ideal world, but the demiurge is unique to the *Timaeus*, and his identity was a subject of unquenchable debate among the Platonists.[7] The first objection seems to have been addressed to the very status of the narrative: if the ideas are immutable, there is nothing either transient or arbitrary in their operations, and if these traits belong only to the demiurge, he is not so good as they. Either, then, the demiurge himself is deficient in goodness, or he creates the world eternally; Plato has no right to speak of the world as generated (or *genetos*), if this implies that it came to be in time.

One solution, found by his earliest pupils,[8] was to say that temporal order is germane to the narrative form, but not to the truths that it expresses; even in the dialogue, Timaeus styles his speech an *eikos logos* (30b), thus forewarning us that it is (at best) an image of the real. Time itself is iconic in the *Timaeus*, being defined as the 'eternal moving image of eternity':[9] this means, we must presume, that it is 'eternal' in so far as it has neither end nor origin, but 'moving' in accordance with the laws of a contradictory and penumbral mode of being. As a measure of motion, time reveals that even motion itself is regulated by a constant, and therefore has some share in the repose of the ideas; yet this very regularity, this cycle of becoming which depends on the complementarity of destruction and generation, negates the everlasting simultaneity of the ideal realm, and is thus itself a measure of the distortion and dispersion of these ideas in the mirror of the world.

Time is the precondition of the universe, but soul is its immediate creator in the *Timaeus*. Fashioned by the demiurge from two 'periods' or cycles, the Same and the Other (38c10 etc.), it shares the paradoxical complexity of all generated being and the cyclical or periodic character of time. Yet in the *Phaedrus*, Socrates maintains that soul is naturally immortal and ingenerate (245c), and acceptance of this teaching is for Platonists the chief argument against a temporal origin of the universe.[10] This is not to say that the reality of time has been abolished with the concept of creation; for in the great myth of the *Phaedrus* temporality supervenes upon eternity for every soul that fails to sustain its quest for an unmediated vision of the Good. For causes as obscure as they are regular, souls fall at stated periods to earth,[11] where, if they do not learn philosophy, they are prisoners for 10,000 years (248e–249a).

According to the *Phaedrus*, the soul forgets its past, but not completely, and is stirred to recollection by the beauty of mortal bodies, from which it can ascend to a new discernment of the glory that it sought above the world (249d–256e). In the dialogue, Phaedrus learns to put away apparent for real beauty, as the progress of the argument recapitulates its myth. Socrates woos his pupil with an erotic tale – by classical convention, a means of stimulating reciprocal desire.[12] Torn between his two 'companions', the speaking Socrates and the absent Lysias who is present in his book, Phaedrus is induced to choose the less prepossessing orator, whose mobile disquisition will reveal to him the source and proper object of his passion. The second-century Platonist Albinus finds this pedagogic structure in the whole corpus when he recommends that the dialogues be studied in the order that conduces to the maturing of philosophy.[13] A later author seems to take the *Timaeus* as his paradigm when he claims that every dialogue is an icon of the world.[14]

The progress of the reader is the deliverance of his soul and the self-disclosure of the real, as Plato intimates in a well-remembered simile.[15] We are to think of men in a cave who are bound so fast that they see nothing but the shadows which appear on the wall before them. The source of these is a fire, before which images are carried, some by speaking, some by silent porters (*Republic* 514a–b). The freeing of the captive's head enables him to turn back from the shadows to their originals, but then he is released to the upper world, where he is overwhelmed by light, until the gradual education of his senses allows him first to look at shadows, then at objects and at last upon the sun (516a–b). Neither in this passage nor in its sequel, the divided line,[16] are we shown a continuous passage from the lowest to the highest grades of vision. The porters in the cave are best interpreted as the poets and rhetoricians who delude the state with counterfeits of justice, truth and beauty. In the cave we see the emancipation of the public from its teachers, in the upper world the restoration of primordial understanding to the soul. The cave (or its description) is styled an icon by one speaker (515a), and the relation holds, not only between the metaphor and its subject, but between the first conversion and the second. The parable of turning from the shadow to an object is the shadow of a parable of turning from the shadow to the sun. The fire which in the first has no plain analogue is intelligible as the image of that sun, which yields the hermeneutic key to both conceptions: the antidote to falsehood, both in politics and in personal salvation, is the vision of the Good.

The progress from the cave is thus the ascent from less to more complete analogy, and the process brings the reader to a deeper understanding of the truth, hence a more intimate communion with the Good. Proclus shows his thorough comprehension of the master when he associates the literary method of analogy with the soul's desire for union with its first principle; philosophy recognizes in this the plainer, though the less adequate, of two routes to the One:

> For because of its likeness to it, there exists in every order of beings a monad analogous to the Good . . . and the cause of this likeness in every case is the reversion (*epistrophe*) of everything to [the One]. . . . The procession of all things reveals to us the ascent back to the First by way of negations, the reversion that by way of analogies.
>
> *Theol. Plat.* II.5

According to Plato's Seventh Letter, the dialogue itself is an example of negation, a refusal by the author to determine any question in his own

14

person.[17] In the irony of Socrates, it may perhaps put forward another model of negation; Parmenides, however, takes the lower route by returning on his argument in accordance with the principle of reversion to the One: 'But again he turns back from this point to the origin (*arkhe*), and imitating the reversion of all things, he separates the One from the highest gods, I mean the intelligibles' (*Theol. Plat.* II.12).

The discernment of analogy is thus a form of spiritual discipline; as the reader penetrates the formal trope, he experiences the same ascent from darkness to illuminated clarity in his own nature, and the allegory of spiritual progress will induce the analogous progress in himself. The tuition of the soul resembles, not so much the imposition of forms on empty matter, as the leading of the captive from his dungeon to a world for which his senses have already been prepared:[18]

> For he does not liken the soul to an unlettered tablet, so as to inscribe things on it when it does not possess them, but as if leading it to the light and simply prompting its recollection, he purifies it in the manner of those who wipe away sores that have become attached to the eyes.[19]

Atemporal truths are thus conveyed in dialogues that unfold in time and often take a narrative as the leading metaphor. We have seen that time in Plato is the medium of creation and of narrative; his followers have a name for the receptacle that holds the temporal image of the paradigm. Matter is the mirror into which the soul projects eternal beauty – though the mirror is little more than the vanishing-point of this projection, and the formula 'moving image of eternity' could as well be applied to matter as to the soul.[20] For the Neoplatonists, as for Plato, time is that participant in eternity which divorces the mundane from the eternal, and Plotinus can distinguish between the time which is the life of the soul in the theatre of the senses and the timeless base which constitutes its unity.[21] Truth – philosophic truth – pertains to eternity, which is the life of intellect, but narratives addressed to our deficient understanding must confer a temporal sequence on the postulates which the intellect embraces in an instant and as one:

> But myths, if they are to be such, must divide temporally what they say, and divide from one another many things which are simultaneous, but distinguished by order or powers. In this case words assign generations to the ingenerate, and themselves divide the things that are simultaneous, and teaching according to their ability leave it to the intelligence to synthesize.
>
> *Enn.* 3.5.9.24–30

Thus Plotinus, commenting on a myth from the *Symposium*, which in his view simultaneously depicts the source of being and of love.[22]

II

Logos is among the most frequent terms in Origen: he believes, like other Christians, in the Logos as the agent of divine creation and governance, but, unlike most before him,[23] he avers that its existence is not merely economic and instrumental to a temporal creation, but eternal and intrinsic to the Godhead. Scripture shows, he argues, that the expression of the Father through his hypostatic wisdom is essential to his nature, as light is to the sun:

> Let him who assigns a beginning to the Word of God or the wisdom of God beware lest he utters impiety against the unbegotten Father himself, in denying that he was always a Father, and that he begat the Word and possessed wisdom in all previous times or ages or whatever else they may be called.
>
> *Peri archon* I.2.3

The Spirit is coeval with the others, though it seems to be permissible to distinguish him from both by the word *genetos*, since he depends for his existence on the Father through the Son.[24] The Trinity is none the less economic, in so far as it subserves the Father's will to create a universe.[25] Since this disposition is eternal, it is not fulfilled in the temporal creation, but in the *logikoi*, the intelligible paradigms, and these, although eternal, are also creaturely, for they subsist by no necessity in themselves, but as the ideas of the Son: 'And certainly, if "all things have been made in wisdom", then, since wisdom has always existed, there have always existed in wisdom, by a pre-figuration and pre-formation, those things which afterwards have received substantial existence' (*Peri archon* I.4.3).

The Logos is thus the receptacle of the *logikoi*, begotten, though eternally, for the purpose of creation. Since the *logikoi* govern all the orders of existence, a philosopher would have argued that our knowledge of concrete being presupposes an ability to comprehend the intelligible archetype, and thus a strong affinity between our minds and God's. Origen is happy to declare that mind is the substance of the Godhead, and even pursues the analogy so far as to suggest that it is determined by the intelligible forms, and so incapable of mastering an infinite variety of objects. This tenet would be at home in Platonism, and in his trinitarian speculation the nomenclature of Origen is often reminiscent of the second-century Platonist Numenius, who posits as his first god the *autoagathon*, a mind at rest which generates the second mind, the *agathos*, as the repository of forms.[26] The Father is superior to the Son and the Holy Spirit in so far as it is they who meet the saint in the present life, and must prepare him for the reception of their own first principle: 'it is the work of wisdom to instruct and train them, and lead them on to perfection, by the strengthening and unceasing sanctification of the Holy Spirit, through which alone they can receive God' (*Peri archon* I.3.8).

Origen combines with this a view of trinitarian economy that echoes (or perhaps anticipates) a fertile axiom in the Platonism of the later Empire. The Father has dominion over all created beings, the Son over animated creatures only, and the Spirit over the rational elect (*Peri archon* I.3.5 = Fr. 9 Koetschau). Thus he who is most remote from understanding, who holds the highest rank in the scale of essence, is the member of the Trinity whose energies are present in the lowest; Proclus the Neoplatonist was to argue in the same way that the first principles can be found below the second, since the greatest power is the widest in extent.[27]

For all that, the first great Christian philosopher does not agree that man can be united in his essence with the Godhead, or can come to know it by his own desire. The essences of creatures are eternal and consubstantial with the Logos, but the subsistence of these creatures as single entities depends on matter (*Peri archon* I.6.4), and this is neither an effluence of the deity nor a coeternal substrate, but a creation out of nothing by his will.[28] Matter is not an icon, not so much as a distant shadow of divinity; it is the principle of differentiation which ensures that there is something other than God. Though Origen states in one place that the essence of man consists in his incorporeal rationality (*Peri archon* I.7.1), he does not allow the soul to live without a body of some kind either before or after its sojourn in the present universe. The adjective *homoousios* may be used to express the unity of the Godhead or the generic homogeneity of mankind; but to suggest that it can apply to the relation between the human and the divine is Valentinian heresy.[29]

Is there a revelation of the Trinity through a natural communion with the human intellect? For the Father at least, this appears to be precluded on the occasions when he is said to be, not a mind, but rather above all mind and being.[30] Origen contradicts himself to follow (or maybe once again to prophesy) the current of Platonic speculation. Spirit is constitutive of God, both in himself and in his relation to the creature, and the same term is interchangeable with *nous* as the name of the ruling and discerning power in humans; yet we are warned, no less in the remnants of his Greek than in the Latin of Rufinus, that the spirit of man is not the Spirit of God.[31]

An analogy can certainly be drawn between the structure of man and the trinitarian being of his Maker. God is mind, the Logos as his demiurgic instrument may be styled his soul (*Peri archon* II.8.5) and the Spirit is his matter when he makes himself present in us (*Comm. John* II.62); Paul and Plato have persuaded Origen that man too is a triple bond of body, soul and mind.[32] Soul and spirit are naturally convertible, as either can acquire the

17

moral properties of the other (*Peri archon* II.8.3), but body, while it can undergo a parallel transformation,[33] is divorced from both by its indefeasible corporeality. To borrow a distinction from a later Christological controversy, it is not a substantial but a moral union that is spoken of when body, soul and mind are said to become 'one spirit' with God:

> For the soul and the body of Jesus formed, after the *oikonomia*, one being with the Logos of God. Now if, according to Paul's teaching, 'he that is joined unto the Lord is one spirit', everyone who understands what being joined to the Lord is, and who has been actually joined to him, is one spirit, with the Lord; how should not that being be one in a far greater and more divine degree, which was once united with the Logos of God?
>
> *Contra Celsum* II.9[34]

Some scholars have been troubled unnecessarily by the word *oikonomia*.[35] There is no contradiction here of the assertion, at *Peri archon* II.6.4, that the soul of Christ was lovingly united with the Logos before it entered Mary's womb. Although the soul will already have possessed a material vehicle, like all others, it was only once, by a gracious inclination, that it joined itself to a tangible and visible carnality, which could not be everlasting or enjoy a natural union with God. Human nature does not become one with God, or even one within itself, except by mutual love and voluntary obedience; Christian thought enjoins on us the analogy of virtue, but cannot go so far with the philosophers as to equate participation and desire.

Another passage, also addressed to Celsus, states that our participation in the Saviour's work is effected by his teaching, which is always analogous to the incarnation:

> condescending occasionally to him who is unable to look upon the splendours and brilliancy of Deity, he becomes as it were flesh, speaking with a literal voice, until he who has received him in such a form is able, through being elevated in some slight degree by the teaching of the Word, to gaze upon what is, so to speak, his real and pre-eminent appearance.
>
> *Contra Celsum* IV. 15

Seeing is thus a metaphor for knowing, the incarnation a metaphor for inward transformation. But hearing alone is literal, while vision remains symbolic. Against the Platonic notion, endorsed by Celsus, that the knowledge of God is a timeless possibility which discloses itself in time to the instructed conscience, Origen sets the Christian belief in revelation periodically vouchsafed through human organs, and perfected by the teaching of the Lord:

> Who then are those wise men and philosophers . . . for whom we are to give up Moses the servant of God, the prophets of the Creator of the world, who have spoken so many things by a truly divine inspiration, and even Him who has given light and taught the way of piety to the whole human race?
>
> *Contra Celsum* VII.41

Analogy of itself will not suffice, if the material is not imparted by the Word of God:

> Celsus supposes that we may arrive at a knowledge of God either . . . after the methods which mathematicians call synthesis and analysis, or again by analogy, which is employed by them also . . . but . . . no-one can know God but with the help of a certain divine grace coming from above, with a certain divine inspiration.
>
> *Contra Celsum* VII.44

Christ's words were spread abroad by the Apostles, just as in ancient Israel he dispersed his inspiration through the prophets; though he has few dealings with the pagans, the eternal Logos chooses to address the human race throughout the course of history. Origen can even surmise the earthly career of Jesus was not the first to exhibit the conjunction of the Logos with a soul: 'That he is Adam, Paul affirms: "The second Adam was made a life-giving spirit" ' (*Comm. John.* I.18).

This sentence was persuasively interpreted by Origen's accusers in the sixth century as a statement that the soul of Adam was also that of Christ.[36] The biblical formula 'image of God' is reserved in Origen's writings for the Logos and for the soul united with it. Of time he speaks only casually, and of matter as an instrument, not an icon; but in his doctrine of Christ's person we find everything that Platonists distinguished in their study of temporality. The Logos is eternal and the seat of eternal essences; his soul, though linked with temporal becoming, transcends the intervals of history, and the bodies which it inhabits are restricted to the span of human life.

III

Origen may owe something to the Aristotelian precept that to teach and to be taught are a single energy, though the subjects of the operations differ (*Phys.* III.202b etc.). It is, however, in scripture that his panegyrist found a fitting paradigm of the sympathy that obtains between a pupil and his tutor, a paradigm which, as he himself observes, he would not have found without the experience of Origen's tuition:

'The soul of David was knit with that of Jonathan.' I read this after, but I felt it before with no less clarity than the annunciations of the clearest oracle. For Jonathan was not knit with David in the literal sense, but it was their souls, which hold the place of highest dignity; these, even when those parts that are apparent to men are separated, cannot themselves be compelled to part by any force, and certainly in no way against their will.

Gregory Thaumaturgus, *Panegyric* 6

As is the rule in Origen, the application of hermeneutic methods to this passage makes it a symbol of and a sanction for the art of commentary. All truth is revelation, but our nature is such that it cannot apprehend the word of God without a conversion of the intellect: to know is to be changed and thus to be morally united with the known. Origen was acquainted with philosophies that supported this belief, but he was even more familiar with the idiom of the New Testament, which speaks synonymously of making holy, of instruction in the Spirit, and of begetting by the Word.[37]

The means of transformation, according to Origen, is an intellectual union of the pupil and his preceptor. We must understand that our universal teacher is the Bible, which contains in itself the goal of our discipleship, a perfect intimacy with the Word:

The whole Word of God indeed, that which was with God in the beginning, is not many words, for it is not words; for it is one word subsisting under many notions, every one of which notions is a part of the whole word.

Philocalia V.4[38]

Just as for the Platonist every being sustains its character through aspiring to its source, so Origen holds that no word in the scriptures would have any meaning for us were it not a discrete expression of the One. This speculation sanctifies the premise on which Origen grounds his numerous expositions of the scriptures: this, affirmed explicitly in the prologue to his commentary on the Song of Songs, is that the sacred Word does not use homonyms. Words that appear synonymous refer sometimes to the outer, sometimes to the inner man, and, as we know, the one may be subsumed into the other. The difference between two contexts, like the difference between the sinner and the saint, is one of spiritual fullness. Once we have established the diversity of usages for any word, we must then attempt a taxonomy, according to which some contexts will say partially what is fully developed in others, and the synthesis of all contexts will comprise the total meaning of the term.[39] Biblical exegesis is an ascent through grades of knowledge; Origen maintains, in a famous chapter of his most philosophic treatise, that this process is determined by the tripartite constitution of the reader: 'For just as man consists of body, soul and spirit, so in the same way does the scripture, which has been prepared by God to be given for man's salvation' (*Peri archon* IV.2.4). Here we should note a point that is all too frequently neglected in discussions of allegory: the hermeneutic canon must be grounded in at least one proposition that is not supposed to lend itself to a figurative reading. Origen's position rests on his literal belief that the human person is compounded of three natures, and upon an eschatology that requires the full, substantial coalescence of soul with spirit and the attenuation of body to the finest state permissible for a vehicle of the soul. Only a moral chastisement, which is also an essential transformation, will equip us to behold the eternal mysteries: since body is the shadow of the soul, and the companion of its destiny, the spiritual construction of the Gospels strikes no bargains with the weakness of the flesh.[40]

The allegorical method in Alexandria had favoured more indulgent practices. The Valentinians boasted of having moved from a material or hylic to a spiritual or pneumatic understanding of the scriptures, but without (it seems) any necessary progress in the correlated virtues.[41] Salvation is not accomplished by renouncing the dominion of our lower selves for that of the higher faculty that all men have in common; matter, soul and spirit are the three classes of humanity, and to feel oneself a member of the third is to be saved. It is possible that, like their admirer Clement, the Valentinians gave a metaphorical turn to their ontology; but even Clement falls below the rigour of his successor when he contends that a higher reading of the most difficult commandment will permit us to maintain the material use of our possessions if we cultivate detachment in the soul (*Quis dives salvetur* 18, 20 etc.).

Is this theory of discipline Platonic? Does Origen agree that the emancipation of the highest faculties will put one in command of all that is requisite for salvation? His hermeneutic theory and that of the Platonists has at least a common basis in analogy, or rather in the transcendence of analogies; as we pass in Plato from the simile of the cave to a higher image, so in Origen we rise from a comparison of the text with human nature to a correlation of that human nature with the Trinity. The levels of understanding are iconically related, in that the soul is called a shadow of the spirit and the body is called a shadow of the soul. Nevertheless, we have already seen that Origen has countervailing principles: analogy in him does not entail participation, and he insists that God is present to us only through the historical epiphanies of his word. For the redeemed this presence is transparent and known through spiritual senses, whose relation to our own is one of transcendence rather than likeness.[42] But in the present life, the revelation of the Father is conditioned by his instruments, and even the incarnate Christ is not directly known. Phrases that other exegetes apply to a sacramental or even mystical communion with the resurrected Saviour are for Origen the proof-texts where the Word proclaims the word:

21

For the names of the organs of sense are often applied to the soul, so that we speak of seeing with the eyes of the heart, that is of drawing some intellectual conclusion by means of the faculty of intelligence. So too we speak of hearing with the ears when we discern the deeper meaning of some statement. So too we speak of the soul as being able to use teeth, when it eats and consumes the bread of life who comes down from heaven.

Peri archon I.1.9

The last remark glosses metaphor by metaphor, but nowhere does Origen say that the commandment to eat Christ's flesh can be obeyed by our attendance at the Eucharist, or that we can rise by any means above the scriptures to a direct illumination of the mind. At all times he employs a double criterion in interpreting the scriptures. On the one hand, we cannot hope in the present life to advance *beyond* the scriptures in our intuition of divinity; on the other, we have a new capacity to advance *within* the text to the highest level of reflection, since the Logos has united his divinity with the human spheres of body, soul and spirit. The person of the incarnate Lord is the source of revelation; the narrative in the Gospels is for us the prime disclosure of that person; yet it is faith in this disclosure, in the Gospel story itself, that frees theology from the literal construction of the text.

Origen believes as firmly as any theologian in the earthly life of Jesus, in his virgin birth, his death, his resurrection and the Pentecostal mission of the Spirit; but he urges from discrepancies in the Gospels that the reader is not to repose his faith in any scheme of time: 'For their goal was, wherever possible, to tell the truth both corporally and spiritually, but where both were not possible, to prefer the spiritual, frequently preserving spiritual truth in the corporal form that some might call a lie' (*Comm. John.* X.4). In assigning the purification of the Temple to an early point in Jesus' ministry, John departs from precedent and from history, to admonish us that chronology is not his main concern. Time is rather the substrate of divine communication, as necessary and irksome to the evangelists as matter to the demiurge in a Greek cosmogony. For humankind, all knowledge has its origin in learning, hence in time, but it is only by divorcing time from knowledge that we apprehend the nature of the Logos, who, combining temporality and eternity, is the origin of reflection and existence in humanity, and also of the eternal truths that inhabit the mind of God:

He is the beginning (*arkhe*) as to generation . . . and he is the beginning as to learning . . . a twofold beginning as to learning, in his nature and with respect to us. Thus if we should speak with regard to Christ, his beginning by nature is his divinity, but with regard to us . . . his humanity.

Comm. John. I.17–18

Faith in the historicity of events is not false knowledge, but it is only potential knowledge. Christ has deigned to assume our lower faculties so that we may rise above them. To adopt a modern simile,[43] we rise from carnal knowledge to a spiritual perception of the Saviour only by pulling up the ladder that has raised us. Origen of course prefers a Pauline metaphor (Gal. 3.24), one that both exemplifies and vindicates the treatment of the text itself as a sempiternal metaphor, an image of the principle by which images are read:

> Just as he dwelt in the perfect before his manifest sojourn in the body, so, after his prophesied appearance, for those who are still immature and are as it were under guardians and stewards, not yet having attained to the fullness of time, the words that precede Christ dwell in the juvenile souls to which they are fitted, and might reasonably be called schoolmasters (*paidagogoi*).
>
> *Comm. John.* I.9

If Origen learned the use of allegory from the Platonists, the premises and eductions were his own. For Platonists there is a natural and permanent analogy between the realms of intellect and matter; the iconic representation of eternal truth in narrative is possible only on the supposition that the narrative, in its superficial aspect, is untrue. For Origen the world becomes significant of divine things only when it has been invaded by the Spirit; time for him is not the emanation but the creature of eternity, and the world derives from nothing, not from God. The Word, not time or matter, is the image of the Father, and it is only its embodiment in time that can establish the analogy of grace.

Origen is often said to have treated propositions as the characteristic form of revelation; he is also said to have treated the propositions of the Bible with intolerable freedom.[44] Neither claim is wholly true, for the axiom of his hermeneutic method is that the author of the written word is also its only subject. To be a Christian is to believe, on the evidence of the text, that the author himself has entered the interpretative process; only by obedience to the precepts given at this point of history can we judge the historicity of the narrative that embodies them. Thus Christian hermeneutics, which addresses only scripture, will conclude with what can only lie beyond the word of scripture. The incarnation marries exegesis with anthropology and confirms the place of both within the economy of God.

NOTES

1 The most influential Lutheran attack on Christian Platonism is probably that of Anders Nygren, *Agape and Eros*, tr. P. S. Watson, Chicago, University of Chicago Press, 1982 (orig. 1953). Typical of modern Anglican work is J. Macquarrie, *In Search of Deity*, London, SCM Press, 1984, which maintains that the (allegedly

Platonic) preoccupation with transcendence is now an anachronism in Christianity.

2 In this summary I am assuming, as the Neoplatonists would, a convergence between the views of Plato and those of Aristotle. For a defence of this position see I. Crombie, *An Examination of Plato's Doctrines*, London, RKP, 1962–3; G. Fine, 'Aristotle's Criticisms of Plato', *Oxford Studies in Ancient Philosophy*, supp. 1992, pp. 13–43.

3 See L. Robin, *La théorie platonicienne de l'amour*, Paris, F. Alcan, 1964.

4 See F. D. White, 'Love and Beauty in Plato's Symposium', *Journal of Hellenic Studies* 109 (1989), pp. 149–57.

5 See *Rep.* 509b, and J. Halfwassen, *Der Aufstieg zum Einem*, Stuttgart, 1992, p. 24. Aristotle's use of a similar metaphor for the relation of the active reason to the passive reason at *De anima* III.4–5 was also fertile in late antiquity.

6 See *Timaeus* 29e on the goodness of the demiurge and 92c on the world as icon.

7 See A.-J. Festugière, *La revelation d'Hermes Trismegiste*, Paris, Les Belles Lettres, 1953, vol. 4, pp. 271–92.

8 On Xenocranes see J. M. Dillon, *The Middle Platonists*, London, Duckworth, 1977, p. 33.

9 *Timaeus* 37d; for the reading and an early appreciation of the significance of this passage, see R. D. Archer-Hind (ed.), *The Timaeus*, London, 1888, pp. 119–20. For a discussion of the relation of Plato's views on time to those of modern philosophy, see the commentary of A. E. Taylor (Oxford, 1928), pp. 678–91.

10 See H. F. Cherniss, *Aristotle's Criticism of Plato and the Academy*, Baltimore, Johns Hopkins Press, 1944, vol. 1, pp. 423ff.

11 Note the uncertainties of Plotinus, *Enneads* IV.8.1. For a modern discussion of the myth, see A. Lebeck, 'The Central Myth of Plato's Phaedrus', *Greek, Roman and Byzantine Studies* 13 (1972), pp. 267–90.

12 On the erotic and dramatic content of this dialogue, see M. Nussbaum, *The Fragility of Goodness*, Cambridge, Cambridge University Press, 1986, pp. 200–234; D. M. Halperin, 'Plato and the Erotics of Narrativity', *Oxford Studies in Ancient Philosophy*, supp. 1992, pp. 93–130.

13 See C. F. Hermann's edition of Plato, vol. 6 (Leipzig, 1974), pp. 147–51 Albinus is now customarily distinguished from Alcinous, the author of the longer and more famous *Didascalicus*.

14 See the anonymous Prolegomena in Hermann, ibid., p.209.3ff.

15 For comments and bibliography see J. Annas, *An Introduction to Plato's Republic*, Oxford, Clarendon Press, 1981, pp. 242–71. My own interpretation here is necessarily of a length that precludes any detailed reference to her opinions.

16 *Rep.* 509d–51le; see Annas, *An Introduction*, pp. 242–71. My interpretation, which posits an analogy between two forms of conversion analogically represented, makes sense of the fact that the ratio between the two major divisions of Plato's line is the same as the ratio between the parts into which each of these is subsequently divided.

17 See *Epistle* VII.340bl–345c3, cited as a leading text in H.-J. Krämer, *Plato and the Foundations of Metaphysics*, New York, 1990 (Eng. edn), pp. 194–8. The authenticity of this letter would not be disputed by a Neoplatonist any more than by Krämer, who defends their assumption of a metaphysical system in the dialogues.

18 The author may have in mind Plato's disparagement of writing at *Phaedrus* 274–6.

19 Hermann, ibid., p.206.20ff.

20 See J. Simons, 'Matter and Time in Plotinus', *Dionysius* 9 (1985), pp. 53–74.

21 See P. Manchester, 'Time and the Soul in Plotinus, III,7 [45],11,' *Dionysius* 2 (1978), pp. 101–36.

22 *Symposium* 201a–204b; for ancient and modern interpretations, see Robin, *La théorie platonicienne*, pp. 101–8.

23 See H. A. Wolfson, *The Philosophy of the Church Fathers*, Cambridge, MA, Harvard University Press, 1970, pp. 192–8.

24 See Jerome, *Ad avitum* 2; Origen, *Comm. John.* II.10, which makes it clear that temporal generation is not in question, only dependence on the Father.

25 See M. F. Wiles, 'Eternal Generation', *JThS* n.s. 12 (1961), pp. 384–91.

26 Cf. Origen, *Comm. John.* II.3 with Numenius, *Frs* 16, 17, 20 Des Places.

27 See J. M. Dillon, 'Origen's Doctrine of the Trinity and Some Later Neoplatonic Theories', in D. J. O'Meara (ed.) *Neoplatonism and Christian Thought*, Norfolk, VA, State University of New York Press, 1982, pp. 19–23.

28 According to *Peri archon* IV.8.6, which ought to have been considered by R. Sorabji in his quest for the 'origins of idealism' in *Time, Creation and the Continuum*, London, Duckworth, 1983, pp. 187–96. A treatise maintaining similar views has been ascribed to Origen, to Methodius and to a certain Maximus. It may be significant that the last is the name of an interlocutor in the *Dialogue with Heraclides*.

29 See G. C. Stead, *Divine Substance*, Oxford, Clarendon Press, 1977, pp. 190–216.

30 See P. Widdicombe, *The Fatherhood of God from Origen to Athanasius*, Oxford, Clarendon Press, 1993.

31 See *Dialogue with Heraclides* 6.30 etc.

32 See 1 Thess. 5.23 and *Peri archon* IV.2.4 below (p. 21). On Plato's tripartite soul see Annas, *An Introduction*, pp. 109–52.

33 See M. J. Edwards, 'Origen's Two Resurrections', *JThS* n.s. 46 (1995), pp. 502–18.

34 Translation, as for all quotations from *Contra Celsum*, by F. Crombie (Edinburgh, 1872).

35 E.g. G. C. Stead, 'Arius in Modern Research', *JThS* n.s. 45 (1994), p. 32.

36 See Photius, *Bibliotheca* 117. *Peri archon* IV.3.7 is a more faithful paraphrase of 1 Cor. 15.45.

37 See especially John 14.6ff., where the coming of the Spirit and the imparting of the Word are almost interchangeable.

38 The *Philocalia* is a collection of Greek excerpts assembled by Origen's admirers Basil and Gregory. This excerpt is from Book 5 of the commentary on John.

39 This notion of *psychagogia* makes Origen's theory more refined than its modern counterpart in Northrop Frye, *The Great Code*, London, Routledge, 1982.

40 Hence the stories of Origen's desire for martyrdom and self-castration in Eusebius, *HE* VI.8.

41 On allegory in Alexandria before Origen see D. Dawson, *Allegorical Readers and Cultural Revision in Ancient Alexandria*, Berkeley, University of California Press, 1992.

42 See K. Rahner, 'The "Spiritual Senses" according to Origen' in *Theological Investigations* 16, London, DLT, 1979, pp. 83–101.

43 L. Wittgenstein, *Tractatus Logico-Philosophicus* 6.54.

44 See H. U. von Balthasar, *The Glory of the Lord: A Theological Aesthetics. I: Seeing the Form*, tr. E. Leiva-Merikakis, Edinburgh, T. & T. Clark, 1982, pp. 266–7; R. P. C. Hanson, *Allegory and Event*, London, SCM Press, 1959, p. 365, where Origen is said to hold the axiom that 'history could never be of significance'.

3

ALLEGORICAL READING AND THE EMBODIMENT OF THE SOUL IN ORIGEN

David Dawson

In *Agape and Eros*, Anders Nygren argues that Origen made the allegorical meaning of scripture equivalent to the 'eros motif', thereby compromising the authentic teaching of Christian love as self-giving *agapê* by combining it with Greek conceptions of love as acquisitive desire.[1] Many have observed that Nygren's assessment rests on a one-sided conception of Platonic *erôs*. But in addition, by linking *erôs* so exclusively to the meanings of Origen's allegorical readings, Nygren also fails to examine the process of allegorical reading as itself an act of *erôs*. Just as Platonic *erôs* can be understood as the striving of the world of particulars for the forms of the Good and the Beautiful that would complete them, so allegorical reading can be seen as the striving of a reader confronted with incomplete or 'thin' literal meanings for the fuller or deeper meanings that would complete them.[2] Platonic *erôs* is the very desire to see the world of particulars as it really is by seeing its 'other-worldly' dimension as one that constitutes the fulfilment or completion of its altogether worldly being. Similarly, allegorical reading enables one to see the allegorical (which is to say, the *real*) meaning *of* – not *in place of* – the letter. In this chapter, I suggest that Origen's theory and practice of the allegorical reading of the 'letter' or first story of scripture reflects his double evaluation of the embodiment of the reader's soul. The allegorical reader's necessary departure from the first story of scripture parallels that reader's resistance to the fall of her soul, away from contemplation of the logos into body, history and culture. The equally necessary reliance of the second story on the first story's 'literal sense' parallels that reader's redemptive use of her soul's embodiment (by virtue of the enabling self-embodiment of the divine logos). For Origen, allegorical reading is the peculiar literary form taken by the soul's effort to live through its embodiment as both fall and redemption.

I

Origen begins his *Commentary on the Song of Songs* by making a distinction between what Solomon wrote (a 'little book') and what he sang (a 'marriage-

26

song'): Solomon 'wrote in the form of a drama' a song that he 'sang under the figure of the Bride' (*Cant.* Pro. 1).[3] Origen first highlights the character of Solomon's song as a written, narrative drama by pointing out how the various speakers (Bride, Bridegroom, friends of both) interact with each other – such is what is meant by saying that the song 'was written in dramatic form' (*Cant.* Pro. 1). But along with the comings and goings of various characters, presented 'one by one in their own order', the 'whole body' of the work also 'consists of mystical utterances' (*Cant.* Pro. 1).[4] Just what sort of relation does an allegorical reading of the Song of Songs forge or discern between the written text as sequential narrative ('drama') and the text as a 'whole body' comprised of mystical utterances ('song')? What is the relation between its 'horizontal' character as narrative sequence and its 'depth dimension' as mystical utterance?

Following his opening account of the double character of Solomon's Song as a work about love, Origen describes the double way it can be read. Before sketching out productive and counter-productive readings, he describes a neutral, unproductive encounter with the text. If the text is to be read productively, the reader must bring to it his or her own passion of love. But if one is like a pre-pubescent child as yet unaffected by this passion, one will 'derive neither profit nor much harm, either from reading the text itself, or from going through the necessary explanations'; it will not be given to such a passionless reader 'to grasp the meaning of these sayings' (*Cant.* Pro. 1).

But the passionate reader may be of two very different kinds. Origen first describes the improperly passionate reader – a reader who 'lives only after the flesh'. Such a reader, suffering from a misdirected *erôs*, 'will twist the whole manner of his hearing' of the text 'away from the inner spiritual man and on to the outward and carnal; and he will be turned away from the spirit to the flesh, and will foster carnal desires in himself, and it will seem to be the Divine Scriptures that are thus urging and egging him on to fleshly lust!' (*Cant.* Pro. 1). Origen then offers a contrasting account of the properly passionate reader. At first glance, this account seems to conflict with the idea of emotional neutrality he has just ruled out: Origen warns that one who is 'not yet rid of the vexations of flesh and blood and has not ceased to feel the passion of his bodily nature' should refrain both from reading the work and from hearing its interpretation (*Cant.* Pro. 1). But clearly this cannot mean that the ideal reader must somehow return to an a-erotic state. Instead, Origen means that one must enjoy a redirected eroticism; one must give heed to that mode of *erôs* that directs one towards spiritual reality. Such a person will be able to 'hear love's language in purity and with chaste ears', not because he himself cannot love, but precisely because his love has been purified.

Is it possible to relate Origen's distinction between dramatic narrative and mystical utterance to his contrast between the two modes of *erôs*? The great temptation, to which Nygren succumbs, is to line them up in this fashion:

Song as mystical utterance = allegorical sense = 'heavenly' *erôs*
Song as written drama = literal sense = 'vulgar' *erôs*

But such a dualistic and hierarchical scheme that pits spirit against letter and sublimated against unsublimated love misses Origen's essential point about the unity of the text and the unity of the reader's *erôs*. Origen faces a specific hermeneutical dilemma in his commentary on the Song of Songs: he must find a way to read a text about physical love so that it becomes a text about a spiritual love that can be understood only through a form of reading that is itself an enactment of spiritual love. Yet the spiritual love that is both impetus to, and reward of, allegorical reading, while not carnal, must also not be disincarnate. Achieving a spiritual love that is neither carnal nor disincarnate is parallel to discerning an allegorical meaning that is neither 'literalistic' nor 'anti-literal'.

II

This hermeneutical dilemma takes a parallel form in Origen's appropriation of Stoic 'name theory' as an aid to interpreting scriptural names. The names in scripture refer to non-textual 'things' or meanings, yet those meanings seem to be linked to the text by way of the spoken qualities of language. The 'depth' dimension of scriptural names lies in the way their spoken features build a bridge from textual signifiers to non-textual meanings. A meaning that is not reducible to language alone without being essentially non-linguistic is the paradoxical goal.

In his reflections on the nature of human language, Origen frequently draws on the categories of Stoic logic.[5] One of the three parts of Stoic philosophy, along with ethics and physics, Stoic logic was a far-ranging discipline that embraced not only the formal principles of valid inference, but also rhetoric and much of what we would call epistemology, semantics and linguistics. Like Stoic ethics, Stoic logic presupposed the entire range of Stoic physics. Sextus Empiricus reports that the Stoics distinguished three basic components of language: the 'sign' or that which signifies (*to semainon*), the 'meaning' or that which is signified (*to sêmainomenon*) by a sign, and the object (*to tynchanon*) to which the sign-user referred by using the sign (*Adv. Math.* 8.11ff.). The sign was first of all human speech (*phônê*) – the vibration of air – and hence both the sign and the object to which the sign referred were material bodies (*sômata*); both my utterance 'Dion is walking' and the actual walking person Dion are physical realities. But my meaning – the thing I am saying about Dion, namely that he is walking – is non-corporeal (*asômaton*). A 'meaning' was, then, a strangely non-material reality that seems to fit uneasily within the materialist Stoic world view (but such non-material 'meanings' might have had a special appeal to Christian philosophers intent on distinguishing spiritual from material realities). The meaning of the sign might also be called *to lekton* – literally, 'what is said' – or simply *pragma* – the 'thing (said)'. Since *pragma* is also the ordinary Greek word for a material thing, event or 'fact', the Stoic use of *pragma* as a synonym for the non-material *lekton* is somewhat specialized.[6]

In the following passage, Origen uses such Stoic technical terms to describe the components of language:

> The one who distinguishes for himself between the expression [*phônê*], the meanings [*sêmainomena*], and the realities [*pragmata*], on which the meanings are based, will not take offense at the incorrect use of expressions when he searches and finds that the realities [*pragmata*] of which the expressions are used are sound. This is especially so when the holy writers confess that their words and message are 'not in persuasive words of wisdom, but in the demonstration of the Spirit and power' [1 Cor. 2.4].
>
> *Comm. John.* 4.1[7]

As both Platonist philosopher and Christian theologian, Origen needs to distinguish material objects from the non-material, intelligible realities that were the proper object of theological knowledge. In this passage, *pragmata* appear to denote such non-material realities; those realities, rather than the the Bible's phonetic expressions or its meanings, make its teachings 'powerful'.

However, another passage seems to locate that power differently: 'Thus it is not the meanings associated with the realities [*ta sêmainomena kata tôn pragmatôn*] that have a certain power to do this or that, but the qualities and characteristics of the sounds [*hai tôn phônôn poiotêtes kai idiotêtes*]' (*Contra Celsum* 1.25).[8] Like the passage just cited, this passage rules out meanings as the source of the power of biblical language. But whereas the first passage suggests that the referents of language are the source of its power, here we are told that the power resides in 'the qualities and characteristics of the sounds'. But the contradiction is only apparent. Origen shares a standard ancient etymological assumption that 'the primary sounds [of language] imitate things' (*SVF* 2.146). There is an isomorphism between verbal utterance and spiritual reality such that to have the first is to have the second.

Hence Origen objects to Celsus's 'cultural relativist' position that 'it makes no difference whether one calls the supreme God by the name used among the Greeks, or by that, for example, used among the Indians, or by that among the Egyptians' (*Contra Celsum* 1.24). Instead, with respect to proper biblical names, especially names for God, Origen endorses the position that such names naturally 'imitate' the things to which they refer: biblical names get their power from the realm of the creator, but that power, as we have seen, also resides in the spoken character peculiar to the particular language in which they are cast. The pronunciation of that language is not random, but proceeds according to a sequence (*heirmos*) that is 'natural' to the names (*Contra Celsum* 1.24).

There is a basic duality in all scriptural language that reflects the difference between sensible and intelligible reality (*Contra Celsum* 7.31). Origen's theory of the powerful effect of the phonetic qualities of divine names is, then, part of a larger distinction in value between names (indeed all of language) and the realities to which language refers. The power that names convey is central, and this power, while distinguishable from language (so that it cannot simply be neutralized by a grammatical mistake) is nonetheless linguistic, linked to the specific qualities of spoken language. By appealing to the spoken qualities of language, Origen builds a bridge from specific textual details to the spiritual 'force' of the extra-textual referents. Yet while it is true that the diverse names for God in different cultures should not be disregarded just because usage is different (as Celsus suggests), the particularities of the names should not be valued over what they signify:

> Let everyone, then, who cares for truth, care little about 'names and words' [1 Tim. 1.4], for different kinds of speech are customary in different nations. Let him be more anxious about that which is signified than about the words by which it is signified [*quod signifi-catur, quam qualibus verbis significetur*].
>
> *Peri archon* 4.3.15

In the case of names for God, 'what they signify' is unitary, despite the multiplicity and diversity of the names themselves (*Contra Celsum* 8.37). When properly interpreted, the words of scripture convey a power that remains imbedded in, even as it exceeds, human language.

III

The interpretation of names represents part of Origen's understanding of the 'depth dimension' of scriptural language. He also thinks that the non-literal realities to which names refer are themselves combined into larger, horizontal or syntactical units, and that the resulting sequential or narrative structures are also spiritually meaningful. When Origen turns from the vertical depth dimension of names with second meanings to the horizontal narrative dimension of first and second stories, he draws on Stoic ideas about language and about the logical and metaphysical connections between items in the cosmos in order to describe three things: the sequence of scriptural narrative; the sequential character of that narrative's second, allegorical story; and the intimate connections between the two stories. A term Origen frequently uses to point to this set of interrelationships is *akolouthia* ('following' or 'connection').

The centrality of the concept of *akolouthia* to Stoicism is underscored by its appearance in all three of its branches: logic, physics and ethics.[9] In logic, a conclusion is said to 'follow from' its antecedent (*akolouthei tôi A to B*), just as 'a falsehood fails to follow from a truth' (*alêthei pseudos ouk akolouthei*). Human beings are able to recognize such 'consequences and contradictions' (*ta akoloutha kai ta machomena*) by virtue of an 'internal speech' (*endiathetos logos*). This ability derives from the fact that, according to the Stoics, correct human thought mirrors reality. It is, then, no surprise that the term *akolouthia* is also used to speak of the tight connection between causes and effects in the cosmos, for, according to the Stoics, in that cosmos, all events are fated and occur 'according to order and sequence' (*kata taxin kai akolouthian*) or 'according to causal connections' (*kata tên tôn aitiôn akolouthian*). When human beings think – which is to say, when they think logically – they recognize and put into concepts how aspects of the world are truly interrelated. The ability to do so is characteristic of the Stoic sage. As the only truly wise and good person, the sage is able to live in congruence with *logos*, 'according to nature' (*akolouthôs têi physei*), 'conformed to the law' (*akolouthêtikos tôi nomôi*). In doing this, the sage's every action is 'in accordance with his own nature' (*akolouthôs têi heutou physei*) as well.

The success of the sage in living according to nature depends on his ability to recognize the signals that nature provides of its inner coherence and on his ability to make correct inferences from those signals. Sextus reports that the Stoics thought that both animals and human beings receive 'simple presentations' (*haplêi phantasiâi*) from the world and produce 'uttered speech' (*prophorikoi logoi*). But only human beings possess 'internal speech' (*endiathetoi logoi*), by means of which complex presentations are generated by inference and combination (*metabatikêi kai synthetikêi*). This means that a human being possesses an idea of 'logical consequence' (*akolouthia*) and 'grasps the way of thinking by signals' (*sêmeiou noêsin*), that is, inferentially, because of this. 'For signal itself is of the following form: "If this, then that." Therefore the existence of signal follows from the nature and constitution of man' (Sext., *Adv. math.* 8.275ff.).

These signals (*semeia*) that are the basis for making inferences must be distinguished from linguistic signs (*sêmainonta*) that give expression to meanings. As we have already noted, linguistic signs are corporeal: they are the significant sounds that rational beings utter, the material of which rational speech (*phônê sêmantikê*) is composed. But the signals that take the form 'if this, then that' are incorporeal because they are propositions (*axiômata*), and propositions are one of the species of incorporeal meanings (*lekta*) signified by linguistic signs. What we have, then, is a double system of meaning and inference. If I say, 'If smoke, then fire,' my uttered nouns 'smoke' and 'fire' are linguistic signs. What these material signs signify in the utterance 'If smoke, then fire' is an incorporeal (*asômaton*) meaning, a *lekton*. This particular *lekton* happens to be a complex proposition, the first half of which is called a signal because a signal is 'a true antecedent proposition in a valid conditional which serves to reveal the consequent' (*Adv. math.* 8.245). In sum, corporeal signs express incorporeal meanings, some of which turn out to be incorporeal signals which can be the basis of inferences. According to Sextus, the Stoics distinguished two sorts of signals, commemorative (*hypomnêstikon*) and indicative (*endeiktikon*). The distinction turned on whether the consequent was 'temporarily unseen' (*pros kairon adêla*) or 'naturally unseen' (*physei adêlon*). The signal 'If smoke, then fire' was commemorative because fire, though temporarily unseen, had in the past been customarily seen with fire. But the signal 'If bodily movements, then soul' was indicative, because the soul is naturally unseen and has never been observed in conjunction with motions of the body.

As an allegorical reader, Origen regards many of the events and phenomena to which the Bible refers as indicative signals signifying spiritual (and hence non-apparent) realities. The 'signs' given by Moses to Pharaoh were divinely given signals of this sort, as were Jesus' miracles. Recognition of the indicative rather than merely commemorative character of these signals is the basis of an allegorical rather than literal reading of the scriptural signs that represent them. If the reader infers from scripturally recorded events only a temporarily non-apparent sensuous object, he would be reading literally and would be engaged in the process of merely sensible understanding (Origen regularly uses *aisthêtos* to denote a 'literal' reading). This literal reader would then be regarding the signals signified by scripture as commemorative: if God is said to display wrath, such a reader would recall to mind concepts (*ennoiai*) representing the physical features of wrathful persons he had previously seen. On the other hand, if the reader infers from the scriptural sign a non-sensuous (and thus inherently non-apparent) signification, such a reader would be reading allegorically and would be engaged in a process of *noêsis* or intellectual understanding, for which *ta noêta* rather than either *ta aisthêta* or *hai ennoiai* are the proper objects.

Origen's conception of allegorical reading reflects Stoic ideas about how to make valid inferences from historical events and natural phenomena regarded as signals. It is not simply a theory of reading or interpreting the language (i.e. sign character) of scripture as such; instead, it is a way of reading those signs in order to discern the interconnections among the elements of extra-textual reality. The scriptural text consists of signs that signify various modes of divine presence in nature and history that are themselves signals by which readers might make true inferences about spiritual reality.

Origen believed that scripture was composed by human beings who expressed in written form their special knowledge (*gnôsis*) of those spiritual

realities (*Comm. John.* 2.10). This knowledge is not the result of sense
perceptions. Instead, Moses 'sees' God by 'understanding him with the
vision of the heart and the perception of the mind' (*Peri archon* 2.4.3). This
kind of vision or perception is 'a certain generic divine sense' (*theias tinos
genikês aisthêseôs*) that is different from the ordinary five senses, a 'sense that is
not sensible' (*aisthêsei ouk aisthêtêi*), but one that takes the form of a spiritual
correlate of the ordinary senses: one can speak of a spiritual tasting or
touching, for example (*Contra Celsum* 1.48). Spiritual vision is the special
skill of the prophets and, though not originating in any sense perception, it
manifests itself as such: the *logos* that 'comes to be' with the prophets,
'enlightens them with the light of knowledge, causing them to see things
which they had not perceived before his coming as if they saw them before
their eyes' (*Comm. John.* 2.10). Just as prophetic writings detail marvellously
physical theophanies and revelatory moments, so even the seemingly physical, sensible activities of Jesus bear witness to other, spiritual realities:
Ezekiel is said to have eaten the roll of the book given to him and Israel to
have 'smelled the scent of his son's spiritual garments':

> in the same way as in these instances Jesus touched the leper spiri-
> tually rather than sensibly [Matt. 8.3], to heal him, as I think, in
> two ways, delivering him *not only*, as the multitude take it, from
> sensible leprosy by sensible touch, *but also* from another leprosy by
> his truly divine touch.
>
> *Contra Celsum* 1.48, my emphasis

Note that the two 'touches' are not separate events but two dimensions of a
single event, a point I will develop below in reference to the erotic language
of the Song of Songs. This passage makes clear that the process of human
scriptural authorship and that of allegorical interpretation are aspects of a
single process: human authors, via revelation and inspiration, turn their
spiritual perceptions into sensible representations; subsequent allegorical
readers discover in those sensible representations underlying spiritual meanings.

But scripture is authored by God as well as by writers like Moses. This
does not mean that the human author is simply a passive vehicle for the
spirit's dictation; rather, the spirit transforms and heals the would-be author,
granting him special knowledge of the divine (the prophets who 'tasted and
smelt, so to speak, with a sense which was not sensible', were able to do so
because 'they touched the Word by faith so that an emanation came from
him to them which healed them' (*Contra Celsum* 1.48)). So Moses can be
called a 'distinguished orator' because he writes a text with morally useful
legislation for the multitude of Israelites, but also conceals a deeper meaning
for those few 'who are able to read with more understanding' (*Contra Celsum*
1.18). For example, Moses' account of the division of nations in Genesis is

for the masses, but the educated few will understand it as an account of how souls become embodied (*Contra Celsum* 5.29). But the divine spirit is perhaps a more 'distinguished orator' than Moses, for in writing in such a rhetorically sophisticated way, Moses is simply executing the spirit's own compositional intention.

Origen presents his most detailed account of scripture's proper allegorical interpretation from the perspective of its composition by its divine author, the Holy Spirit. This spirit has produced the text of scripture as a means of achieving two specific aims (*skopoi*): first, to enlighten (= to inspire) the souls of the prophets and apostles with mysteries (or 'doctrines') concerning human souls so that a reader who is 'capable of being taught' can discover these mysteries (*Peri archon* 4.2.7); second, to hide these mysteries in surface narratives so that readers unable to 'endure the burden' of seeking out the deeper meaning might nonetheless be edified (*Peri archon* 4.2.8).

The spirit has in effect written a single text for two different audiences: the small elite group of Christian seekers of *gnôsis* (e.g. people like Origen and his patron Ambrose), and the larger 'multitude' of simple believers. But the spirit's goal was not to produce a single text susceptible of two utterly different readings, providing the occasion for two distinct readerships; instead, the goal was to provide the opportunity for two readings of a single text that could nevertheless finally cohere as a single, harmonious, integrated reading by a single community. The 'most wonderful thing' about the spirit's composition of the Bible is that it enabled just those often unappealing surface accounts of narratives and laws simultaneously to provide 'secret truths' to the elite and moral profit to the multitude (*Peri archon* 4.2.8).

While in principle there need be no inner relationship between elite and common meanings, Origen claims that there is. Here I arrive at the heart of the question I posed at the outset: just what sort of relation does allegorical reading forge or discern between the written text as sequential, dramatic narrative and the text as a 'whole body' composed of mystical utterances? Origen declares that there is an inner principle or logic that relates the outer, bodily, sensible dimension of the text to its inner, spiritual, intellectual meaning. In addition to using the term *akolouthia*, Origen often uses the term *heirmos* ('series' or 'connection') to refer to this coherence: in scripture, seemingly inappropriate or unedifying narratives and laws have been 'recorded in a series [*heirmôi anagegrammenôn*] with a power which is truly appropriate to the wisdom of God' (*Peri archon* 4.2.8). Origen links the notion of the text's 'power' with the idea of a series or sequence; there is a logic that shows how the seemingly inappropriate text is in fact appropriate, and its appropriateness is a function of the power of divine authorship. There is an 'order' or 'coherence' to the text that embraces and makes compatible these two dimensions of meaning.

However, the common reader does not perceive this deeper coherence of apparent and non-apparent scriptural meanings. In many cases, this produces no problem, for 'it is possible to derive benefit from the first, and to this extent helpful meaning', as do 'multitudes of sincere and simple believers' (*Peri archon* 4.2.6). But the potential for danger remains, lying in 'the sheer attractiveness [or 'seductiveness', as in the Song of Songs] of the language' of the text. If one attends only to the surface narrative, there are two likely outcomes: one will either find the narrative satisfying as it stands, and learn nothing truly divine, or one will find the narrative repellent, and learn nothing worthy of God (*Peri archon* 4.2.9). Simple-minded Christians are the typical victims of the first sort of literalism, gnostics of the second. One communal threat of literalism is clear: simple Christian literalists are prime candidates for conversion by gnostic exegetes able to show that literal scriptural accounts of God are morally repugnant (see *Contra Celsum* 4.48).

The following diagram of Origen's conception of the contents and structure of scripture will help show in more detail how he conceives of the interrelationship of the text and the two orders of reality to which it refers. The diagram has two basic divisions: (I) the non-sensible realm of intellectual realities (*ta noêta*) and (II) the sensible realm of material realities (*ta aisthêta*), a realm that includes both the text (IIa) and all historical events and natural phenomena to which the text might refer (IIb).

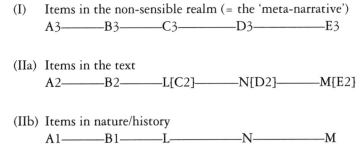

(I)   Items in the non-sensible realm (= the 'meta-narrative')
      A3———B3———C3————D3—————E3

(IIa) Items in the text
      A2———B2———L[C2]————N[D2]———M[E2]

(IIb) Items in nature/history
      A1———B1———L————N————M

A3, B3, C3, etc. in the non-sensible realm (I) stand for the intellectual or spiritual realities that constitute the final allegorical referents of scripture. They occur in a 'sequence' (*akolouthia*), represented here by their alphabetical order, and they are linked to one another by dashes to show their inner 'connection' (*hiermos*). Level IIa shows elements in the text of scripture (A2, B2, etc.), which may be words, sentences, complete stories or images. The loss of alphabetical fullness (between B and L) and the disruption of alphabetical order (between L, N, M) show that the scriptural text either lacks or subverts obvious sequence and connection at certain points. Level IIb displays the historical events and natural phenomena represented by scripture (i.e. *pragmata* as material things or events in the world of space and time). The letters in brackets on level IIa (i.e. [C2], [D2], [E2]) represent textual items that the divine spirit leads human authors to insert into scripture. If taken as representing sensuous realities, these items are falsehoods, impossibilities or improbabilities (i.e. no correspondents for them can be found at level IIb). But when read allegorically, they represent intellectual realities needed to complete the sequence of IIa and simultaneously to represent important elements in the sequence of level I.

Discerning the deep coherence of the sensible (II) with the non-sensible aspects of scriptural narratives and laws (I) is the allegorical reader's proper task. Whether or not these different dimensions of reality cohere is determined solely by the non-sensible realm, which consists of the interrelationships of intellectual realities. The divine author's compositional task was to bring the accounts of temporal, sensible realities into alignment with this meta-narrative: 'The principal aim [*skopos*] [of the divine author] was to announce the connection that exists among spiritual events [*ton en tois pneumatikois heirmon*], those that have already happened and those that are yet to come to pass' (*Peri archon* 4.2.9). The allegorical reader must read the narrative of scripture in order to discern this intellectual or spiritual meta-narrative (which is the deepest 'meaning' of the text) and its inner coherence: 'For how can one be said to believe the Scripture in the proper sense, when he does not perceive the meaning [*nous*] of the Holy Spirit in it, which God wants to be believed rather than the intent of the letter' (*Comm. John.* 10.300). The reader is alerted to the need for a deeper, allegorical reading by the divine composer, who has intentionally disrupted narrative coherence (indicated in the diagram by the insertion of the series L, N, M following A, B, in IIa). If the surface narratives of scripture displayed an immediate and obvious 'connection' and 'sequence' (A, B, C, D, E) or if the usefulness of scriptural laws was everywhere apparent, readers would be taken in, naively embracing the obvious reading. To counter such a naive reading, the divine author has inserted 'certain stumbling-blocks' (*skandala*) into the text, alerting readers that something 'beyond the meaning at hand [*para to procheiron*] is hidden there' (*Peri archon* 4.2.9).

As for the rest of the scriptural narrative and the concrete (i.e. natural or historical) realities to which it refers, the divine author used both text and realities in so far as they could be brought into relation with the authoritative sequence of the meta-narrative. If it was possible to harmonize historical events reported in scripture with the sequence of that meta-narrative of 'mystical events', the divine author did so (as in the case of A1, A2, A3 and B1, B2, B3 above). In other cases, the divine author was faced with narratives composed by human authors not in order to report historical events, but to express mystical meanings. But if those meanings 'did not correspond with the sequence of the intellectual truths [*tês peri tôn noêtôn akoluthias*]' (as L, N, M fail to correspond to C3, D3, E3), the divine author then 'wove into the story something which did not happen ([C]), occasionally something which could not happen ([D]) and occasionally something which might have happened but in fact did not ([E])' (*Peri archon* 4.2.9). All of these falsehoods, impossibilities and unrealized possibilities, which are meaningless and false on an empirical level, are true on the level of the intellectual meta-narrative – indeed, they are vital to the inner coherence of this narrative. How much of scripture contains such interpolations varies: 'sometimes a few words are inserted which in the bodily sense are not true, and at other times a greater number' (*Peri archon* 4.2.9). The meta-narrative consists, then, of intellectual truths connected in their own precise series or sequence (A3—B3—C3 etc.). A number of elements in the meta-narrative are represented by portions of scripture that the composing spirit has added to the text – [C], [D], [E], which, when understood literally, are untrue, irrational or impossible. The allegorical reader must read the text so that the added material coheres perfectly with the meta-narrative of which it is part, producing a single, unified and unifying reading of the entire biblical text.

The principal task of the allegorical reader is to read the text so that the added material coheres perfectly with the meta-narrative of which it is part, producing a single reading of all portions of the biblical text. What follows is one of Origen's fullest and most nuanced accounts of this reading process:

> When, therefore, as will be clear to those who read, the passage as a connected whole is literally impossible [*adynatos men ho hôs pros to hrêton heirmos*], whereas the principal part [*ho proêgoumenos*] of it is not impossible but even true, the reader must endeavor to grasp the entire meaning [*nous*], connecting [*syneironta*] by an intellectual process [*noêtôs*] the account of what is literally impossible with the parts that are not impossible but are historically true, these being interpreted allegorically together [*synallêgoroumenois*] with the parts which, so far as the letter goes, did not happen at all. For our contention with regard to the whole of divine scripture is, that it all has a spiritual meaning, but not all a bodily meaning; for the bodily meaning is often proved to be an impossibility.
>
> *Peri archon* 4.3.5

An allegorical reading is, then, both a linguistic and philosophical process that connects literal impossibilities, historical realities and literal fictions, producing a single coherent narrative. These elements can be interrelated when one 'interprets them allegorically together', that is, when one ignores those literal aspects of the story that fail to contribute to the intellectual meta-narrative (L, M, N on IIa).

When read allegorically, the biblical text reveals a surprising and total isomorphism with the very structure of spiritual reality; to read this text properly is to be brought into direct relation with the way things – in their deepest reality – actually are. When scripture is read allegorically, the scripture reader's soul 'makes room' for the reception of the knowledge of spiritual realities needed for the fashioning of his soul. This 'powerful' result of reading comes to those with the 'power' to read the text properly. The process is, of course, finally circular: a divine rhetorician produces words that are powerful, and those able to read them properly are 'empowered' to do so because they have been inspired by the same spirit that animates the very words they seek to understand.

IV

How does Origen's philosophical account of language, scripture and inter-pretation relate to the more biblical, metaphorical and mystical idioms of his commentary on the Song of Songs? It appears that the kind of links that Origen finds between names and their deeper meanings, or between biblical stories and the second stories told by the spirit through them, is the same sort of relation an allegorical reader of the Song of Songs seeks to achieve by transcending 'carnal love' without simply repudiating love's bodily senses. Origen's view of allegorical *erôs* as transforming but not rejecting bodily love is consistent with his confidence in the persistence of personal identity in the resurrected 'spiritual body'.

In the commentary Origen refers to the need to interrelate the 'order and sequence' of spiritual and textual realities in the allegorical reading process:

> For he [the allegorical reader] will add to the others [i.e. other songs in the Bible] the fifteen Gradual Songs and, by assessing the virtue of each song separately and collecting from them the grades of the soul's advance, and putting together the order and sequence of things with spiritual understanding [*spiritali intelligentia ordinem rerum consequentiamque componens*], he will be able to show with what stately steps the Bride, as she makes her entrance, attains by way of all these to the nuptial chamber of the Bridegroom, passing 'into the place of the wonderful tabernacle, even to the House of God with the voice of joy and praise, the noise of one feasting'. So she comes, as we said, even to the Bridegroom's chamber, that she may hear and speak all these things that are contained in the Song of Songs.
>
> *Cant*. Pro. 4

Here Origen indicates that the allegorical reader is obligated to understand spiritually the sequence of the textual narrative, discerning at the level of spiritual reality or meta-narrative the syntax represented at the level of the immediate story. Origen offers a biblical rationale for those two orders of reality, invoking the double account of creation in Genesis, as well as Paul's distinction between the 'inner' and 'outer' man. He observes that biblical terms like 'child', 'adult', 'womb' and 'eye', if they denote spiritual as well as bodily meanings, must be homonyms:

It is perfectly clear that in these passages the names of the members can in no way be applied to the visible body, but must be referred to the parts and powers of the invisible soul. The members have the same names, yes; but the names plainly and without any ambiguity carry meanings proper to the inner, not the outer man.

Cant. Pro. 2

Origen indicates that the two meanings of a biblical homonym must be kept distinct, for corruption is the opposite of incorruption: 'The same terms, then, are used throughout for either man; but the essential character of the things is kept distinct, and corruptible things are offered to that which is corruptible, while incorruptible things are set before that which cannot be corrupted' (*Cant.* Pro. 2). It is the hallmark of a non-allegorical, literalistic reading that it fails to see that the term is a homonym and that the second meaning is about incorruptible realities:

It happens in consequence that certain people of the simpler sort, not knowing how to distinguish and differentiate between the things ascribed in the Divine Scriptures to the inner and outer man respectively, and being deceived by this identity of nomenclature, have applied themselves to certain absurd fables and silly tales. Thus they even believe that after the resurrection bodily food and drink will be used and taken – food, that is, not only from that True Vine who lives for ever, but also from the vines and fruits of the trees about us.

Cant. Pro. 2

At this point, the contrast between literal and non-literal meanings seems absolute. But this is not the case. The scriptural homonyms, though denoting meanings which in one respect – corruption and incorruption – contrast absolutely, do not do so with respect to all of their connotations. For example, one can be a 'child' either with respect to the age of the incorruptible soul, or with respect to the age of the corruptible body. Soul and body contrast absolutely with respect to corruptibility, but there is similarity with respect to age, since the childlike soul will progress in time towards the 'perfect man', even as the actual child will grow into an adult. Hence the contrasting meanings of the homonym rule out corruption without ruling out temporal progression: the soul, though incorruptible, will develop in time. And, as we shall see, to develop in this way, the soul will require a body – though not a corruptible one.

Origen is clearly concerned to preserve specific links between the meanings of biblical homonyms, such that the spiritual meaning cannot be entirely separated from all bodily meanings. He defends such a procedure in the following passage:

Because of certain mystical and hidden things the people is visibly led forth from the terrestrial Egypt and journeys through the desert, where there was a biting serpent, and a scorpion, and thirst, and where all the other happenings took place that are recorded. *All these events, as we have said, have the aspects and likenesses of certain hidden things.* And you will find this correspondence not only in the Old Testament Scriptures, but also in the actions of Our Lord and Savior that are related in the Gospel.

If, therefore, in accordance with the principles that we have now established *all things that are in the open stand in some sort of relation to others that are hidden*, it undoubtedly follows that the visible hart and roe mentioned in the Song of Songs are related to some patterns of incorporeal realities, *in accordance with the character borne by their bodily nature.* And this must be in such wise that we ought to be able to furnish a fitting interpretation of what is said about the Lord perfecting the harts, by reference to those harts that are unseen and hidden.

Cant. Pro. III.12, my emphasis

My previous discussion of the way the homonym 'child' preserves temporal development even as it drops corruption is an example of what Origen might mean by discovering a spiritual meaning that is 'in accordance with the character borne by their bodily nature'. He also gives an example to illustrate his point about the roe or deer; in this case, the spiritual meaning is intrinsically related to the alleged physical capacity of the roe both to see acutely and to generate a physical substance that enhances the vision of others:

For those who are skilled in medicine assert that there is a certain fluid in the vicera of this animal which dispels dimness from the eyes and stimulates defective vision. Deservedly, therefore, is Christ compared to a roe or fallow deer, since He not only sees the Father Himself, but also causes Him to be seen by those whose power of vision He Himself has healed.

Cant. Pro. III.12

Scripture consists of synonyms as well as homonyms. A most important example for Origen in the Song of Songs commentary are the terms *erôs* and *agapê* (translated by Rufinus as *amor* and *caritas*). Origen insists that the reader of scripture 'must take whatever Scripture says about *caritas* as if it had been said with reference to *amor*, taking no notice of the difference of terms; for the same meaning is conveyed by both' (*Cant.* Pro. 2). But one must carefully distinguish true synonyms and closely derived usages (i.e. as God is 'love', so must one 'love' one's neighbour) from improper and false usages ('love' applied to money or harlots is an improper usage; 'love' applied to the devil is false). Here Origen is making a distinction between two applications of love: love for God versus love for all that is not God. On the one hand, he wants to insist that the faculty of love has been 'implanted in the human soul by the Creator's kindness' and that 'it is impossible for human nature not to be always feeling the passion of love for something' (*Cant.* Pro. 2). On the other hand, one can 'pervert' this divinely given capacity for love, debasing it by directing it towards earthly and perishable objects. The result is that 'the love that is of God' should not 'be esteemed to be in our every attachment' (*Cant.* Pro. 2).

Origen is not suggesting that, in one's love for God, one rejects or ignores the body: rather, the bodily realm necessarily informs one's love for God while not being the object of that love. The bodily realm has such a role because it is divinely created. The soul that loves spiritually is able to behold clearly the beauty and fairness of the Word of God, falling deeply in love with the Word's beauty and receiving in turn from the Word 'a certain dart and wound of love' (*Cant.* Pro. 2). How does one perceive the Word's beauty? Where is it found? The Word is the image of the God who creates, and for Origen, it is to the creation's beauty – the realm of matter and the body – that one must look to discern the beauty of the Word:

> For this Word 'is the image' and splendour 'of the invisible God, the Firstborn of all creation, in whom were all things created that are in heaven and on earth, seen and unseen alike'. If, then, a man can so extend his thinking as to ponder and consider the beauty and the grace of all the things that have been created in the Word, the very charm of them will so smite him, the grandeur of their bright- ness will so pierce him as with 'a chosen dart' – as says the prophet – that he will suffer from the dart Himself a saving wound, and will be kindled with the blessed fire of His love. (*Cant.* Pro. 2)

The concept of creation through the Word revalues the bodily realm – otherwise understood in Origen's system as the penalty/consequence of that 'cooling off' (becoming 'ensouled') of the mind's (or spirit's) ardour that constitutes its fall away from contemplation of the Word – making it the soteriologically necessary vehicle for the soul's recovery of its former status as mind or spirit (*Peri archon* 2.8.3). That return cannot bypass the body, but rather must work through it, or more deeply into it – into its inner depths, its true origin in the spiritual realm from which the soul that it embodies fell. This may require a radical transformation of body, but it cannot entail its replacement, even as an allegorical reading must entail a reconstrual, not a replacement, of its literal meaning.

We saw earlier that Origen can heap scorn on those non-allegorical readers who thought that after their resurrection they would continue to eat and drink ordinary food. That makes it look as though he thought that the soul's return to God demanded its radical disembodiment. But just as understanding Paul's language of being a child in faith required dropping the connotations of corruption while retaining a very literal conception of time's unfolding, so too does a proper grasp of the resurrected life require dropping some, but not all, aspects of ordinary embodiment. Referring to the heavenly bodies, Origen observed elsewhere that 'it would be exceedingly stupid if anyone were to think that, like statues, it is only their outward appearance which has a human form and not their inner reality'.[10] Soul, to be soul, requires an appropriate body. It seems as though, despite the claims of later theological opponents, Origen did not teach that resurrection bodies of human beings would be spherical. Henry Chadwick makes a good case that Origen's real views are best preserved by Methodius:

> So the body has well been called a river, since strictly speaking its primary substance does not perhaps remain the same even for two days; yet Paul or Peter are always the same, not merely with respect to the soul . . ., because the form (*eidos*) which characterizes the body remains the same, so that the marks which are characteristic of the physical quality of Peter and Paul remain constant; it is because of the preserving of this quality that scars caused in our youth persist in our bodies, and so with other peculiarities, moles and similar marks.[11]

Chadwick goes on to summarize the import of Origen's views in a way that highlights how Origen's discussion of the resurrection body relates to the preservation of temporality without corruption that I noted above:

> It is this same physical form (that which characterizes Peter and Paul) which the soul will again possess in the resurrection, though the form will then be much improved; but it will not be exactly as it was on earth. *For just as a man has roughly the same appearance from infancy to old age, even if his features seem to undergo much change, so also there will be the same sort of relation between the earthly form and that to come.* It will be the same although it will also be vastly improved. The reason for this is that wherever the soul is it has to have a body suitable for the place where it finds itself; if we were going to live in the sea we should need fins and scales like fishes; if we are to live in heaven, then we shall need spiritual bodies. *The earthly form is not lost*, just as the form of Jesus did not become quite different on the mount of the Transfiguration.[12]

Chadwick concludes that Origen 'held to the continuance of personal identity in some form'.[13] I have suggested that, for Origen, allegorical reading enacted for the reader both sides of the tension in the passage Chadwick cites: on the one hand, the allegorical reader's commitment to the textuality of scripture corresponded to a commitment to the body; on the other hand, that reader's hope for an incorruptible (but not asomatic) existence meant that such embodiment, though it would endure, would do so 'in some form' unlike that with which the reader was more usually accustomed. The transformation of the reader's own embodiment from penalty to therapy was enacted precisely by means of this sort of allegorical reading of scripture, a reading in which the reader's misdirected *erôs*, like the text's seemingly unedifying letter, became redirected to that which would properly complete it.

NOTES

1 Anders Nygren, *Agape and Eros*, tr. P. S. Watson, Chicago, University of Chicago Press, 1982 (orig. 1953). See especially Part One, Chapter One, section VI: 'The Eros Type in Alexandrian Theology', pp. 349–92.

2 L. A. Kosman, 'Platonic Love', in W. H. Werkmeister (ed.), *Facets of Plato's Philosophy*, *Phronesis* supp., Assen, Van Gorcum, 1976, pp. 53–69.

3 *Origen: The Song of Songs, Commentary and Homilies*, tr. R. P. Lawson, Ancient Christian Writers, vol. 26, New York, Newman Press, 1956; Latin text in *GCS* 33.

4 Quae singula suo ordine scriptura haec continet totumque eius corpus mysticis formatur eloquiis.

5 My understanding of Stoic logic is based on A. A. Long's discussion in his *Hellenistic Philosophy: Stoics, Epicureans, Sceptics*, 2nd edn, Berkeley and Los Angeles, University of California Press, 1986, especially chapter 4, part III.

6 J. M. Rist, 'The Importance of Stoic Logic in the Contra Celsum', in H. J. Blumenthal and R. A. Markus (eds), *Neoplatonism and Early Christian Thought: Essays in Honor of A. H. Armstrong*, London, Variorum, 1981, p. 67.

7 *Origen: Commentary on the Gospel According to John Books 1–10*, tr. Ronald E. Heine, The Fathers of the Church, vol. 80, Washington, DC, Catholic University of America Press, 1989; Greek text in *GCS* 4. I have occasionally modified Heine's translation in order to highlight Origen's use of specific Greek terms.

8 *Origen: Contra Celsum*, tr. with introduction and notes by Henry Chadwick, Cambridge, Cambridge University Press, 1965. Greek text in *GCS* 1–2. I have occasionally modified Chadwick's translation in order to highlight Origen's use of specific Greek terms.

9 The following summary of Stoic thought is derived from A. A. Long, 'Language and Thought in Stoicism', in *Problems in Stoicism*, London, Athlone Press, 1971, pp. 75–113, esp. pp. 95–6.

10 Origen, *On Prayer* 31.3, quoted in Henry Chadwick, 'Origen, Celsus, and the Resurrection of the Body', *Harvard Theological Review* 41 (1948), p. 96.

11 Origen, ap. Method., *De resurrectione* 1.22, quoted by Chadwick, 'Origen, Celsus, and the Resurrection of the Body', p. 98.

12 Chadwick, 'Origen, Celsus, and the Resurrection of the Body', p. 99, my emphasis.

13 Chadwick, 'Origen, Celsus, and the Resurrection of the Body', p. 102.

Part II

READING THE FOURTH CENTURY

4

THE FOURTH CENTURY AS TRINITARIAN CANON

Michel René Barnes

RE-EVALUATIONS OF ARIANISM

The last fifteen years or so have seen a major re-evaluation of 'Arianism'; not the least of these re-evaluations is new doubt about the authenticity of the traditional category and designation 'Arian(ism)'. Arius' theology is now rehabilitated to this extent: it is clear that Arius' theology was not an alien theology, but a Christian theology which would have appeared familiar even to those who profoundly disagreed with it. It was a theology with antecedents and roots in earlier theologies. Arius' theology was, to use an over-worked metaphor, a late point along a 'trajectory' that went back at least two hundred years. This is not an altogether recent observation. French Augustinians in the first half of the twentieth century thought that fourth-century Logos theology was very much part of anti-Nicene ('Arian') theology, and in their eyes such providence fortuitously delayed the development of a real Logos theology – happy wound! – until Augustine, who could then offer Logos theology without fear of Arian taint. Pre-Augustinian Logos theology, then, was one trajectory along which Arian subordinationist theology travelled.[1]

My work in this chapter is intended to offer a synthetic account of the trinitarian debates following the Council of Nicaea 325 through to the Council of Constantinople 381. The first half of this chapter is largely synthetic since my purpose is to present the current understanding in scholarship of the development of canonical trinitarian theology in the midst of the 'Arian' controversy; thus the first half of the chapter is concerned with reporting the understanding of the path from Nicaea 325 to Constantinople 381 now current in research, an account which pivots on the status of Marcellus of Ancyra and the issue of 'Nicene' modalism. The general conclusions of this section are, I think, accepted at least generally by those whose field of research is fourth-century trinitarian controversies (which does not mean that everyone agrees on all the details). It is not until the second half of this chapter that I offer any original insights into the way in which Nicaea did and did not function as normative in the latter half of the fourth century.

47

This chapter is written with other issues in mind beyond those presented directly by recent scholarship on the fourth-century trinitarian controversies. Such contextual concerns include a pressing regard among some theologians for the content of an orthodox Christian faith. Such a regard is now trans-denominational, as some recent writings on both sides of the Atlantic make clear.[2] An almost apologetic concern for the substance of orthodoxy has led to a renewed interest in Christian tradition, especially the tradition of the early or patristic church. This concern is lent apologetic motivation by the end-trajectory of 'liberal' Christianity and by an encounter with the prob-lematic of 'pluralism' (insofar as these two are distinguishable).

NICAEA 325 AND THE CONDEMNATION OF ARIUS[3]

It has been typical until quite recently that accounts of the development of fourth-century trinitarian theology were built around two fundamental dramas: the first climaxed at Nicaea, the second climaxed at Constantinople. In between was a puzzling excursus if not a doctrinal intermission. A recent general history like Stuart Hall's exemplifies the effects of new scholarship on fourth-century trinitarian theology: his account is divided into four stages.[4] In the present account of the fourth-century trinitarian debates I will speak in terms of three stages in the debate (though without a fair or equal attention to each): first, the condemnation of Arius and Nicaea 325; second, the post-Nicaea assault on Marcellus; and third, the invention of Arianism. My account of the 'invention of Arianism' will serve as the oppor-tunity to discuss the re-interpretation of Nicaea 325 in the second half of the fourth century and its reception of a normative status in 381.

I will not rehearse the details of the events of the disagreement between Alexander, bishop of Alexandria, and one of his presbyters, Arius, that led to the Council of Nicaea. The origins of the creed that the council eventually promulgated are given scholarly description in J. N. D. Kelly's *Early Christian Creeds*[5] and R. P. C. Hanson's *The Search for the Christian Doctrine of God*. Broadly speaking, a text was produced which articulated in a general way the kind of beliefs the council participants felt to be at issue. To this credal text was added a list of anathemas, some of which condemn doctrines which are recognizably Arius' (from some stage of his career), and some of which have nothing whatsoever to do with doctrine. The council was concerned to express the doctrines that the Son has the same kind of exis-tence as the Father has, and that the Son takes his origin from the Father, but that nonetheless the Son is eternal and he is not a creature. These last two points show the pressure of the disagreement with Arius, as does the overall guiding principle of the theological language of the creed, namely the emphasis on the unique character of the origin of the Son from the Father. It is within this context that the term *homoousios* appears.

The earliest accounts of the process involved in selecting the word *homoousios* date from the mid to late 350s. Popular modern accounts attributing the term to either the Western Ossius or the Emperor now seem unlikely.[6] The fourth-century account puts the term squarely in the context of emphasizing the unique character of the origin of the Son from the Father. Alexander first sought out scriptural terms such as 'power of God', 'son of God' etc., and in each case Arius and Eusebius were able to offer exegesis which rendered the title equivocal, that is, one which applied to both the second person and all saved humans. When the Eusebians understood how completely Alexander meant to portray the unique character of the origin of the Son, they sought to identify Alexander's position with the universally condemned modalist position of a century earlier, which remained captioned in the tradition with the word *homoousios*. Alexander, finding at last a term that Arius had shown he could not equivocate on, must have jolted Arius and the Eusebians when he accepted the term, and thus *homoousios* made it into the creed.[7] Yet the connotations of the term would later prove to be the lightning rod which would attract all the residual uncomfortableness with the council. *Homoousios* had three strikes against it. First, it had a modalist history of use, and indeed figured in a third-century conciliar condemnation of a modalist theology. Second, and not unrelatedly, in its limited use it had had materialist connotations.[8] Third, it was nowhere to be found in Scripture. The context of the Nicene use of *homoousios* added yet a fourth strike, as it were.

Although Arius' epistolary invocation of the name of Lucian of Antioch has been used by scholars to argue that Arius' theology was fundamentally 'Antiochene' over against the Alexandrian theology of Alexander and (later) Athanasius,[9] what little we know of Lucian's theology suggests his own debt to Origen and re-enforces the conclusion that one takes directly from reading Arius' limited writings, namely, that Arius' theology is as Alexandrian as anyone's.[10] What such a statement means is that the argument between Arius and Alexander is an argument between two kinds of 'Origenists'.[11] Both Arius and Alexander deserve this classification to the extent that they both believed in the eternal, separate existence of the second person (unlike, for example, Justin or Hippolytus). It is this feature of Origen's trinitarian theology that is most significant for the fourth-century debates, namely the reality of the eternally separate existence of the second person. Origen's trinitarian theology has anachronistically been called 'Arian before Arius' precisely because Origen was willing to sacrifice unity language for the sake of maintaining individuality language. Yet the Nicene creed had very little to say about the reality of the separate existence of the second person; indeed, it anathematized a term that sometimes seemed to be associated with a theology of this separateness, namely *hypostasis*.[12] We know that the silence of the creed on this issue, coupled with the strength of its modalist associations, left queasy a number of those bishops who otherwise agreed that Arius had to be stopped. The bishops could accept the modalist-sounding creed for the sake of condemning Arius, but having succeeded at condemning him they envisioned no wider application of the creed. When Arius was indeed exiled, and the doctrine that 'the Son is a creature' was condemned, these bishops felt that the time was over for the extreme measures represented in the creed's language. The idea that the creed might have a wider application despite its modalist connotations was turned on its head when the creed was promoted by Marcellus of Ancyra, seemingly because of its modalist connotations.[13]

In order to suggest what might have seemed modalist about the creed of Nicaea, let me offer the following analysis of the creed, an analysis somewhat simplified because of its use of thematic categories rather than the categories strictly of the era and the literature. First, let us allow that there exists in Christianity two insights about God; the first is God's unity or singularity, articulated above all in the prayer 'Hear, O Israel, your God is one'; the second insight is that there is a diversity about God, manifested, for example, in events such as the baptism at the Jordan or Pentecost, or even when Scripture says 'Let *us* make . . . ' or 'The Lord said to my Lord . . . '. By the fourth century – if not much earlier – each of these two insights finds expression is a certain use of language when speaking about the Trinity. Doctrines of the unity in God are expressed using the *same* language of Father and Son: the Father is God, the Son is God; the Father is creator, the Son is creator; and the Father is Life, the Son is Life, etc. The *diversity* in God is expressed using *relational* language: original, image; creator, first creature (or, more piously, a creature unlike any other creature); and lord, servant (or messenger).[14]

Each insight, with its associated language, is not always valued equally with the other, and too emphatic use of one language triggers concern among those whose sympathy lies with the other insight and the other language. Arius' sympathy is clearly in the 'diversity' camp, with its accompanying strong preference for relational language. The original crisis in Alexandria seems to have been triggered when Arius heard his bishop going too far in applying the 'same' language: Arius thought that by saying 'Always Father, always Son' Alexander was calling both the Father and the Son 'unbegotten' or 'uncaused', while, in fact, Alexander was anxious to attribute at least the 'same' language of 'eternal' to both. Another example may be found in Eunomius' *Apology*, chapter 19. Eunomius recognizes the authority of the traditional attribution of the same titles 'Light' and 'Life' to Father and Son, and to refute the claim to unity implied by the use of the same titles for both persons he re-interprets these titles as (implied) relational titles: if Father and Son are both called 'Light' it is only because 'Light' applied to the Father really means 'Unbegotten Light' and 'Light' applied to the Son really means 'Begotten Light'. In this way Eunomius restates 'same' trinitarian language, with its implicit theology of divine unity, as 'relational' trinitarian language, with its implicit theology of divine diversity.

When one turns to the creed of Nicaea one finds precious little 'relation-ship' language expressing divine 'diversity': the creed looks like a document from the 'same' and unity-emphasizing camp – not surprisingly so, since it is precisely that, written to exclude an unacceptable doctrine of divine diver-sity expressed in some equally unacceptable language of divine relationality. The creed says that both Father and Son are 'God', both are 'Light', and both are 'true God'. Moreover, in the creed the unity theology of God typically articulated in what I am here calling 'same' language is expressed explicitly in *ousia* doctrines: 'of the *ousia*' may sound now to express a relationship (*'from* the essence') but it was at the time universally taken by supporters and critics alike to express divine unity. An identical understanding attaches to the famous phrase '*homoousios* with the Father' and may fairly be judged to have been the intention behind the phrase: the unity theology intimated in the use of the same language – God, Light, true God – of both Father and Son is expressed and explained in the creed's *ousia* language.[15] The creed was intended to be a strong statement of divine unity, and the kind of language it uses reflects that intention.

THE POST-NICAEA ATTACK OF MARCELLUS

The theology of Marcellus made explicit the very implications feared by most of those who had condemned Arius and signed the creed, with the result that the immediate problem after Nicaea was not the subordina-tionism of Arius' theology but the modalism seemingly condoned by the language of the creed. We have evidence – for example, Eusebius of Caesarea's *Ecclesiastical Theology* and *Against Marcellus* – to suggest that the Marcellan position became a problem very quickly. Similarly, we have evidence – Athanasius' *On the Incarnation* – that with the condemnation of Arius even Nicenes considered the issue of Arius settled and so moved on to other topics as if he no longer existed. After Nicaea the object of concern and condemnation is Marcellus, not Arius. The long litany in the East of conciliar condemnations of Marcellus, appearing almost annually and stretching into the early 350s, makes clear the depth of the antipathy towards a Marcellan reading of Nicaea. Such conciliar condemnations also reveal the enduring suspicion that Nicaea's theology was modalist after all.

Marcellus was the spokesman for those whose theology owed almost nothing to Origen. Marcellus, a 'Greek', emphasized the unity of the divinity over all else, and he seems to have asserted his doctrine most purely in a denial of any attribution of 'two' (much less 'three') to the godhead. Marcellus denied that we could speak of two *ousiai*, two *hypostases* or two *dunameis* in God; to use any such language was to imply that there were two divine things, two Gods. Marcellus' trinitarian theology is wholly centred in a Logos theology, in which divine unity is described by analogy to the unity between a speaker and the speaker's word: the word exists 'within' and then it 'goes out' – is uttered. That 'going out' was a moment of creation, not – most emphatically a 'not' – because the Logos is created, but because creation is an act of the Logos, or more precisely, an act of God via His Logos. First Genesis puts it rather succinctly: 'And God said "Let there be ... " '. The title 'son' only applies at the incarnation and only to the incarnated Logos. Marcellus' trinitarian theology begins with a divine Monad and ends with that Monad restored: in the time between the initial and final divine Monad – that time known as the *oeconomia* – is the temporary activity of the divine as Son and Spirit. Marcellus' theology was captioned – at least by his opponents – by the slogan that the reign of the Son would come to an end, just as his separate existence would come to an end. The desire to condemn Marcellus' infamy left its trace in the creed of 381, where the belief is affirmed (pace Marcellus) that the Son's 'kingdom will have no end'. The unstated corollary is that neither will the Son's separate existence 'have an end'.

The Marcellan claim on Nicaea seems not to have been simply a development after the fact, as though Marcellus made a claim on an event which was otherwise unconnected to his sphere of theological influence. Recent scholarship comparing the creed of the Council of Antioch, early in 325 (which promulgated doctrines favourable to Alexander and condemned Arius), with the creed of the Council of Nicaea, late in 325, has suggested that the very wording of the creed of Nicaea bears the theological fingerprint of Marcellus.[16] Alastair Logan's conclusions to this effect are worth quoting in full: the creed of Constantinople,

> in an attempt to remove any hints of Sabellianism in the creed of Nicaea, not only replaced the Nicene wording [of 'begotten of the Father before all ages'] with the traditional form ... but equally removed the associated gloss *ek tes ousias*. The two belong together and imply, at least to Marcellus and his party, that there is one *hypostasis* or *ousia* in the Godhead.[17]

The argument in support of Marcellan background to Nicaea depends in part upon the 1857 discovery of a letter from the Emperor revealing that originally the council was to be held at Ancyra, the episcopal see of Marcellus, but the site was changed to Nicaea.

In this century historians of dogma have had trouble explaining the way that Nicaea disappeared so quickly from the theological stage after 325. There is an odd doubling here – for there has been a similar lack of awareness of the significance of Marcellus. The works written against Marcellus by Eusebius of Caesarea, which are foundational for the doctrinal consciousness of the Eastern church from 330 to 357, even now have not been translated from the Greek (although, happily, we at least have a critical edition of *Ecclesiastical Theology* and *Against Marcellus*). The reason why the years from 330 until 362 are described so oddly is because until recently – and by 'recently' I mean in the last fifteen years – Athanasius' post-355 accounts of the controversy have been taken literally.

THE INVENTION OF ARIANISM AND THE REINTERPRETATION AND NORMATIVE STATUS OF NICAEA 325

The idea that there was a post-Nicene 'Arian conspiracy' run by closeted Arians who secretly believed that the Son was a creature seems initially to have been promoted by Marcellus in his polemic against those who opposed him. The earliest example we have of this kind of argument being made is Marcellus' letter to Julius of Rome, written in 341, while the exiled Marcellus was in Rome appealing for the Bishop's support. By coincidence Athanasius was also in Rome at the same time, seeking help against his own exile at the hands of Eusebius of Nicomedia. While Marcellus may have consistently understood Nicaea and *homoousios* to have a broad normative intention, a careful reading of Athanasius' works reveals that it took him almost twenty years to come to this understanding of the significance of Nicaea, while he took almost another ten years to fasten upon *homoousios* as the *sine qua non* of Nicene theology. If it seems striking for contemporary scholars to propose that Nicaea slowly acquired its authority only after shedding its modalist associations, then the suggestion that that paragon of Nicene theology, Athanasius, did not always regard Nicaea as authoritative is breathtaking. But a very strong case can be made for this position, and I would say that this judgement is now accepted among most of those who specialize in this field.

The presupposition that one tests for the relative orthodoxy of fourth-century Greek trinitarian theology by comparing its content to Athanasius' as the 'norm' for this theology has had a rich manifold of expressions. Harnack, of course, made Athanasius' interpretation of Nicaea the normative one, and set about unfavourably comparing the Cappadocian Constantinople of 381 with the Athanasian Nicaea of 325. His infamous conclusion was that the faith of Nicaea had been hijacked by the 'semi-Arian' theology of Basil of Ancyra and Gregory of Nyssa.[18] This fundamental positioning of Athanasius by Harnack remains with us, I think, in the assumption that the distinctive substance of Athanasius' theology must have been known by the Cappadocians and that it must have directly influenced their own theology, such as one sees in works by T. F. Torrance.[19] This presupposition is a scholarly commonplace; unfortunately we have no real basis for this judgement since we have no detailed understanding of what (and when) the Cappadocians had read of Athanasius (if they had read anything).[20] Prestige's claim that *Letter* (*Ep.*) 9 is evidence that Basil was influenced by a reading of Athanasius' *De synodis* can hardly be regarded as proven.[21]

A related expression of the presupposition of Athanasius' centrality is the tendency to represent theology in the first half of the fourth century in the person of Athanasius at the expense of Eusebius of Caesarea. For our purposes here the most important effect of the promotion of Athanasius' significance at the expense of Eusebius' is the way in which, until recently, authority has settled on Athanasius' understanding that the immediate post-Nicene trinitarian crisis was occasioned by Arius' theology instead of Eusebius' understanding that the immediate post-Nicene trinitarian crisis was occasioned by Marcellus of Ancyra's theology. Among Athanasius' greatest polemical triumphs was his development of and promulgation of the rhetorical strategy of identifying his opponents as 'Arians'. It is this very distinctive feature of Athanasius' polemical theology that I will turn to now.

Athanasius' preferred argument against his opponents had two related parts. First, Athanasius identified the varieties of Origenist theology (as I defined it above) in the 340s and 350s with the theology of Arius; second, Athanasius promoted Nicaea generally (and later, *homoousios* specifically) as the touchstone of trinitarian orthodoxy as intended by the Church in 325. The strength of Athanasius' polemic (as articulated by Epiphanius) has meant that until recently polemically charged terms like 'semi-Arian' and 'neo-Arian' passed largely unchallenged into the vernacular of dogmatic history. The recognition that the roots of the characterization of non- and anti-Nicenes as 'Arians' lie in Athanasius' polemic is a fruitful one because it allows us to see that the doctrinal connection between the theology of Arius in the 320s and those who strongly opposed Nicaea in the 350s is neither obvious nor certain. If one does not *assume* Arius' influence it suddenly becomes very difficult to *prove* Arius' influence, particularly if one is suggesting a consistent pattern of Arius' influence on later generations. This is not to suggest that there is no connection whatsoever between Arius and those later called 'Arians', but that whatever connections there are give little support for the idea that anti-Nicene theology descends from, or develops out of, Arius' theology, as if homoian and heterousian theologies are later stages in 'Arian theology'.

The second of Athanasius' arguments against his opponents has to do with the emphasis he came to place, over time, on the creed of Nicaea as the canon of trinitarian theology. Within the general development of Athanasius' understanding of Nicaea there is the specific feature of his attachment to the term *homoousios*. Athanasius' earliest polemical text against Arius and the 'Arians' is the *First Oration Against the Arians*, which was written not less than fifteen years after Nicaea. In the intervening years Athanasius had been concerned primarily with ecclesiastical matters: his own elevation to the see of Alexandria occurred with difficulty, and there remained the enduring local problem of the Melitians. The success of Nicaea in suppressing Arius personally, as well as the most distinctive and egregious of his doctrines, left the field open for many bishops to reject the implicit modalist connotations of the language of the creed, especially as these connotations were made explicit by Marcellus. Both Athanasius and Marcellus turned to Rome in the aftermath of Eusebius of Nicomedia's renewed ascendancy, their own exiles and the polarization that occurred after Constantine's death. As already noted above, while in Rome Marcellus wrote an epistolary defence of his faith for bishop Julius.

Rome is thus the site for the development of the fundamental features of anti-Arian polemic. Most of these features are found in Marcellus' letter to Julius, where he casts his opponents as those who are out to overturn Nicaea.[22] The salient doctrines of these anti-Nicenes are recognizably Arius': that the Son is not God's very Word, Wisdom or Power, that the Father pre-exists the Son, that there was a time when the Son was not, and that the Son is a creature and a thing made. This letter must stand as the first polemic against 'Arian' (so-called) anti-Nicenes. Athanasius' *First Oration* takes the apologetic categories Marcellus utilizes but sets them in an explicitly anti-Arian context.[23] According to Athanasius, he is opposed, for doctrinal reasons, by followers of Arius, who, like Arius, believe that there was a time when the Son was not, that the Son is not God's very Word, Wisdom or Power, and that the Son is a creature and thing made – a list that very much resembles Marcellus'. We may note in passing that at this time Athanasius, like Marcellus, characterizes his opponents as anti-Nicenes without ever actually feeling himself compelled to embrace or even hardly mention *homoousios*. Athanasius' time in Rome completes a transformation begun, I suggest, at the council in Tyre in 335, where he had been condemned and exiled. Tyre was not concerned with doctrinal issues, but the result of Tyre was, we might say, to radicalize Athanasius' theology, for at Tyre Athanasius suffers at the hands of two young central European bishops, Valens and Ursacius. I will return to these two bishops shortly.

Marcellus' letter also deserves recognition for one other feature beyond its articulation of the premise of an enduring anti-Nicene Arian theology, namely, the immediate success of the letter: Julius not only buys Marcellus' argument, he acts upon his purchase. Rome is on the side of Marcellus and Athanasius, and they are all on the side of Nicaea. This almost obvious fact should be emphasized, for it needs to be taken seriously, if only to provoke an explanation of why exactly Marcellus' argument works with Julius.[24] Hanson remarks, apropos of Athanasius' appeal to Julius, that the bishop of Rome had always supported the bishop of Alexandria when he could; unfortunately Hanson's remark stands without explanation.[25]

With Marcellus and Athanasius we have significant representation in Greek theology of an understanding of the Trinity that strongly emphasized the unity of God even to the point – in the case of Marcellus – of sacrificing the reality of the distinct persons. We can make such a statement without collapsing the differences between Marcellus' and Athanasius' trinitarian theologies at least because Athanasius was unable to bring himself ever to condemn Marcellus, a fact which fed the fears of those (such as Basil of Caesarea) who supported Nicaea but saw its difficulties. The positions of Marcellus and Athanasius were not accepted by most Greek bishops: Marcellus' doctrines were consistently condemned. Athanasius' reputation as the defender of orthodoxy depends in part upon later developments: the doctrines that he accepted at Alexandria 362, changes in Imperial favour and the continued support of the bishop of Rome allowed Athanasius' theology to be identified with the received theology of Nicaea–Constantinople. Other Western theologies, such as Hilary's, resembled Athanasius' in their polemical form, but not necessarily in their content (as I will show shortly). If we talk about an East–West division in fourth-century trinitarian theology we must include Alexandria with Rome and the West (so that 'West' cannot equal 'Latin').[26] Moreover, we cannot locate the emphasis on divine unity (so often associated with Augustine) as a later development; it already belongs to the first stage of the life of the creed (but not to the first stage of the life of the controversy: Alexander's theology was not modalist, and Nicaea did not originally mean what Marcellus – and perhaps Athanasius – said it meant).

WESTERN AND EASTERN ANTI-ARIAN POLEMICAL FORMS

As my final comment on the two 'Roman' works by Marcellus and Athanasius, I note that from this time onwards we can be sure that something concrete and specific of Arius' doctrines was known to the Roman Church and indeed to many of the Western churches.[27] There was a pronounced literary hunger for Arian texts in the Western Church which results in the interesting fact that Arius' writings, specifically his letters, are better attested to in Latin polemical writings than they are in Greek (other than in Athanasius' writings). Phoebadeus in Gaul knows at least part of Arius' *Letter to Alexander of Alexandria*;[28] Hilary quotes this letter *in toto* twice in his *De trinitate* (*De fide*).[29] Marius Victorinus, writing at about the same time, has Arius' *Letter to Eusebius of Nicomedia* and most of Eusebius of Nicomedia's *Letter to Paulinus of Tyre*. Last but not least is the fact that even Augustine knows passages from Arius and likes to show that he knows them (as at *De trinitate* VI.1). This kind of quoting of Arius is characteristic of the way Athanasius and Latin Nicenes write trinitarian polemics.

The same cannot be said for Eastern pro-Nicene polemicists generally, of which the Cappadocians may serve as the most important examples: they almost never quote from Arius, nor do they find it useful to use 'Arian' texts to identify their opponents with an earlier stage of anti-Nicene theology. Gregory of Nyssa, for example, argues at length that Eunomius' theology owes to Manichaeism, but he never works through Eunomius' theology to show that it resembles Arius'. The Cappadocians do not need to be the authors of the *Contra Sabellianos et Arium et Anomeos* and *Adversus Arium et Sabellium* for these writings to serve as useful evidence of polemical texts where Arius' writings are not quoted.[30] Instead these two works treat Arius only in terms of the need to avoid the opposite errors of Sabellianism and Arianism. Gregory of Nazianzus speaks of the 'Arians' in same way in the only reference to Arianism in his five *Theological Orations*.[31] This kind of rhetorical or formal pairing off of Arius and Sabellius as two opposite heresies to be avoided appears consistently in pro-Nicene literature from one end of the Empire to the other: Phoebadeus uses it in France, in 358,[32] and the Cappadocians use it twenty (and more) years later. The fact that the Cappadocians show no knowledge of anything beyond stereotypical expressions of Arius' doctrines leads me to conclude that the Cappadocians had never read anything by Arius. Arius' few writings, in particular the *Thalia*, may have had very limited circulation east of Alexandria.[33] Indeed, I doubt that the *Thalia* had any significant circulation outside of Athanasian polemical redaction of that text.

By contrast, we find in Athanasius' *De synodis* what can serve as the prototype of the mature development of his 'Western' style of anti-Arian, pro-Nicene polemic. Its form includes providing a dossier, with running commentary, of text(s) by Arius, a reduction of non-Nicene conciliar theologies to Arius' theology, an emphasis on Rome's (often Julius') role in recognizing orthodoxy, and an identification of the Nicene faith with *homoousios* through a sustained defence of that term. We can say that just as the primitive redaction of Arius' *Thalia* in the *First Oration* mirrors Athanasius' groping with a polemical form and a positive restatement of Nicene theology (with only a symbolic or partial appropriation of that creed), so the sophisticated redaction of Arius' *Thalia* in *De synodis* mirrors Athanasius' successful development of a comprehensive polemical form and a textually grounded interpretation of Nicene theology through a complete appropriation of the creed by identifying it with the theology of *homoousios*.

However, one distinctive feature of Western anti-Arian polemic emerges if we go one step further and begin to compare Athanasius' polemic in *De synodis* with Hilary's polemic in his work of the same title. Hilary's purpose in his *De synodis* seems at first glance to be almost the opposite of Athanasius': Hilary does *not* want to reduce the authors of the various conciliar creeds to 'Arians' – rather, he wants to find something like anonymous Nicenes in their theology. But, as is well known, he does ultimately base his articulation of the Nicene doctrine on a correct understanding of *homoousios* (which is not to imply that Hilary's understanding is the same as

Athanasius'). Yet the most important common feature between Hilary's *De synodis* and Athanasius' is the way their arguments begin. Athanasius' *De synodis* begins by describing the creed of the Council of Rimini as an expression of *the Arian theology of Valens and Ursacius*. Similarly, Hilary's *De synodis* begins by describing the creed of the Council of Sirmium as an expression of *the Arian theology of Valens and Ursacius*. If, as seems likely, Hilary wrote his *De synodis* independently of Athanasius, then the common attack on Valens and Ursacius as 'Arians' is striking and suggests just how important yet another council – Serdica, 343 (342?) – was for the formation of Western pro-Nicene polemics. Why the mention of Valens and Ursacius should lead us to think of the anti-Arian Council of Serdica will be clear shortly.

First we must note that the link made by Athanasius and Hilary between Valens and Ursacius and Arius is not mere fantasy: Arius was exiled to Illyrica, the home region of Valens and Ursacius. The demonstration of a doctrinal genealogy going back to Arius by uncovering the mediating influence of Valens and Ursacius is a feature of Western pro-Nicene polemic in several sources from the fifties: aside from Athanasius and Hilary one thinks of Phoebadeus and Marius Victorinus. There is a certain power if not irony in Athanasius' use of this genealogy, since it plays to his own humiliation at their hands at Tyre, but interestingly it is not a connection he made all along, since these two bishops are not referred to in the *Orations* against Arius. What intervened between the *Orations* and *De synodis* was the Western creed from the Council of Serdica, which describes Valens and Ursacius as 'two vipers begotten from the asp of Arius'. Serdica was not a pro-Nicene council, and thus represents another tradition of Western anti-Arian polemic which pro-Nicene polemicists later adapt for their own purposes. Yet Serdica, like the twin *De synodis* of the 350s, reminds us that the use of Valens and Ursacius as types of Arius is a feature of the Western pro-Nicene, anti-Arian polemic of the fifties and early sixties, and no later: even polemicists from the seventies as indebted to Athanasius as the Latin-speaking Ambrose and the Greek-speaking Epiphanius no longer refer to Valens and Ursacius in this way. Epiphanius is the most interesting example, given his clear polemical interests and his overwhelming debt to Athanasius: although Epiphanius writes in detail of the roles of Valens and Ursacius at the Council of Tyre, he does not mention them as links in the doctrinal chain of Arianism.

THE NORMATIVE STATUS OF *HOMOOUSIOS*

The final general point I want to treat in this context lies in an account of the origin of the term *homoousios* in the Nicene creed that is commonly found in Western pro-Nicene polemic. Athanasius tells the story that the word was used in the creed after Arius and Eusebius of Nicomedia used it themselves to describe what they could not accept in the doctrines they heard being suggested by Alexander.[34] This story is told to counter the effective anti-Nicene criticism that *homoousios* is unscriptural; the critique from Scripture loses credibility over time as anti-Nicenes of a wide variety settle their own theologies on an equally unscriptural term, *agennetos*.[35] I rehearse Athanasius' account of the credal use of the term *homoousios* because of what the account reveals about the development of positive interest in the term, namely that pro-Nicene anti-Arian interest in the term *homoousios* is in reaction to the way in which anti-Nicenes so clearly, consistently and vigorously rejected the term. Hanson directly relates Athanasius' interest in *homoousios* to his reaction to the Second Creed of Sirmium (357), 'which explicitly denied the propriety of using ousia in connection with the Son's relation to the Father'.[36] I want to generalize Hanson's observation. While positive polemical discussions of *homoousios* are limited to the sphere of Athanasius and Latin pro-Nicenes, anti-Nicene criticism of the term *homoousios* abounds across the Empire continuously throughout the trinitarian controversies.

The attacks on *homoousios* in Athanasius' milieu are evident, so I will illustrate the enduring character of anti-Nicene attacks on *homoousios* through examples from the other end of the Mediterranean, during the years from 360 to 380. First, Eunomius' rejection of *homoousios* is clear and emphatic in his *Apology* of 360 (a text we can regard as functionally homoian), even though it would be rare to find anyone in that part of the Empire who was actually promoting a *homoousios*-based theology at the time. However, the most dramatic example of the point I am making can be found by examining the only reference to *homoousios* in Book 1 of Gregory of Nyssa's *Contra Eunomium* (written in three books dated from 380 to 383). This use of *homoousios* occurs in Gregory's story of his brother Basil's confrontation with an emissary from Valens, the homoian Emperor. Valens, the emissary says, wishes for peace and would be satisfied if the one word, *homoousios*, were removed from the creed. Here, as is typical in Cappadocian polemics, the word *homoousios* enters the text in the mouth of those who oppose it.[37] But unlike the Greek Westerner Athanasius and the Latins, the Cappadocians do not respond to anti-Nicene attacks on *homoousios* by making the term the centrepiece of their own polemic; indeed, *homoousios* makes almost no appearance in the Cappadocian writings devoted to anti-Eunomian polemic. A quick analysis of the incidence of key words in Gregory of Nyssa's writings will make this point plainly.

The word *homoousios* occurs twenty-five times in Gregory's corpus now indexed from the GNO;[38] by contrast, *homoousios* occurs almost three times as often in Athanasius' *De synodis* alone. Of the twenty-five appearances, twelve of the citations are in Gregory's work against Apollinarius; nine are in the *Contra Eunomium*. Of these latter nine, three references are in the voice of an anti-Nicene, Eunomius or Valens, and four are used without any trinitarian connotations at all. That leaves two, which occur together in Book 3.

The use of *homoousios* by Gregory in his argument in Book 3 can be summarized thus: *homoousios* appears in a *reductio ad absurdum* argument by Gregory to show that Eunomius' thought leads not only to the Son being *homoousios* with the activity that produced Him, but all of creation being *homoousios* with that same productive activity. A similar pattern of use can be observed in Gregory's references to the Council of Nicaea: Gregory mentions Nicaea only five times in all of his writings; three of these references are in his polemic against Apollinarius, none of them are in a polemical text against Eunomius. No doctrinal use of *homoousios* is made in Gregory's texts belonging to the genre of a polemic against Eunomius, and, similarly, Nicaea is never invoked in these texts as the norm. However, both *homoousios* and Nicaea do figure in Gregory's other writings, such as his letters and his polemics against Apollinarius, showing that Gregory did not avoid this kind of language entirely. Let me note in passing that this reticence on Gregory's part cannot simply be attributed to the time separating him from Nicaea. Gregory's Western contemporary, Ambrose, regularly invokes Nicaea in his *De fide*, where he identifies its theology with *homoousios*, and where he continues the polemical tactic of reducing contemporary anti-Nicenes to Arians by mixing quotations from Arius and from contemporary anti-Nicenes.[39]

The significance of a similar ambivalence about *homoousios* that can be found in Basil's *Contra Eunomium* (dated to 363) has largely passed unnoticed.[40] Prestige argued for the Basilian authorship of *Ep.* 361 and 362 on the basis of the similarities of language between *Ep.* 361 and *Contra Eunomium* I.15, yet what is striking about those passages is that *Ep.* 361 includes a use of *homoousios* while *Contra Eunomium* does not.[41] Given that *Ep.* 361 is dated to 360–362 by those who accept its Basilian authorship, that is to say, that it is dated precisely to the time immediately before Basil published his *Contra Eunomium*, then their hypothesis requires us to conclude that Basil accepted a *homoousios* theology and then declined to apply it to his polemic against Eunomius, that is, the *Contra Eunomium*. I have argued this very point, that Cappadocian polemical theology does not build upon the Nicene use of *homoousios* (unlike Athanasius and Latin pro-Nicenes). The question still remains for further study as to whether the circular letter sent eastward from the Council of Alexandria, 362, had any significant readership in the East at all. It would have arrived just as Basil of Caesarea was writing his *Contra Eunomium*, yet that text shows no awareness of the letter.

In short, while I do not mean to deny that the Cappadocians recognized and expressed their own theological allegiance to the creed of Nicaea, including the use of *homoousios*, their polemical writings in favour of this theology do not bring into play either the creed in general or *homoousios* in particular. Furthermore, the rhetoric of their polemics makes no significant and detailed use of Arius' theology or literary output. Cappadocian polemic is unlike the Western Nicene polemics typified by Athanasius and various Latins in both these regards. We have then at least two models or genres of pro-Nicene polemic, namely, the Western Rome-Alexandria genre, and the Eastern, typically Cappadocian, genre. I would expect that the Cappadocian model of polemic will be found to be basically characteristic of Eastern pro-Nicene polemics, especially wherever Athanasius' writings have limited (or no) circulation.[42]

There is no reason to assume that the use or non-use of *homoousios* in polemical texts can function as a universal indicator of the presence or absence of 'pro-Nicene' sentiments.[43] Ignoring for the moment the difficult and unsettled question as to what objective links exist between the theology of Arius and Eusebius of Nicomedia, on the one hand, and anti-Nicenes of the 350s and thereafter, on the other, we cannot assume that the title 'Arian' is operative even rhetorically in all controversies with anti-Nicenes. Contemporary scholarship's own reflexive sympathy as Westerners for the Roman-Alexandrian account of fourth-century trinitarian controversies has led scholars to give the terms of this account a universality that they never had in the original controversies.

The standard commonly accepted division of Latin–Greek cannot still be given credibility. Yet to know exactly what constructive possibilities the loss of the cliché of the Latin and Greek models of trinitarian theology opens up first requires an understanding of how the existence of the contrasting paradigms have served as a necessary presupposition for modern theology. How is the modern understanding of trinitarian theology predicated upon the opposition dramatized (fictionalized?) in the Greek and Latin epitomes? We are almost at the point where we can say that modern theology, needing the doctrinal opposition between 'Greek' and 'Latin' trinitarian theologies, invented it. Forensically then, what was (is) that need? Rather than treating de Régnon's paradigm as a description of fourth- and fifth-century trinitarian theologies, we should imagine it as a symptom or a structural prerequisite of modern thinking about trinitarian theologies.[44]

The loss of the divisions of trinitarian theology into the two models, Latin and Greek, means, as a minimum, that we have to give up any account of the development of trinitarian doctrine which takes literally a rhetoric of logical succession or sequential replacement – a point Hanson has already made on other grounds.[45] When an Eastern reinterpretation of Nicaea in the 370s was added to a Western reinterpretation of Nicaea in the 360s[46] and to the vigorous pro-Nicene polemic of Alexandria and the churches in Rome and Gaul, these together produced a dominant consensus in favour of a rein-terpreted Nicene creed.[47] In 380/381 the Western component of the consensus obtained support for a faith descriptively attached to the creed of Nicaea, particularly in its use of *homoousios*. The Eastern component of the consensus obtained support for a faith that in content went beyond Nicaea, particularly in the doctrinal significance of *hypostasis*.[48] The West got the official language; the East got the official interpretation. In the end, Nicaea 325 became orthodoxy only when its potential cost to real distinctions was contained at Constantinople 381, and I would argue that this is how it should be understood today. Fourth-century trinitarian orthodoxy was the net product of rejecting modalism's claim as the necessary cost for defeating subordinationism.

THE SIGNIFICANCE OF THE PROCESS

More than perhaps any other comparably important texts, the creeds of Nicaea and Constantinople present substantial difficulties for any serious reader. So much of their meaning, their sense, is carried 'off the page', as it were, in the context. The key to grasping the correct reading of the texts must be found in words that do not appear in the creeds at all. Indeed, another way of describing the process that I have been outlining here is to describe how the term *hypostasis* changed from being a term Nicaea anathematized to be the term necessary for an orthodox understanding of the creed of Nicaea – all without ever appearing in the creeds of Nicaea or of Constantinople. Anyone with even a minimal knowledge of trinitarian theology knows that the orthodox formula is 'three persons in one nature'. Finding the doctrine – much less the language – of 'three persons' in the creed is more tenuous than one might imagine beforehand. Without a good sense of the context within which these creeds were produced, without a sense of how the words that *are* there relate to the word which is *not* there, the doctrine these texts came to embody and symbolize cannot be read off them. For example, when, at a much later time, Thomas Aquinas wanted to anchor in holy tradition 'person' as a trinitarian term he had to turn to Augustine as his most ancient authority, since orthodoxy presupposed the term but did not supply it in the creeds.[49] The need for a correct reading of these creeds leads us, at least, to seek out that context, those words, that tradition, which the authoritative transmission of those creeds presupposes. The creeds function 'canonically' only when they communicate not simply the literal terms of the creeds themselves but, as well, when they communicate and mandate the interpretation which, over time, lifted these creeds out from among their 'peers' and made them normative.

Nothing that I have said in this chapter removes the significance of the creeds of Nicaea and Constantinople generally or the place of *homoousios* specifically as a canon of Christian belief. I have argued that these creeds and *homoousios* have to be understood in a way which excludes the simple 325 modalist understanding, since the Nicene creed became normative only through the process of excluding the modalist content. Any application or development of the creed which omits the dialectical content (between unity in God and the reality of distinction in God) is false to the canonical creed.

NOTES

1 A related judgement has been argued in R. P. C. Hanson's last work, *The Search for the Christian Doctrine of God*, Edinburgh, T. & T. Clark, 1988: Nicene theology put an end to a long and honoured way of speaking when it turned from Logos theology. As a quick glance comparing the creeds of Antioch 325 and Nicaea 325 will reveal, the title Logos is conspicuous by its absence in the Nicene symbol. As this chapter makes clear, Logos theology was not solely the possession of anti-Nicene theology; Marcellus of Ancyra had an equal investment in a trinitarian use of Logos.

2 See, for example, S. Mark Heim (ed.), *Faith to Creed*, Grand Rapids, MI, Eerdmans, 1991; Frederick Norris, *The Apostolic Faith: Protestants and Roman Catholics*, Collegeville, MN, Liturgical Press, 1992; Thomas C. Oden, *Systematics*, 3 vols, San Francisco, Harper & Row, 1987–92; and Robert L. Wilken, *Remembering the Christian Past*, Grand Rapids, MI, Eerdmans, 1995. In the United Kingdom there has been a highly visible interest in the normative character of early Christianity, as one sees in the spectrum of theology typified by the writings of, for example, T. F. Torrance, Maurice Wiles and Rowan Williams. For a new approach in Britain to traditional sources for a renewed understanding of orthodox Christian faith, see John Milbank, *The Word Made Strange*, Oxford, Blackwell, 1997.

3 For the approach that I take in summarizing the triumph of Nicaea at Constantinople, i.e. Nicaea's canonical status via Constantinople, I am particularly indebted to four articles (alphabetically): Patrick Gray, ' "The Select Fathers": Canonizing the Patristic Past', *SP* 22 (1989), pp. 21–36; André de Halleux, 'La réception du symbole oecuménique, de Nicée à Chalcédoine', *Ephemerides Theologicae Lovanienses* 61 (1985), pp. 5–47; R. P. C. Hanson, 'The Achievment of Orthodoxy in the Fourth Century AD', in R. Williams (ed.), *The Making of Orthodoxy*, Cambridge, Cambridge University Press, 1989, pp. 142–56; and A. H. B. Logan, 'Marcellus of Ancyra and the Councils of AD 325: Antioch, Ancyra, and Nicaea', *JThS* n.s. 43 (1992), pp. 428–46.

4 Stuart Hall, *Doctrine and Practice in the Early Church*, Grand Rapids, MI, Eerdmans, 1991. Hall treats the trinitarian controversies in the four consecutive chapters entitled 'Arius and the Council of Nicaea', 'Councils and Controversies: 327–361', 'Towards Synthesis: 361–378' and 'Theodosius I and the Council of Constantinople'.

5 J. N. D. Kelly, *Early Christian Creeds*, 3rd edn, London, Longmans, 1972.

6 The thesis that the term *homoousios* owes to the Emperor (directly or indirectly) seems unlikely in light of the fact that its Western pro-Nicenes defenders never turn to such a defence when faced with four decades of anti-Nicene criticism of the word.

7 See *De decretis* V.20 (as well as the 'Athanasian' *Ad Afros* VI). We have no reason to suppose that Alexander or any Alexandrian originally proposed the term: Alexander's letters, for example, never use the term *homoousios*.

8 Hilary of Poitiers rehearses these objections to *homoousios* in his *De trinitate* IV.4. In the second half of this chapter I will return to the larger polemical significance of the fact of Hilary's interest in *homoousios*.

9 A theory developed by John Henry Newman in *Arians of the Fourth Century*, promulgated by Gwatkin, and articulated in modern scholarship by T. E. Pollard.

10 This is Rowan Williams' argument in *Arius: Heresy and Tradition*, London, Darton, Longman and Todd, 1987, although Maurice Wiles laid the groundwork for it in 'In Defence of Arius', *JThS* n.s. 13 (1962), pp. 339–47, by

arguing that Arius' theology had to be understood first in terms of its local setting, i.e. Alexandria.

11 Hanson pointed out that Origen's influence on fourth-century trinitarian theologies is not a direct influence, but rather an influence mediated by Eusebius of Caesarea. The 'Origenism' of those involved in the controversies from 341 onwards is the 'Origenism' of Eusebius. See 'The Influence of Origen on the Arian Controversy', in L. Lies (ed.), *Origeniana Quarta*, Innsbruck and Vienna, Tyroli-Verla, 1987, pp. 410–23.

12 A helpful account of the different theologies precisely in terms of their understanding of *hypostasis* will be found in Joseph T. Lienhard, 'The 'Arian' Controversy: Some Categories Reconsidered', *TS* 48 (1987), pp. 415–36. It should be noted that Lienhard regards the trinitarian insight that Marcellus' theology represents more sympathetically than I am here treating it.

13 Most studies of Marcellus are in German, e.g. Gerhard Feige, *Die Lehre Markells von Ankyra in der Darstellung seiner Gegner*, Erfurter Theologische Studien 58, Leipzig, St Benno, 1991; Klaus Seibt, *Die Theologie des Markell von Ankyra*, Arbeiten zur Kirchengeschichte 59, Berlin, de Gruyter, 1994; and Theodore Zahn, *Marcellus von Ancyra: Ein Beitrag zur Geschichte de Theologie*, Gotha, Andreas Perthes, 1867. However, there are a few English-language treatments, including the two previous cited articles by A. (Alastair) H. B. Logan as well as Joseph T. Lienhard's presently unpublished Habilitationsschrift, *Contra Marcellum: The Influence of Marcellus of Ancyra on Fourth-Century Greek Theology*, and his 'Marcellus of Ancyra in Modern Research', *TS* 43 (1982), pp. 486–503.

14 The appeal of Logos trinitarian language almost seems to be its ambiguity: either it sounds like a title expressing a relationship, but it really carries a theology of divine unity (as with the case of Marcellus), or it sounds like a title expressing unity, but it really carries a theology of divine diversity (as with the case of Eusebius of Caesarea).

15 A contemporary reader of the creed of Nicaea might object that 'Father' and 'Son' are relational titles in the creed which support a theology of real diversity in the godhead. Such a reading anachronistically imposes the results of the process this chapter documents onto the early creed, for the title 'son' is, in the creed, used of Jesus Christ and not of any pre-incarnate second divine existence. Marcellus' theology lies precisely in this point: 'son' refers only to the Logos incarnated, and to nothing else.

16 See Logan, 'Marcellus of Ancyra and the Councils of AD 325'.

17 Logan begins this comment by noting that 'it is the merit of Stuart Hall's review of Hanson's book to have pointed to the dominant Marcellan (and Eustathian) influence in the drafting of the creed of Nicaea' ('Marcellus of Ancyra and the Councils of AD 325', p. 444).

18 Adolph Harnack, *History of Dogma*, tr. Neil Buchanan, seven books in four vols, New York, Dover, 1960, vol. 4, pp. 84–8. For a recent work which shows very clearly the continuing impact of Harnack's judgement, see Cornelis P. Venema, 'Gregory of Nyssa on the Trinity', *Mid-America Journal of Theology* 8 (1992), pp. 72–94.

19 See especially 'The Doctrine of the Trinity in Gregory Nazianzen and John Calvin', *Sobornost* 12 (1990), pp. 14, 15, 17; and *The Trinitarian Faith: The Evangelical Theology of the Ancient Catholic Church*, Edinburgh, T. & T. Clark, 1988, pp. 311–13, 319–22.

20 The initial occasion for pursuing the question of what exactly the Cappadocians knew of Athanasius' writings was a conversation with Rowan Williams, whose influence I must acknowledge. Williams has recently referred in passing to the

question of Basil's knowledge of Athanasius' theology in 'Baptism and the Arian Controversy', in Michel R. Barnes and Daniel H. Williams (eds), *Arianism After Arius: Essays on the Development of the Fourth Century Trinitarian Conflicts*, Edinburgh, T. & T. Clark, 1993, pp. 149–80. After describing, in pp. 156–7, similarities between Athanasius' and Basil's understanding of the implications of the baptismal liturgy for the controversy, Williams remarks that '[w]hether Basil knew the *contra Arianos* is disputable', but specific similarity of doctrine 'suggests a fairly direct connection' (p. 157).

21 G. L. Prestige, *St. Basil the Great and Apollinaris of Laodicea*, London, SPCK, 1956, p. 17. Prestige makes no argument for his judgement that Basil read Athanasius' *De synodis* after he wrote *Ep.* 361 and before he wrote *Ep.* 9. In particular he fails to address two necessary questions: first, how did a text addressed to monks in Egypt end up in Cappadocian Caesarea? And second, why does thematic similarly constitute textual influence?

22 Marcellus' *Letter to Julius* is extant in Epiphanius, *Panarion* 72.2.1–3, 4.

23 Joseph Lienhard has already suggested the influence of Marcellus on Athanasius there in Rome. See his 'Did Athanasius Reject Marcellus?' in Barnes and Williams (eds), *Arianism After Arius*, pp. 65–80.

24 Logan has argued, with a thesis similar to mine, that it was 'as a result of his sojurn in the West and appreciative discovery of the universal tradition of the apostolic faith represented in Rome and defended by Tertullian, that Marcellus, developing the heresiological thesis . . . wrote *De santa ecclesia*'. See 'Marcellus of Ancyra and Anti-Arian Polemic', *SP* 19 (1987), p. 196. I find Logan's conclusions supportive, but I cannot quite accept his precise account of Western influences on Marcellus.

25 Hanson, *The Search*, p. 272. Hanson explains Julius' support for Athanasius very well; what remains unexplained is the remark that the bishop of Rome had always tended to support the bishop of Alexandria.

26 As we explore the Christian roots of Marius Victorinus' theology, we may find that some Western theology of the early 350s was anything but 'orthodox', even if it attached itself to Nicaea and *homoousios*.

27 See Gustave Bardy, 'L'occident et les documents de la controverse arienne', *Revue des Sciences Religieuses* 20 (1940), pp. 28–63.

28 *Contra Arrianos* VIII.7 (CCL 64 32.27–9).

29 First at *De trinitate* IV.12–13, and again at VI.5–6.

30 At one time Lienhard suggested tentatively that the Ps. Athanasian *Contra Sabellianos* should be understood as an earlier draft by Basil of Caesarea of what later became his *Contra Sabellianos et Arium et Anomeos*; see his 'Ps. Athanasius, *Contra Sabellianos*, and Basil of Caesarea, *Contra Sabellianos et Arium et Anomeos*: Analysis and Comparison', *VC* 40 (1986), pp. 365–89. Lienhard seems not to think this anymore. In any case both ancient texts have the same significance for this study: whoever the author(s) may be, neither text shows any substantial or textual knowledge of Arius' doctrines.

31 See *Or.* 31.30.

32 *Contra Arrianos* XIV.3 (CCL 64 39.10).

33 Rowan Williams similarly notes that 'We have no knowledge of later Arian use of the *Thalia*, and the paucity of information of it in orthodox historians suggests that – in contrast to some of the letters – . . . it never formed part of a regular dossier on Arianism, at least after 360 or thereabouts; which suggests that it was not to the fore in the debates of the mid-century' (*Arius: Heresy and Tradition*, p. 65). I am suggesting that polemical use of the *Thalia* was indeed limited precisely to Athanasian anti-Arian circles.

34 Athanasius' recollections may be found in *De decretis* V.20 and *De synodis* 18; they are repeated in the 'Athanasian' *Ad Afros* V.

35 Anti-Nicene emphasis on unbegottenness as a divine trait is found among both Eastern and Western homoians and among heterousians ('Eunomians') in the East.

36 *The Search*, p. 438. Those who condemned all uses of *ousia*-based formula may have actually facilitated the removal of differences between *homoousios* and *homoiousios* theologies.

37 Or again, many of the references to *homoousios* in Gregory of Nazianzus' *Theological Orations* of 380 are in the voice of the fictional Eunomian interrogator, and Gregory's defence of the term is usually couched as a response to the initial Eunomian attack. For example, the interrogator says, 'Whatever is *homoousios* are counted together . . . but whatever is not *homoousios* are not counted together. [If God is *homoousios* he must be counted together as three.] We run no risk here, since we deny that they are *homoousios*' (*Or.* 31.17). There are thus four references (the literal fourth is at 31.18) to *homoousios* in *Oration* 31, and they are all by the Eunomian.

38 GNO I and II. The incidence of *homoousios* (etc.) in Gregory's writings was determined by consulting Cajus Fabricius and Daniel Ridings (eds), *A Concordance to Gregory of Nyssa, Studia Graeca et Latina Gothoburgensia* 50 (1989) (whole issue).

39 In *De fide et symbolo*, written in 393, Augustine refers to several Arian doctrines while in the process of 'refuting' a succession of heresies, including Sabellianism and Manicheaeism, yet I do not find in this text either a polemical motive or the polemical form I have been describing. First, the Arian citations are not identified as such, but are rather clearly part of a formula denunciation of a variety of heretical exegeses. Second, the word 'Arian' does not appear in Augustine's text. Third, in this text Augustine is not at all comfortable with the term *homoousios*.

40 See *Contra Eunomium* I.20.11, where *homoousios* is introduced on the basis of Heb. 1.3. Bernard Sesboüé, in *Contre Eunome*, SC 299, p. 244, n. 1, remarks about this use of *homoousios* that it is the 'first but only time *homoousios* is used of the Trinity in the *Contra Eunomium*'. He goes on to say that in the four other occasions where *homoousios* is used it describes either the consubstantiality between humans, or the consubstantiality between a person and their works – the same kind of use Gregory finds for the term (as described above).

41 Interestingly, it is the very similarity of expression in these two texts that causes Paul Fedwick to doubt the authenticity of *Ep.* 361. See his 'A Chronology of Basil' in P. Fedwick (ed.), *Basil of Caesarea: Christian, Humanist, Ascetic*, Toronto, Pontifical Institute of Mediaeval Studies, 1981, vol. 1, p. 7, n. 23.

42 That is, among authors such as Didymus the Blind, Theodore of Mopsuestia, Diodore of Tarsus and Theodoret of Cyrus.

43 For example, in his *De trinitate* I.9 Augustine does not use the Latin version of Nicene *homoousios*, '*consubstantialis*' but instead he uses '*eiusdem substantia*'; nonetheless his trinitarian theology is Nicene and anti-Arian.

44 See my 'Augustine in Contemporary Trinitarian Theology', *TS* 56 (1995), pp. 237–50.

45 *The Search*, pp. xviii ff.

46 The most important of such 'Western' reinterpretations would be Alexandria, 362. I include the writings of Hilary of Poitiers among these 'Western reinterpretations in the 360s' even though specific relevant texts may date from 359. Eastern reinterpretations from the seventies are primarily Cappadocian (especially Basil's), although we do not see the full fruit of that reinterpretation until

the turn of the decade (after Basil has died), when the Imperial wind shifts
clearly in favour of a 'Nicene' solution.

47 See, for example, de Halleux's 'La réception du symbole oecuménique, de Nicée
à Chalcédoine', p. 15: 'Mais ce triomphe de l'homéisme, soutenu par Constance,
devait être de courte durée, car il allait provoquer chez adversaires de l'arianisme
un ralliement décisif au nicaeum.'

48 It is interesting to note the West's continued puzzlement over *hypostasis* and its
role in Nicene theology as evidenced, more than forty years after
Constantinople, in Augustine's *De trinitate* V.10.

49 Athanasius may say that the Father is not the Son, but he says precious little
beyond that. He does not say 'person' – *hypostasis* – until very late in the game,
and only then with his teeth clenched.

5

THE DOG THAT DID NOT BARK[1]

Doctrine and patriarchal authority in the conflict between Theophilus of Alexandria and John Chrysostom of Constantinople

Susanna Elm

The subject of the following chapter is somewhat unusual: it is about something that is missing. It is about accusations of doctrinal irregularity that could have been made by the protagonists but were not, and argues that this was not an oversight, but a deliberate choice. In other words, this chapter makes an argument not so much from silence as about silence, in particular about silence as an argumentative tool. Because in this case the silence regards doctrinal questions that involved two patriarchs, this chapter is also about the relationship between authority, doctrine and the rivalry between the sees of Alexandria and Constantinople. The rhetoric of orthodoxy and heresy that we find in the sources should thus be read as part of a developing language of ecclesiastical power.

The confrontation of Theophilus of Alexandria with John Chrysostom, which culminated in the 'Synod of the Oak' in 403 and John's subsequent exile, provides the context of this silence. Scholars have usually discussed this episode in terms of the precise unfolding of events and the disentangling of the forces at play. My focus is on the way in which the sources nearest to the events have represented the protagonists, especially Theophilus, and what arguments they have used – or left out – to fashion their presentation. By choosing this focus I hope to provide a more comprehensive explanation of Theophilus' attitude towards doctrine in his conflict with John than the usual one, according to which Theophilus was a Machiavellian opportunist who simply used doctrine as a means to his ends.

Theophilus of Alexandria (ca. 345–412) is one of the more puzzling of the bishops and patriarchs who made history during the fourth and fifth century AD. A contemporary of John Chrysostom, Ambrose, Augustine and other leading lights, he never made it to centre stage, despite his position as patriarch of Alexandria from 385 to 412. Indeed, Theophilus is not a sympathetic character. A ruthless politician for whom the end justified all means,

Theophilus as he appears in both the ancient and modern record is a thug.[2] Regardless of Theophilus' alleged shortcomings, however, this record is not entirely complete. What remains largely absent from both the ancient and modern characterizations of Theophilus are discussions of his doctrinal position, a most surprising omission considering that he was one of the leading figures during the Origenist controversy.[3]

Leaving modern scholarship aside for the moment, the issue at hand is precisely the ancient sources' treatment of the doctrinal aspects of the conflict: the moment Theophilus and John Chrysostom, the two protagonists, enter the scene, none of the sources closest to the events mentions doctrinal positions, as if Theophilus and John were operating in a 'doctrine-free zone'. Instead, both Theophilus and John Chrysostom are accused of administrative misconduct. Origenist charges and counter-charges are made, but they are brought only against those who were 'second-in-command', such as Heraclius, bishop of Ephesus, and Palladius, bishop of Helenopolis. Furthermore, more or less veiled allusions in our sources leave no doubt that matters of doctrinal irregularity loomed just beyond the surface.[4] Given the obvious presence of Origenist concerns, what caused our ancient authors to become suddenly so doctrinally tongue-tied when dealing with the protagonists?[5]

I would like to suggest that one reason for such reluctance on the part of our sources was the relationship between the sees of Alexandria and Constantinople at the beginning of the fifth century. Since these were the two most important sees in the Eastern empire, and Theophilus and John Chrysostom the two most powerful patriarchs, any conflict between the two men would have far reaching consequences. Outright accusations of doctrinal irregularity could thus not be made easily, unless clear-cut heresy could be proven.[6] It was more effective, and also more appropriate, to resort instead to charges of a more limited and personal nature, namely those of administrative misconduct, especially if such charges also happened to be true.

THE HISTORICAL BACKGROUND PRIOR TO THE 'SYNOD OF THE OAK'

The ordination of John Chrysostom in 398 signalled a new phase in the development of the Constantinopolitan patriarchate, during which it solidified and expanded its position *vis-à-vis* Alexandria and Rome.[7] The council of Constantinople of 381 had already attempted to further clarify the boundaries of episcopal administration first established by canons 4 and 5 of Nicaea, by stipulating that:

> bishops of another diocese (*uperdioikasin*) must not confuse the churches. According to the canons, the bishop of Alexandria must

occupy himself solely with the affairs of Egypt; those of the Orient administer (*dioikein*) only the Orient . . . those of Thrace only the affairs of Thrace. Bishops must not ordain or perform any other administrative act outside their diocese without appeal.[8]

These measures were in part a response to years of Arian crisis, during which frequent collusion between Alexandria and Rome had led to a number of direct interferences in the internal affairs of Constantinople.[9] Under Nectarius, Gregory's successor, Constantinople had progressed to where relations with Alexandria had reached a stable though highly precarious equilibrium. Both patriarchs were now called upon to act as mediators and judges between different bishops within their sphere of influence, whereby the exact dimensions of this sphere were constantly renegotiated.[10] With John Chrysostom this equilibrium broke down.

Already events surrounding his ordination signalled the impending disruption of the delicate balance of power. The Antiochene John Chrysostom had been ordained by Theophilus, who had been forced to abandon his own candidate, Isidore, under pressure from the court in Constantinople in the person of the eunuch Eutropius, at that point the leading power behind Arcadius' throne.[11] With full support of the court, John began to expand the radius of his episcopal see well beyond the boundaries stipulated by the canons of Constantinople. He enlisted imperial support in the fight against 'heresies' and 'pagans'; he initiated a neutralization of Antioch by mobilizing Theophilus of Alexandria to effect a reconciliation between Flavian of Antioch and the pope in Rome through the emissaries Acacius of Beroea and Isidore; he formulated the first systematic policy regarding the conversion of the Goths to orthodoxy; and he made a number of direct interventions in jurisdictions other than his own. In ca. 400–401, John ordained one of his deacons, the Origenist Heraclides, as bishop of Ephesus against local opposition, deposed several other Asian bishops and reorganized the entire diocese in a flagrant transgression of canonical procedure which resulted in an expansion of his territorial base directly prior to the events culminating in the 'Synod of the Oak'.[12]

THE 'SYNOD OF THE OAK'

At the 'Synod of the Oak', assembled on the outskirts of Constantinople in the year 403, thirty-six bishops under the leadership of Theophilus of Alexandria ousted John Chrysostom from his see as bishop of Constantinople.[13] Ostensibly this was a moment of triumph, but Theophilus' victory proved to be a Pyrrhic one that eventually sealed his fate.[14] The discord led to a serious rift between Theophilus and Pope Innocent, the first significant rupture in the relationship between Rome and

Alexandria since Theodosius I made the alliance between those two sees the basis of the Nicene faith.[15] As a result, Rome's position was ultimately strengthened at the expense of both Alexandria and Constantinople.[16]

However, as far as Theophilus is concerned, what proved truly decisive for posterity was the fact that John Chrysostom's followers and their sympathizers wrote the history of these events and thus shaped Theophilus' reputation. His picture, in addition to deriving from hostile sources, has further been impaired by the fact that modern debates about the events surrounding the 'Synod of the Oak' often uncritically reflect these ancient sources, and thus centre on John Chrysostom and the concerns of Constantinople. Missing are evaluations of Theophilus beyond his function as the villain, and, as a direct consequence, of the significance of the patriarchate of Alexandria during the first part of the fifth century.[17]

Theophilus is usually considered the agent of larger forces whose confluence caused John's downfall.[18] These forces have been variously identified as Eudoxia, wife of the emperor Arcadius;[19] a disenfranchised Constantinopolitan clergy and monastic elite;[20] hostile members of the Eastern capital's aristocracy, disturbed by John's pro-barbarian leanings;[21] his overly zealous recruitment of wealthy aristocratic women;[22] or his all-too-intimate ties to the Western aristocracy at the Theodosian court.[23] In all this, the focal point remains Constantinople, whereas the position of the Alexandrian patriarchate prior to Cyril is rarely described, even less explained.[24]

By examining the ways in which the sources most significant for the 'Synod of the Oak' shaped the picture of Theophilus of Alexandria, and how they treated doctrine in the process, this discussion begins a reassessment of Theophilus' status and, by implication, that of Alexandria.

THE SOURCES

Palladius

The first and most significant source shaping the picture of Theophilus is Palladius of Helenopolis' *Dialogue on the Life of St John Chrysostom*.[25] It was written in 408 and purports to be an eye-witness account of the tumultuous events leading to John Chrysostom's deposition. The *Dialogue* was conceived perhaps in response to a pamphlet by Theophilus himself, and under the influence of Palladius' own mission on behalf of John Chrysostom to Pope Innocent of Rome between 404 and 405.[26]

According to Palladius, Theophilus of Alexandria was the engineer of a 'conspiracy' that led to Chrysostom's spectacular downfall. In his portrayal, Theophilus was particularly suited to the task because of his character, reflected not only in his anti-Chrysostom machinations, but in his entire style of episcopal rulership. Thus, when John's enemies, driven by envy, sought to harm John, they chose 'the reckless' Theophilus as their ringleader, because 'he was very clever at engineering projects like this'.[27]

Theophilus – according to Palladius – was a 'weather cock',[28] prone to change from overbearing 'gentility and sweetness' to uncontrolled rage in an instant, a master of double talk, whose words seldom matched his thoughts, a schemer, driven by hunger for unlimited power and greed for money, who invented endless tricks to get his way.[29]

In Palladius' rendering, the one episode that most strikingly represents Theophilus' nefarious character and actions, is that of the Egyptian monks he expelled from Nitria because of their Origenist doctrine, and whose reception by John Chrysostom directly resulted in the 'Synod of the Oak' and John's subsequent downfall. Consequently, Palladius devotes significantly more space to these events, which are so revealing of the wolf in sheep's clothing, than to the entire affair of the 'Synod of the Oak'.[30]

In Palladius' account, at issue are not questions of doctrine, but acts of improper comportment and misuse of authority on the part of Theophilus. This is succinctly exemplified in Palladius' description of Theophilus' behaviour at a key moment, namely when John received the expelled Egyptian monks in Constantinople. Theophilus flew into uncontrolled rage, defying all customary rules of proper decorum and respect, giving John no opportunity to admit a mistake whilst saving face:

> Would he not have been less obstinate when dealing with pious bishops to have said 'Brother John, have you not done this without due consideration?' And then John in excusing himself could have said that he was unaware of having done wrong.[31]

This lack of decorum reveals Theophilus' true motives which are dominated by lust for power. The crisis itself was precipitated by Theophilus' self-aggrandizing *mania*, his *lithomania*, to construct superfluous churches in the fashion of the Pharaohs as monuments to his ego.[32] Because of that he misappropriated moneys donated to the Church by a widow and intended for the poor, which were held in trust by his deacon Isidore, who, in sharp contrast to his superior, was a true 'gentleman'. After disguising his intentions for some months, 'like a dog that bites you when you least expect it', Theophilus suddenly deposed Isidore on grounds of a patently trumped up charge of sodomy, and forced him to leave Alexandria for the desert. But this was not enough. 'With a dragon's blood-shot eyes', 'glaring like a bull', Theophilus proceeded to direct his fury against the Nitrian monks who had given Isidore shelter.[33]

At that point, and only at that point, doctrine comes into play – as the epitome of Theophilus' deviousness. Attempting to hide his true motives, namely greed, self-aggrandizing *huperbia*, rage and lust for power,

Theophilus resorts to doctrinal issues as a decoy. According to Palladius, Theophilus produced on the spur of the moment an anathema of Origen as a pretext to expel all the monks who supported Isidore on charges of heresy. Palladius claims that this was done in direct violation of canonical prescripts and on false charges garnered through bribery of other clergy, carried out by the army and some Ethiopian slaves. In short, 'in his overweening pride, Theophilus not only spoke as a god, but even imagined he was a god'.[34]

This is the leitmotif which dominates Palladius' description of Theophilus' conduct throughout the remainder of the affair: violation of episcopal authority, falsification of charges with the help of bribery, misappropriation of funds, slander and persecution of upright clergy, breach of the rules of hospitality and disregard of decorum made manifest through fits of uncontrolled rage, improper display of gluttony, disdain and lack of respect towards the Church and its representatives.[35] Palladius says not a word of doctrine except in the pivotal description of the expulsion of the Nitrian monks, and here only to underscore Theophilus' reprehensible conduct.[36]

Enter John Chrysostom, whose reception of the refugees ostensibly brought the crisis into the open. It will come as little surprise that John Chrysostom as Palladius portrays him is the exact opposite of Theophilus. Where Theophilus is double tongued, John shines through 'the frankness of his speech' (parresia);[37] where Theophilus is an inconsistent changeling at the whim of his passions, John is in perfect mastery of body and mind, so much so that asceticism ruined his digestion and forced him to eat alone;[38] where Theophilus' hunger for power stoops to bribery, false accusations and sheer terror, John is concerned only with the Church's welfare to the point that his own authority is threatened by those he has thus challenged.[39] Contrary to Theophilus who persecutes those of his clergy who are above corruption and eager to provide for the poor, John introduces stringent reforms and chastises the corrupt. Unlike the profligate Theophilus, John minimizes the expenses of the episcopal household to benefit the sick, the poor and the widows. Where Theophilus interferes with his bishops' pastoral care, John reforms the liturgy; where Theophilus forces his laity into perjury, John calls them to almsgiving and modesty. The list goes on.[40]

Palladius establishes here two diametrically opposed models of episcopal behaviour, the dark side of Theophilus corresponding precisely to the purity in John Chrysostom. The substance of both sides, the positive and the negative one, however, is provided not by questions of doctrine, but by proper and improper use of authority as reflected by each protagonist's character. In other words, rather than seeking to give an accurate portrayal of historical events, Palladius constructs here models of authority, based on the standard typologies of the good and the evil administrator.[41] However, this decidedly rhetorical and indeed strongly apologetic nature of the Dialogue has remained largely overlooked in scholarly debates, and its relevance for the historical reconstruction of Theophilus has not been taken into consideration at all.[42]

The *Acts* of the Synod

The ingredients of Palladius' carefully constructed picture of Theophilus as the diametrical opposite of John the hero gain additional significance when compared to another contemporary source, namely the *Acts* of the Synod itself. As in the case of Palladius' *Dialogue*, the *Acts* of the Synod, too, are a composite of several levels of intentionality. First, they have reached us mediated through Photius in his *Bibliotheca*.[43] This adds an important component in the form of Photius' own editorial perspective, influenced both by his personal fate as well as his intellectual leanings. The *Bibliotheca* was most likely completed in Photius' later years, when he had already been elected and deposed as patriarch of Constantinople at least once, and both his predilection for the Antiochene school and his strong interest in heresies are well documented.[44] The question arises, therefore, whether or not Photius' interests materially affected the content of the *Acts*, and if so how. The *Acts* were originally composed by John Chrysostom's opponents under the leadership of Theophilus of Alexandria. Photius introduces them by calling the Synod illegal and its leaders partial, 'being at the same time judges, accusers and witnesses'. Photius' pro-Chrysostom sentiments are thus made abundantly clear.[45] However, his excerpts must be judged historically accurate, first because they are supported by other sources which corroborate the main accusations,[46] and second, because the John portrayed by the *Acts* fits the negative description given by none other than Theophilus: he was a man 'filled with a passionate love for power (*philarchia pathos spoudasos*)'.[47] Indeed, a survey of the *Acts* yields a significant conclusion: though differing in the specifics, the bishops assembled at 'the Oaks' accused John Chrysostom of exactly the same types of misdemeanours with which Palladius had charged Theophilus.

Like Theophilus, the John emerging from the *Acts* is accused of inconsistency: during the 'soldiers' revolt', that is, the Gothic uprising, John had betrayed the whereabouts of the *comes* Johannes, leading to his capture by the Gothic troops.[48] Furthermore, he was prone to fits of uncontrolled rage to the point of punching a member of his clergy, drawing blood.[49] He consistently violated rules of proper decorum by eating alone (and thus without proper restraint) and by having the baths heated for himself only. He even saw women alone, behind closed doors.[50]

John's behaviour towards members of his clergy, however, truly defied all rules of proper comportment. He treated his clergy 'as if they were men without honour, corrupt, good-for-nothings', and had called 'Saint Epiphanius an "air-head" and little demon'.[51] He accused three deacons of having stolen his *maphorion*, and had the monk John flogged.[52] He engineered a conspiracy against Severian of Gabala,[53] and he bribed clerics to better suppress those who might oppose him.[54]

More egregiously, according to the *Acts*, John Chrysostom frequently violated the procedures of ordination and transgressed the limits of his power. He had ordained clergy against canonical prescriptions and deposed others on false charges. He ruled like an autocrat, without seeking consensus among his peers. And he mismanaged Church finances. Not only did he divert moneys budgeted for buildings to unknown use, he sold off an inheritance, and generally diverted Church revenues to unknown ends.[55]

According to the *Acts* of the Synod, John's accusers, mainly his deacon John and the monk Isaac, charged him with administrative misconduct. He had flagrantly disregarded the rules of proper decorum, in particular *vis-à-vis* his clergy, resulting in disrespect, breaches of hospitality, and generally bad manners. He had violated canonical prescripts through improper ordinations and interference in other bishops' areas of competence; and he had misappropriated Church funds, though, as in the case of Theophilus, not necessarily for personal gains.

In Photius' transmission of the *Acts* of the Synod, several of Chrysostom's accusers, especially the monk John and bishop Isaac, a 'leader of the monks', charge his confidants, Heraclides of Ephesus and Palladius of Helenopolis, with Origenism, and fault John and his second-in-command Serapion for their failure to address the injuries they had personally suffered by the hands of the Origenists. Isaak also adds a *libellum* against Chrysostom, complaining that Origenists have mistreated one of his monks, and that because of the Origenists, the holy Epiphanius has refused to enter into communion with Isaak. Again: the charge is not that John is an Origenist, but that his confidants are and that he himself does not deal with them in the proper manner. To conclude, as portrayed by the first two contemporary sources examined, both Theophilus and John respectively failed to govern appropriately.

(Pseudo-) Martyrius' *Life of John Chrysostom*

A third contemporary source is the so-called *Discourse on the Life of John Chrysostom*, attributed to Martyrius of Antioch.[56] As demonstrated by F. van Ommeslaeghe, this text is in fact an *oratio funebris* composed by an anonymous supporter of John Chrysostom around the time of the latter's death, that is, around 407, and intended for a like-minded audience.[57] The anonymous author, who had been baptized and ordained by John, also purports to have been an eye-witness, and had been part of the deposed patriarch's inner circle.[58]

Indeed, Ps.-Martyrius' intentions are those of Palladius, namely to rehabilitate and defend his mentor with great passion. However, Ps.-Martyrius' tone is more sober and he adheres far more closely to factual details. Whilst Ps.-Martyrius also faults Theophilus' conduct in the affair of the Egyptian monks for the ensuing conflict, he mentions the affair only briefly and in general terms, without implying any long-standing animosity between John and Theophilus.[59]

Indeed, as portrayed by Ps.-Martyrius, Theophilus was an experienced politician and resourceful strategist, who resorted immediately following the eruption of hostilities to classic campaign measures: he sent an advance troop of Egyptian bishops to Constantinople by sea, while he chose the land-route using his journey to lobby all the bishops on the way for his cause. Once arrived in Constantinople, according to Ps.-Martyrius, Theophilus skilfully exploited long rankling animosities harboured by the city's power-brokers to topple his adversary.[60]

The Theophilus portrayed by Ps.-Martyrius is not a likeable character either, but rather than the abject villain portrayed by Palladius, we find here a man who was a shrewd politician and excellent power-broker, quick to forge and dissolve alliances without being overly impeded by scruples.[61] Again, however, the focus is on decorum and modes of governance, not on doctrine. Ps.-Martyrius accuses Theophilus of breaches of hospitality and lack of decorum, as well as transgression of the boundaries of episcopal power.

The same type of arguments are marshalled in Ps.-Martyrius' defence of Chrysostom. Here, too, the issues at hand are procedural irregularities,[62] politically importune efforts of charity,[63] John's non-canonical deposition of Asian bishops, his misappropriation of funds and his disrespectful habit of eating alone.[64]

Doctrine appears only once, and here, as in Palladius' case, only in reference to Theophilus' dealings with the monks. However, Ps.-Martyrius' reference is even more indirect and oblique: Origen himself (rather than Theophilus) is portrayed as some obscure figure emerging from the desert to cast the spell of heresy over the unfortunate monks – an interesting notion given that Ps.-Martyrius is the only source to defend John Chrysostom against accusations of magic.[65]

John Chrysostom's *Letter to Innocent of Rome*

The three contemporary sources discussed so far contain reports of the events and portrayals of the protagonists as fashioned by third parties, either John's ardent supporters, or the formal complaints lodged against him by the 'Synod of the Oak', as preserved by yet another sympathetic party. All three sources concentrate on charges and counter-charges of administrative and personal misconduct, focusing on transgression of episcopal spheres of influence, misappropriation of Church funds and breaches of hospitality and proper comportment. These complaints are also stressed by yet another contemporary source, this time by one of the protagonists himself, namely John Chrysostom's *Letter to Innocent of Rome*.[66]

In this letter John explained the events that led to his first exile after the 'Synod of the Oak', his recall and the calamitous riots prior to his second and final exile, during which fire destroyed the Hagia Sophia, the senate house and adjoining buildings in the Easter night of 404.[67] Rather than composing a formal letter of defence, an *oratio pro domo*, however, John sought here to appeal the sentence of the synod and reverse its decision; in short, rather than responding to individual charges he sought to nullify the validity of the synod as such.[68] For that purpose, he concentrated on identifying and denouncing the driving force behind this sham synod – none other, of course, than Theophilus – whilst at the same time attempting to enhance his own role and to minimize that of a third party, the imperial household.[69]

In these endeavours John, too, circumvented all direct references to questions of doctrine, and highlighted instead issues of decorum, administrative misdemeanours, and especially procedural irregularities. Thus he bitterly criticized Theophilus' refusal to lodge with him upon his arrival in Constantinople, even though the rooms in the episcopal residence had already been prepared, a violation of old customs that caused a public scandal: 'Still we kept inviting them, doing the proper thing for them, trying to find out why he should start such a conflict and bring such insult to our city.'[70]

He then scorned Theophilus for not treating him as an equal, but as an adversary: by citing the example of Theophilus' summons of his second-in-command, his archdeacon John, 'in the manner of one having great authority, as though the Church were already widowed and did not have a bishop', he reversed Theophilus' charges of interference in another's episcopal jurisdiction, levelling it against Theophilus himself.[71]

The principal source of grievance was, however, Theophilus' acts 'against the laws and canons and all regular procedure':[72] Theophilus had called John to judgement prior to having cleared himself of charges brought against him, being himself the most unfit of judges who had to resort to bribes;[73] and more crucially, 'nor was it even fitting to one from Egypt to act as a judge in Thrace'.[74] Then, to top this history of unlawfulness, Theophilus even ignored imperial letters, whilst John, in sharp contrast, continually pressed for 'proper procedure of interrogation and response. We stood ready to assert our innocence and their disregard for law.'[75]

Throughout, allusions to questions of doctrine are veiled at best. Theophilus' refusal of communion and his avoidance of John implies that he treated him as a schismatic or heretical bishop.[76] Furthermore, Chrysostom's insistence on Theophilus' violation of procedure could signify more than meets the modern eye: a contemporary such as Innocent would have known that claims of orthodoxy and heresy were formulated in accordance with the adversarial techniques of forensic Roman law with bishops acting as *causidici*.[77] For contemporary ears, especially those well versed in the art of fighting heretics according to the rules of law, John's insistence on procedure might have had a different ring. Yet, the fact remains that doctrine is never openly mentioned.

To summarize, the Theophilus emerging so far from our sources is the diametrical opposite of John Chrysostom. This Theophilus is furthermore crafted in such a way that the charges levelled against him are the direct inverse of those with which our one hostile source, the *Acts*, accused John Chrysostom. The substance of these accusations and counter-accusations are issues of governance and the appropriate conduct of authority figures: correct observance of procedure (either regarding the conduct of a synod, or modes of ordination); maintenance of proper spheres of influence; appropriate management of funds; and adherence to customary rules of decorum when interacting with equals. If it were not for synods and ordination, one might think that this was a power-struggle between figures of secular authority.

Indeed, all issues of a doctrinal nature are subordinated to the authors' rhetorical construction of the antagonist. Since Palladius portrays Theophilus as a scrupulous and tyrannical ruler, his treatment of issues relating to doctrine has to remain 'in character'. Accordingly, in keeping with his construction of Theophilus as the villain, Palladius can only phrase Theophilus' understanding of doctrine as a means to the end of toppling Chrysostom, never as a genuine concern. Similarly, Ps.-Martyrius' view of doctrinal concerns fits with his description of Theophilus as the Alexandrian politician, enmeshed in his own, nebulous, local doctrinal 'business'. Both Palladius and Ps.-Martyrius were closely aligned with John Chrysostom. Palladius is further known to have been an Origenist.[78] Given that they were writing while John's position was still precarious, their reluctance to engage in doctrinal discussions and their method when doing so needs hardly to be explored further. But this does not explain the reluctance of our one pro-Theophilus source, the *Acts*, to associate John Chrysostom with Origenism. As pointed out above, all charges of that nature in the *Acts* are exclusively directed against John's close associates but never against himself. If Theophilus wanted to depose John, why not simply accuse him of doctrinal irregularities? Instead, John Chrysostom is only charged with the insufficient supervision of his Origenist clergy. John's own letter, not surprisingly, reflects this. His 'defence' is based solely on issues of procedure. Doctrine is seemingly not at stake. Yet, we do know from other sources that questions raised by the so-called Origenist controversy were at that moment hotly debated. In fact, one important witness for that is Theophilus himself. How then did he use doctrine in the period leading up to and surrounding his clash with John Chrysostom?

THEOPHILUS' USE OF DOCTRINE: THE SILENCE SPEAKS

Efforts to reconstruct Theophilus' use of doctrinal issues are determined by the manner in which his writings have been preserved.[79] The majority of the writings relevant to that period have reached us in Jerome's Latin translation, augmented by a number of Greek fragments. In cases in which original fragments of Jerome's translations exist, they confirm that he reflected Theophilus' viewpoint faithfully.[80] However, the complexity of the transmission of Theophilus' writings, including those that reflect his doctrinal development more broadly,[81] makes an occasional recourse to other sources necessary when reconstructing Theophilus' use of doctrinal issues prior to the 'Synod of the Oak'.[82]

Palladius' account of the events leading up to John Chrysostom's downfall made the affair of the Origenist monks the litmus test of Theophilus' attitude towards matters of doctrine. According to him, Theophilus had no sincere doctrinal concerns, but used doctrine only as a front for extending his power. When recounted from Theophilus' side, it becomes evident that Palladius had a point. Theophilus' dealings with the affair of the Origenist monks reveals a continuously escalating series of events, at the culmination of which matters of doctrine, crucial though they had been throughout, took second rank *vis-à-vis* matters of authority. In the final analysis, what mattered most to Theophilus was the fact that John Chrysostom, regardless of doctrinal issues, had violated canon 5 of Nicaea that regulated the boundaries of episcopal authority.[83] By receiving the Origenist monks, Chrysostom automatically questioned Theophilus' competence regarding the doctrinal charges responsible for their expulsion. In so doing, he questioned the legitimacy of Theophilus' actions, and that constituted interference into the internal affairs of the see of Alexandria. What was at stake for Theophilus were three kinds of authority: his authority within the boundaries of his own see; his authority in relation to other sees of equal importance, namely Constantinople and Rome; and his authority with regard to the imperial court. If any one of these three realms of authority was challenged, the other two were automatically affected as well. Issues of a doctrinal nature, raised by readings of Origen's writings, were important in all three spheres, not least since they determined the legitimacy of Theophilus' actions. But when Theophilus refused to accept what he saw as John Chrysostom's serious transgression of boundaries, doctrinal concerns were subordinated to issues of authority – and John Chrysostom's letter to Innocent confirms that he was aware of that.[84]

Jerome's *Letter* 92 is a translation of Theophilus' synodal letter of the year 400 addressed to the bishops of Palestine and Cyprus with Theophilus' own account of the issue of the Nitrian monks.[85] According to Theophilus, his own involvement began when he, as befitting the patriarch, was called upon by local fathers and monastic leaders to mediate a dispute threatening to split the entire monastic community of Nitria. This dispute had originated when certain foreign monks[86] insisted on propagating a reading of Origen's writings that seriously questioned subordination, rendered the resurrection problematic, posited that the heavenly powers, that is, the angels, received their orders through a pre-cosmic fall of angels, and a number of other questionable points, including suspicion of magic.[87] Theophilus had ascertained these dangerous aspects of Origen's teachings independently and in accordance with the 'ecclesiastical rule', by convening a synod composed of local monastic leaders and bishops in ca. 399, who examined Origen's writings and duly found them wanting.[88] This synod did, however, not convince the offending monks of their error. They not only continued to circulate through the Nitrian monasteries, but formed a veritable shock-troop (*facto cuneo*) that attempted to bring violence to Theophilus' see in Alexandria. There, according to Theophilus, they made use of a separate disciplinary suit against Isidore, already before the bishops,[89] as a front to defend their heresy (*sub nomine Isidori haeresem defenderent . . . iste est signifer hereticae factionis*).[90] Faced with such blatant insubordination, and seeing that these monks defended their heresy by sedition, Theophilus was left with no other choice than to expel these monks from the Church. However, as he does not fail to point out, he undertook these measures not because of ill-will towards these monks, but because of his readiness to defend the faith.[91] It is this that compels him now to write. The monks have fled to Palestine, and therefore Theophilus has to carry the matter likewise outside the confines of Egypt, in order to inform his neighbouring brothers of his actions and to warn them of the heretical threat in their midst.

In his own presentation, Theophilus has so far merely fulfilled his role as patriarch of Alexandria. He was asked to mediate a doctrinal dispute troubling his ascetic constituency; he proceeded with an independent investigation of the doctrinal issues at stake; a synod of local leaders assembled by him concluded that indeed one side proposed teachings that questioned the resurrection and denied likeness between Christ and the Father, and which therefore had to be condemned. The losers did not accept their lot, making disciplinary measures inevitable, as a result of which they fled into neighbouring provinces. Only at that point did Theophilus carry matters outside his own diocese by warning his neighbouring bishops of potential doctrinal and disciplinary problems in their midst. The bishops responded by declaring that no such teachings had been observed in their dioceses, thus effectively neutralizing the issue.[92]

After several months had passed, by the middle of 400, some of the expelled monks sailed to Constantinople.[93] In so doing, they carried the dispute onto a much larger stage that included two new players: the patriarch of Constantinople and the imperial court. Theophilus took corresponding measures. He sent a letter to Epiphanius of Salamis, whose position towards Origen he knew, and asked him to assemble his local bishops to compose an official condemnation of Origen's teachings and to inform the bishop of Constantinople as well as those of Asia Minor of the dangers posed by Origenism.[94] He himself had already sent trusted ascetic leaders to Constantinople to inform John Chrysostom, undertaken successful steps to gain the support of Anastasius of Rome for his concerns regarding readings of Origen, and enlisted Jerome to rally further supporters.[95] Theophilus also continued to devote attention to these matters at home. Fragments of letters to the monks in Scetis as well as to the 'Origenist monks' have been preserved in addition to his festal letter of 401, all attesting to his concern with Origen's teachings on the resurrection and subordination.[96]

For the following two years the chronology is difficult to establish; but there seems to have been a certain period of stasis until 402, which could easily be explained by local Constantinopolitan events that commanded centre stage.[97] It seems clear that Theophilus' early attempts to gain John Chrysostom's support on the doctrinal issues neither succeeded nor failed. Although the expelled monks were allowed to remain in Constantinople without being condemned, they were apparently denied official rehabilitation.[98] But by 402, the events had accelerated. In his festal letter of this year, Theophilus again challenged doctrinal issues raised by contemporary readings of Origen, now regarding specifically the Eucharist.[99] In addition, he states that Origenists are now canvassing the rich of the big cities (apparently referring to Constantinople) to stir up hatred against him, even though, as he again reiterated, he personally wished them no harm and would readmit them if they abandoned their mistaken teachings.[100] In the same year, Epiphanius went to Constantinople in person in an attempt to persuade Chrysostom of the dangers inherent in Origen's writings, but to no avail.[101]

Now matters had reached a crisis point. Apparently the monks had succeeded in winning over the emperor Arcadius and his wife Eudoxia as well as John Chrysostom. As a result, Theophilus was summoned to Constantinople to defend himself against the charge of unlawful expulsion of the monks.[102]

The mere fact that Theophilus' judgement in the doctrinal issues of the Nitrian monks was officially questioned and challenged in Constantinople, by the patriarch in co-operation with the court, constituted, at least in Theophilus' eyes, an unacceptable breach of canon 5 of Nicaea and canon 2 of Constantinople, which regulated the boundaries of episcopal authorities.[103] It was a clear interference in the affairs of his own diocese. Hence his accusation of John: Theophilus never challenged John's doctrinal position, he never accused him of being himself an Origenist, but he consistently accused John of having 'accepted Origenists' (*Origenistas in suam recipiens familiaritatem*).[104] This acceptance and toleration of the Origenists undermined Theophilus' authority at home, vis-à-vis Rome and in the eyes of the emperor.[105] So Theophilus had to strike back, and did. Throughout doctrine remained important, first because the doctrinal concerns raised by Theophilus were serious, and second because they formed the basis for his actions against the Origenist monks.[106]

CONCLUSIONS

This discussion attempted not so much a rehabilitation of Theophilus of Alexandria, as a reassessment of his role in the conflict with John Chrysostom and its portrayal in both the ancient and modern literature. To begin with modern studies, Theophilus is repeatedly portrayed as having made a failed attempt at accusing John Chrysostom of Origenism as part of his overall plot to topple the latter.[107] When this attempt failed, according to scholarly opinion, Theophilus resorted instead to 'trivial charges' of administrative misconduct.[108] Analysis of the sources closest to the actual conflict correct this picture. Theophilus did not accuse John Chrysostom of Origenism. He accused him of accepting and receiving Origenists and thereby tolerating their beliefs and activities. This constituted indeed administrative misconduct, but that was by no means a trivial matter. It was instead an issue of central importance: interference in the affairs of another patriarch's see violated canon 5 of Nicaea and seriously jeopardized the co-operation of the most important sees of the Eastern empire, Alexandria and Constantinople. Theophilus' suit brought against John Chrysostom at the 'Synod of the Oak' succeeded in part because it was supported by similar charges unrelated to the Origenist question, namely John's aggressive and improper handling of the reorganization of the Asian sees and the ordination of Heraclides as bishop of Ephesus, discussed above.

The centrality of administrative charges with regard to this case raises further questions of a more fundamental nature. Were administrative charges indeed of a lesser merit, less serious than those of doctrinal irregularity, and if so according to whom? The manner in which Theophilus' actions have been portrayed in modern accounts of secular historians and those of doctrine alike suggests an underlying assumption that whenever authority and doctrine are simultaneously at stake, doctrinal concerns and not matters of governance ought to prevail.[109]

A close reading of the sources nearest to the conflict reveals, however, that the opposite was in fact the case. Even though issues of a doctrinal nature were fundamental to the conflict, in the final analysis it was the question of a bishop's authority within his see that proved to be decisive. As it happened, the doctrinal position of Theophilus carried the day, but that was a consequence not a primary cause. The presupposed primacy of doctrine over authority is in fact the result of the way in which sources hostile to Theophilus have depicted the conflict. It was Palladius and sources sympathetic to John who have determined this reading of the conflict to the present day. Palladius was himself an Origenist, as were the majority of the sources relating the events. He belonged to the doctrinal party that had been seriously impaired by the result of the conflict between John Chrysostom and Theophilus, and he wrote from a defensive position. It is Palladius who places questions of governance, administration and authority in the centre as well – and from a 'historical' point of view accurately so – but who does so with a strongly negative slant. To stipulate the moral superiority of doctrine over administration is Palladius' own defence.

The close analysis of the sources makes yet an additional point. At the level of patriarchs, questions of authority and appropriate governance cannot be disassociated from issues of doctrine. Not only are both closely linked, but this case study has shed some light on how this functions in practice. When the highest level of ecclesiastical power are involved, questions of authority proved more important as well as more effective, in part because such issues had already been codified and canonized. Theophilus does not accuse John of Origenism because he cannot: Origenism does not yet carry the legal value of a heresy since it has not yet been officially declared as such.

This is a chapter about Theophilus of Alexandria as portrayed by sources sympathetic to John Chrysostom. As such, it provides an analysis of the rhetorical strategies used by these sources, and the ways in which they use and do not use issues of a doctrinal nature. The results of this analysis raise many questions about the relationship between Alexandria and Constantinople, and about the use of orthodoxy and heresy, most of which cannot be answered here. It becomes clear, however, that issues of orthodoxy and heresy are never static. They must always be seen in their context: the same doctrinal concerns will be described differently depending on the source, the situation and the status of the accuser and the accused.[110] Questions of orthodoxy and heresy thus illuminate precisely 'the peculiar nature of the exercise of power in late antiquity', shaped by the 'decisive determination of the average bearers of authority' – ascetic bishop, patriarch or (pagan) court official – 'to remain in control of their own world'.[111]

NOTES

1 After A. Conan Doyle, 'Silverblaze'. If this were a book, it would be dedicated to Michael Maas, whose insights and generosity were both equally remarkable.

2 Theophilus is frequently referred to 'as the Church's pharaoh . . . [whose] harsh and authoritarian conduct provoked resentment', M. Dzielska, *Hypatia of Alexandria*, tr. F. Lyra, Revealing Antiquity 8, Cambridge MA, Harvard University Press, 1995, quote 84. Indeed, his activities filled even his modern biographers with dismay: G. Lazzati, *Teofilo d'Alessandria*, Pubblicazioni della Università Cattolica del Sacro Cuore s. 4, 19, Milan, Vita e Pensiero, 1935, and A. Favale, 'Teofilo d'Alessandria (352 c.–412)', *Salesianum* 18 (1956), pp. 215–46, 498–535; 19 (1957), pp. 34–83, 215–72.

3 Following the ancient sources, most modern scholars have dismissed any serious doctrinal motifs behind Theophilus' stance on Origenist questions. The most significant exception is, to my knowledge, E. A. Clark, *The Origenist Controversy: The Cultural Construction of an Early Christian Debate*, Princeton, NJ, Princeton University Press, 1992, pp. 105–21.

4 See the individual discussion of the sources below.

5 In the case of John Chrysostom, scholars have rarely felt it necessary to investigate any potential involvement into the doctrinal aspects of his conflict with Theophilus, because he is generally seen as being either uninterested in matters of doctrine, cf. J. Chrys., *Hom. IV 2 in Joann.* (PG 59 48) and E. Demougeot's remark (*De l'unité à la division de l'empire romain, 395–410*, Paris, Librairie Adrien-Maisonneuve, 1951, p. 299): 'peu lui importaient les controverses', which eloquently summarizes this attitude; or as orthodox beyond question. Authors who discuss potentially Origenist leanings of John Chrysostom are M.-G. de Durand, 'Evagre le Pontique et le "Dialogue sur la vie de saint Jean Chrysostome" ', *Bulletin de Littérature Ecclesiastique* 3 (1976), pp. 191–206; J.-M. Leroux, 'Jean Chrysostome et la querelle origeniste', in J. Fontaine and C. Kannengiesser (eds), *Epektasis: Mélanges patristiques offerts au Cardinal Jean Daniélou*, Paris, Beauchesne, 1972, pp. 335–41, who dismisses the possibility; and C. Pietri, 'Esquisse de conclusion: L'aristocratie chrétienne entre Jean de Constantinople et Augustin d'Hippone,' in C. Kannengiesser (ed.), *Jean Chrysostome et Augustin: Actes du Colloque de Chantilly, 22–24 settembre 1974*, Theologie Historique 35, Paris, Beauchesne, 1975, pp. 283–305. I have not been able to locate the published version of a paper on the subject given by F. van Ommeslaeghe at the 1983 Oxford Patristics Conference.

6 That is, while doctrinal irregularities were still under debate and not yet officially codified as heretical. Origenism was not formally condemned as a heresy until the 5th ecumenical council of 553. J. Dechow, *Dogma and Mysticism in Early Christianity: Epiphanius of Cyprus and the Legacy of Origen*, Patristic Monograph Series 13, Macon, GA, Mercer University Press, 1988, pp. 448–60; F. Diekamp, *Die origenistischen Streitigkeiten im sechsten Jahrhundert und das fünfte allgemeine Concil*, Münster, Aschendorf, 1899, pp. 90–96; A. Guillaumont, 'Evagre et les anathèmatismes antiorigenistes de 553', *SP* 8 (1961), pp. 219–26; R. Lim, *Public Disputation, Power, and Social Order in Late Antiquity*, Berkeley CA, University of California Press, 1995, pp. 217–29.

7 G. Dagron, *Naissance d'une capitale: Constantinople et ses institutions de 330 à 451*, Bibliothèque Byzantine Études 7, Paris, 1974, pp. 454–65; C. Pietri, *Roma Christiana: Recherches sur l'église de Rome, son organisation, sa politique, son ideologie de Miltiade à Sixte III (311–440) 1–2*, Bibliothèque des Écoles Françaises d'Athène et de Rome 224, Rome, École Française de Rome, 1976, pp. 791–884.

8 Canon 2 of 9 July 381; Hefele-Leclercq, *Histoire des concils*, vol. 2/1, pp. 21–2. For Nicaea 4 and 5 (also 6) cf. Hefele-Leclercq, *Histoire des concils*, vol. 1, pp. 539–69; Dagron, *Naissance*, pp. 411–23.

9 A famous example is Peter of Alexandria's favouritism of Maximus against Gregory of Nazianzus, who, however, in turn also violated the same canon by having previously been ordained as bishop of Sasima, Soc. *HE* 5, 7.

10 Dagron, *Naissance*, pp. 410–65.

11 Pall. *Dial.* 5–6; Soc. *HE* 6.2; Soz. *HE* 8.2, 12–19. Dagron, *Naissance*, 464 questions Theophilus' role in the ordination.

12 Theod. *HE* 5.29–31; Pall. *Dial.* 6, 13–15; Soz. *HE* 8.3.3–4 and 8.6; Soc. *HE* 6.11; G. Albert, *Goten in Konstantinopel: Untersuchungen zur oströmischen Geschichte um das Jahr 400 n. Chr*, Studien zur Geschichte und Kultur des Altertums, n.f. 1., Reihe, Monographien 2, Paderborn, Schöningh, 1984, pp. 151–79; A. Cameron, 'Earthquake 400', *Chiron* 17 (1987), pp. 343–60; Dagron, *Naissance*, pp. 465–6; Demougeot, *De l'unité*, pp. 301–3.

13 Theophilus acted in concert with Acacius of Beroea, Antiochus of Ptolemais, Severian of Gabala and Cyrinus of Chalcedon. Photius, *Bibl.* 59.133 speaks of

forty-five, and Pall. *Dial.* 3.12 speaks of thirty-six bishops. Pall. *Dial.*
8.145–9.9; Ps.-Martyrius, *Vita S. J. Chrysostomi*; Soz. *HE* 8.17; Soc. *HE*
6.15–16; Zos. 5.23.3–4. Cf. esp. F. van Ommeslaeghe, 'Que vaut le
témoignage de Pallade sur le procès de saint Jean Chrysostome?', *Analecta
Bollandiana* 95 (1977), pp. 389–414; id., 'Jean Chrysostome et le peuple de
Constantinople', *Analecta Bollandiana* 99 (1981), pp. 329–49. For the location
of the property called 'the Oaks', see R. Janin, *Géographie ecclésiastique de l'empire
byzantin. 3: Les églises et les monastères des grands centres byzantins*, Paris, Institut
Français d'Études Byzantines, 1975, pp. 36–40; and J. Pergoire, 'Rufinianes',
Byzantinische Zeitschrift 8 (1899), pp. 429–77, esp. pp. 437–49.

14 John Chrysostom's exile after the synod was short; he was recalled, but then
exiled again in 404 until his death in 407, and his supporters, the so-called
Johnites, suffered reprisals for a number of years; cf. *C.Th.* 16.4.5–6 and
16.2.37. Cf. esp. T. E. Gregory, 'Zosimus 5, 23 and the People of
Constantinople', *Byzantion* 43 (1973), pp. 63–81; J. H. W. G. Liebeschuetz,
'Friends and Enemies of John Chrysostom', in A. Mofatt (ed.), *Maistor:
Classical, Byzantine and Renaissance Studies for R. Browning, Byzantina
Australensia* 5, Canberra, Australian Association for Byzantine Studies, 1984,
pp. 85–111, here pp. 99–101; id., 'The Fall of John Chrysostom', *Nottingham
Medieval Studies* 29 (1985), pp. 1–31 (= id., *From Diocletian to the Arab Conquest:
Change in the Late Roman Empire*, Aldeshot, Variorum Reprints, 1990, ch. iv);
id., *Barbarians and Bishops: Army, Church, and State in the Age of Arcadius and
Chrysostom*, Oxford, Clarendon Press, 1990, pp. 202–27; F. van Ommeslaeghe,
'Jean Chrysostome en conflit avec l'impératrice Eudoxie: Le dossier et les orig-
ines d'une légende', *Analecta Bollandiana* 97 (1979), pp. 131–59.

15 *C.Th.* 16.1.2 issued in Thessalonica on 28 Feb. 380. For an interpretation of
Theodosius' approach cf. the brilliant chapter by Dagron, *Naissance*,
pp. 454–87.

16 John's immediate successor, Nectarius' brother Arsacius, ordained on 27 June
404, held office only briefly, according to Pall. *Dial.* 11, 18–30, fourteen
months; according to Soc. *HE* 6.20, until 11 November. Atticus, bishop from
406 to 425, was the *de facto* bishop of reconciliation, as well as an excellent
administrator, Soc. *HE* 7.25; cf. Dagron, *Naissance*, pp. 468–70, 492. Already
by 407, while Chrysostom was still alive, Theophilus seems to have initiated a
reconciliation with Rome, which appears to have been successful by 412. By
413, John was posthumously reinstated as bishop into the *diptychs* of Antioch,
by 418 into those of Constantinople, and shortly thereafter even a reluctant
Cyril of Alexandria consented to recognize his episcopal status, thus effectively
declaring a truce between all the parties affected by the results of the 'Synod of
the Oak'; Soc. *HE* 7.25; Theod. *HE* 5.34–5; Atticus, *Ep. ad Cyril.* 75 (PG 77
348–9); *Innoc. ad Acac. Ber. ep.* 21 (PL 20 543–4); J. Ch. Baur, *John Chrysostom
and his Time*, 2 vols, tr. M. Gonzaga, Westminster, MD, Newman Press, 1959,
vol. 2, pp. 445–54; Liebeschuetz, 'Friends', p. 100 dates the rehabilitation to
416. For the relationship between the three sees cf. N. H. Baynes, 'Alexandria
and Constantinople: A Study in Ecclesiastical Diplomacy', *Journal of Egyptian
Archaeology* 12 (1926), pp. 145–56 (= id., *Byzantine Studies and Other Essays*,
London, Athlone Press, 1955, pp. 97–115); J. Meyendorff, *Imperial Unity and
Christian Divisions: The Church 450–680 A.D.*, The Church in History 2, New
York, St Vladimir's Seminary Press, 1989, pp. 1–66; Pietri, *Roma Christiana*,
pp. 1152–1212.

17 Most secondary literature discusses Alexandria during the patriarchate of
Theophilus solely with reference to two episodes: Theophilus' role in the

destruction of the Serapeion, an episode best illuminated by F. Thelamon, *Paiens et chrétiens au IVe siècle: L'apport de l'histoire ecclésiastique de Rufin d'Aquilée*, Paris, Études Augustiniennes, 1981, pp. 159–279; and his conflict with John Chrysostom recounted from the Constantinopolitan or Western point of view, cf. e.g. Demougeot, *De l'unité*, pp. 298–337; S. Mazzarino, *Stilicone: La crisi imperiale dopo Teodosio*, Milan, Rizzoli, 1990, pp. 335–97; Pietri, *Roma Cristiana*, pp. 791–849, 1069–1130, 1152–1212. This holds even for the works of Lazzati and Favale, exceptions being Clark, *Origenist Controversy*, pp. 37–60, 105–21, and Meyendorff, *Imperial Unity*, pp. 113–17.

18 For an overview of the interplay of these forces see now the magisterial chapters by Liebeschuetz, *Barbarians and Bishops*, especially pp. 198–227; for specific details of the circumstances surrounding John's fall cf. Gregory, 'Zosimus 5, 23', pp. 63–81; Liebeschuetz, 'The Fall', pp. 1–31; Ommeslaeghe, 'Jean Chrysostome et le peuple', pp. 329–49.

19 Pall. *Dial.* 8.245–7; Soc. *HE* 6.18.1–5; Soz. *HE* 8.20.1–3; and esp. Marc. Diaconus, *Vita Porph.* 37 (which is according to the editor H. Grégoire [*Marc le Diacre, Vie de Porphyre de Gaza*, Paris, Les Belles Lettres, 1930, lxxxv–lxxxvi], a later insertion). Eudoxia's irritation, supposedly caused by John's too poignant sermons, is most commonly held responsible for his downfall, but see the critical discussion by Ommeslaeghe, 'Jean Chrysostome en conflit', pp. 131–59 and Liebeschuetz, 'Friends', p. 97. Demougeot (*De l'unité*, pp. 305–35) and esp. K. Holum (*Theodosian Empresses: Women and Imperial Dominion in Late Antiquity*, Berkeley, CA, University of California Press, 1982, pp. 69–78), who interprets the conflict as resulting from John's attack 'against the domestic side of the monarchy' (p. 78), give more weight to Eudoxia's role.

20 For the role of monks, their regional identity and aristocratic supporters see G. Dagron, 'Les moines et la ville: Le monachisme à Constantinople jusqu'au Concile de Chalcédoine (451)', *Travaux et Mémoires* 4 (1970), pp. 229–76, here pp. 232–46, 258–65; Liebeschuetz, 'Friends and Enemies', pp. 93–4; J. F. Matthews, *Western Aristocracies and the Imperial Court A.D. 364–425*, Oxford, Clarendon Press, 1975, pp. 126–45.

21 J.Chr. *Hom. cum Saturninus et Aurelianus acti essent in exsilium* (PG 52 413–20); Syn. *De prov.* (PG 66 1267 B); Theod. *HE* 5.33; Zos. *Hist. nov.* 5.23; Albert, *Goten*, pp. 151–79; Cameron, 'Earthquake 400', pp. 343–60; Demougeot, *De l'unité*, pp. 301–3; Liebeschuetz, *Barbarians and Bishops*, pp. 167–70, 188–94.

22 A suggestion made most forcefully by Dagron, *Naissance*, pp. 498–506.

23 In addition to the works regarding the ties between aristocratic, monastic and episcopal circles mentioned above (n. 12), cf. also P. Devos, 'La "servante de Dieu" Pœmenia d'après Pallade, la tradition copte et Jean Rufus', *Analecta Bollandiana* 87 (1969), pp. 189–212; id., 'Silvie la sainte pélerine', *Analecta Bollandiana* 91 (1973), pp. 105–20; E. D. Hunt, 'St. Silvia of Aquitaine: The Role of a Theodosian Pilgrim in the Society of East and West', *JThS* n.s. 23 (1972), pp. 351–73; id., 'Palladius of Helenopolis: A Party and its Supporters in the Church of the Late Fourth Century', *JThS* ns 24 (1973), pp. 456–80; Matthews, *Western Aristocracies*, pp. 107–47, 236–7; Mazzarino, *Stilicone*, pp. 335–97.

24 A notable exception is Baynes, 'Alexandria', passim. The vast majority of works concerned with Egypt in late antiquity end with Athanasius' death and resume with Cyril and the monophysite controversy. Alexandria during the patriarchate of Theophilus tends to receive only a sprinkling of references; cf. e.g. R. Bagnall, *Egypt in Late Antiquity*, Princeton, NJ, Princeton University Press, 1993, pp. 290–91; A. Martin, *Athanase d'Alexandrie et l'Église d'Egypte au*

IVe siècle (328–373), Collection de l'École Française de Rome 216, Rome, École Française de Rome, 1996, pp. 714–19, and the extensive bibliography. For Cyril's period there is little written aside from the monophysite conflict, cf. e.g. T. Gregory, *Vox Populi: Popular Opinion and Violence in the Religious Controversies of the Fifth Century A.D.*, Columbus, OH, Ohio State University Press, 1979, pp. 163–92; J. Leipoldt, *Schenute von Atripe und die Entstehung des national-ägyptischen Mönchtums*, Texte und Untersuchungen 25, Leipzig, Mohn, 1903, pp. 24–6, 177; R. Teja, *La 'tragedia' de Efeso (431): Herejia y poder en la antigüedad tardia*, Santander, Universidad de Cantabria, 1995, passim and for latest bibliography.

25 Pall. *Dial. on the Life of John Chrysostom* 4, 122–4 (SC 341 & 342); tr. R.T. Meyer, Ancient Christian Writers 45, New York, Newman Press, 1985, quotation from pp. 32–3, cited in the following with my own occasional modifications. The impact of the *Dialogue* on the following generations has been enormous. It forms the principal source for both later *Lives*, that by Gregory of Alexandria (*Bibliotheca Hagiografica Graeca* = *BHG* 873), and by Theodore of Trimithontus (*BHG* 872b), both ed. by F. Halkin, *Douze récits byzantins sur saint Jean Chrysostome*, Subsidia Hagiographica 60, Brussels, Soc. des Bollandistes, 1977, pp. 69–285, 7–44. Its impact is rivalled only by Socrates' independent account in *HE* 6.2–23 and 7.25 and 45. Even though Socrates is on the whole less favourably predisposed towards John than Palladius – he devotes an entire chapter, 6.5, to John's shortcomings – his material derives nevertheless primarily from John's supporters, beginning with Ps.-Martyrius discussed below. Sozomen, *HE* 8.2–24, 26, 28 is again a staunch supporter, but adds little to Socrates. Theodoret, Philostorgius and Zosimus have likewise few additions with the exception of certain passages in Zosimus that are drawn from Eunapius. Since this chapter focuses on the earliest sources, the later ones will only be discussed when necessary for the recreation of events. See Baur, *John Chrysostom* 1, xix–xlv; S. Elm, 'Model Bishops: Theophilus of Alexandria and John Chrysostom', *Augustinianum* forthcoming; Favale, 'Teofilo', p. 236; Gregory, 'Zosimus 5, 23', pp. 62–8 and passim; Ommeslaeghe, 'Jean Chrysostome en conflit', pp. 132–9, 153–9; id., 'Le témoignage', p. 389. For an overview of Socrates' and Sozomen's attitude towards Origenism cf. G. Chestnut, *The First Christian Historians: Eusebius, Socrates, Sozomen, Theodoret, and Evagrius*, Macon, GA, Mercer University Press, 1986, pp. 175–212.

26 Palladius' Roman audience included Pinianus and Melania the Younger. Palladius probably wrote the *Dialogue* from exile in Syene, today's Assuam in Egypt, *Dial.* 20, 41–2; cf. Malingrey and Leclercq, *Dialogue*, 15–21. P. R. Coleman-Norton (*Palladii dialogus de vita S. Joannis Chrysostomi*, Cambridge, Cambridge University Press, 1928, pp. xx and xxxvi) suggested that it may have been composed in response to Theophilus' pamphlet against John, preserved in fragments in the R. Devreessee (ed.), *Responsio ad synodo Constantinopoli*. Apud Pelagius Diaconus, *In defensione-trium capitulorum*, Studi et Testi 57, Città del Vaticano, Biblioteca Apostolica Vaticana, 1932, pp. 70–71; also with textual variations in Facundus of Hermiane, *Pro defensione trium capitulorum* 6.5 (PL 67 677–8). See also J. Dumortier, 'Le valeur historique du dialogue de Palladius et la chronologie de saint Jean Chrysostome', *Mélanges de Science Réligieuse* 10 (1953), pp. 53–62; and especially Ommeslaeghe, 'Le témoignage', pp. 389–414.

27 Pall. *Dial.* 6.20–27.

28 Pall. *Dial* 6.24, *amphallax*; cf. Malingrey and Leclercq, *Dialogue*, p. 128, n. 2.

29 Pall. *Dial.* 6.49–117.
30 Chapters 6, 7, 8. See also Ommeslaeghe, 'Le témoignage', p. 403, n. 5.
31 Pall. *Dial.* 6.39–42; cf. J. Straub, *Vom Herrscherideal in der Spätantike*, Forschungen zur Kirchen- und Geistesgeschichte 18, Stuttgart, Kohlhammer, 1939, repr. Darmstadt, 1964, pp. 153–74 with reference to Menander and Themistius.
32 Pall. *Dial.* 6.62–4; cf. also Isid. of Pelusium, *Ep.* 1, 152 (PG 78 285), who calls him 'admirer of money and crazy for stones'. For episcopal building programmes see P. L. Brown, 'Art and Society in Late Antiquity', in K. Weitzmann (ed.), *Age of Spirituality: A Symposium*, New York, Princeton University Press, 1980, pp. 17–27, here 19–22.
33 Pall. *Dial.* 6.125–6.
34 Pall. *Dial.* 6.49–139 and 7.1–60.
35 Pall. *Dial.* 7.53 – 8.90.
36 Pall. *Dial.* 16.205–11, where Palladius accuses Theophilus of having switched sides with regard to Epiphanius, alludes a second time to doctrine, again to prove Theophilus' shiftiness.
37 Pall. *Dial* 5.68 and 18.191–310.
38 Pall. *Dial.* 5.19–29, and 12.1–75.
39 Pall. *Dial.* 18.
40 Pall. *Dial.* 5.100–166.
41 See my forthcoming 'Model Bishops'. For a discussion of such 'Fürstenspiegel' see M. Maas, *John Lydus and the Roman Past: Antiquarianism and Politics in the Age of Justinian*, London, Routledge, 1992, pp. 28–52, 83–95 for administrators, and J. Vanderspoel, *Themistius and the Imperial Court: Oratory, Civic Duty, and Paideia from Constantine to Theodosius*, Ann Arbor, MI, Michigan University Press, 1995, pp. 187–221.
42 Exceptions highlighting the *Dialogue's* rhetorical character are P. Devos, 'Approches de Pallade à travers le *Dialogue sur Chrysostome et l'Histoire Lausiaque*: Deux œuvres, un auter', *Analecta Bollandiana* 107 (1989), pp. 243–66; and Ommeslaeghe, 'Le témoignage', p. 413, who mainly (and correctly) seeks to emphasize the relevance of Ps.-Martyrius' *Life of John Chrysostom*. P. Ubaldi, 'Appunti sul "Dialogo storico" di Palladio', in *Memorie della Reale Accademia delle Scienze di Torino*, seria seconda 16, Turin, 1906, pp. 217–96, provides mainly a stylistic analysis.
43 Photius, *Bibliothèque I. Cod. 59* (SC 342 101–15). Photius introduces the acts with a genitive partitive construction that could suggest a partial excerpting of the acts; however, this is his standard formula. Ommeslaeghe, 'Le témoignage', pp. 392–3, *pace* p. 409, n. 2.
44 The actual dating of the *Bibliotheca* remains debated. According to P. Lemerle (*Byzantine Humanism*, tr. H. Lindsay and A. Moffatt, Australian Association for Byzantine Studies, Byzantina Australiensia 3, Canberra, Australian National University Press, 1986, pp. 204–35, esp. pp. 219–25), the composition of the *Bibliotheca* must be dated to the year 837, i.e. prior to Photius' repeated election to and deposition from the patriarchate of Constantinople. However, N. G. Wilson, *Scholars of Byzantium*, London, Duckworth, 1983, pp. 89–119, conceding that the date is uncertain, favours a much later date of composition. M. Maas ('Photius' Treatment of Josephus and the High Priesthood', *Byzantion* 50 (1990), pp. 184–94, esp. pp. 193–4), not only argues likewise convincingly for a later period of completion, in which case Photius' own fate would doubtlessly have influenced his attitude towards John Chrysostom, but also

gives evidence for the degree to which his own preoccupations influenced his editorial method. K. Ziegler, s.v. Photios, *RE*.

45 Corroborated by his regard for the bishop in general, *Bibl.* 229, 274; Wilson, *Scholars*, pp. 89–119.

46 Especially Ps.-Martyrius, *Life of John Chrysostom*, see below; and Pall. *Dial.* chapter 12, corresponding to 25th accusation of John, and chapters 13, 14, 15 and 19.

47 Pall. *Dial.* 13, 129–131; alluding to Theophilus' pamphlet written after the synod in 405, Pel. Diac. *In defensione* 70–71.

48 Accusation of John the Deacon 11. As mentioned above, John appears to have alienated Aurelianus, Saturnius and Johannes during the Gainas crisis. Ps.-Martyrius P 483a–486b states that John Chrysostom's opponents had falsified rumours of his pro-Gothic stance even prior to Theophilus' arrival on the scene, implying that John had intended to abandon Church and Empire – an even graver betrayal. See also Zos. *Hist. nova* 5.23.2. Ommeslaeghe, 'Le témoniage', p. 403, n. 3; id., 'Jean Chrysostome et le conflit', p. 152. Soc. *HE* 6.6 account of the events is based on Eusebius Scholasticus' lost work *Gainea*; Alberts, *Goten*, pp. 166–7; Cameron, 'Earthquake', pp. 347–50.

49 Acc. of John 27.

50 Acc. of John 23, 25, 15. Isolating behaviour is frequently associated with tyrannical rulers. The seriousness of this charge is underlined by its frequent repetition and by Palladius' efforts to counter it. For the association of isolation and secretiveness with illegal rulership, Albert, *Goten*, pp. 52–3, nn. 196 and 198; Straub, *Herrscherideal*, pp. 22–3.

51 Acc. of John 5, 6. Literally 'nonsense, silly-talker'; *LSJ* s.v.

52 Acc. of John 9, 2.

53 Acc. of John 9. For Severian of Gaballa see Pall. *Dial.* 3.50; and M. Aubineau, *Un traité inédit de christologie de Sévérien de Gabala In Centurionem et Contra Manichaeos et Apollinaristas*, Cahiers d'Orientalisme 5, Geneva, P. Cramer, 1983, pp. 11–17. The function of the *dekanoi* employed against Severian remains debated; Dagron, *Naissance*, p. 491 suggests that 'ils ne sont ni les croque-morts de Constantinople, ni des supérieurs de monastères, ni des clercs de l'economat, comme on l'a cru, mais un corps d'appariteurs ou d'huisseurs à la disposition de l'archevêche.'

54 Acc. of John 29.

55 For the at times intense building activity of bishops cf. Ambr. *De off.* 2.136; *Sermo contra Aux.* 33; Brown, 'Art and Society', pp. 19–22; N. McLynn, *Ambrose of Milan: Church and Court in a Christian Capital*, Transformation of the Classical Heritage 22, Berkeley, CA, University of California Press, 1994, pp. 226–37, and for accusations and counter-accusation of improper use of funds, p. 55.

56 I have not been able to locate the edition of the cod. Parisinus grec. 1519, Bibliothèque national de Paris, announced by F. van Ommeslaeghe, *L'oraison funèbre de S. Jean Chrysostome attribuée à Martyrius d'Antioche*, Subsidia Hagiographica 73, Brussels, Soc. Bollandistes, 1989, nor have I been able to consult id., *De lijkrede voor Johannes Chrysostomus toegeschreven aan Martyrius van Antiochie: Tekstuitgave met Commentaaar*, Hoofdstukken uit de Historische Kritiek, Louvain, 1974. I have had access to the manuscript on microfilm. Parts of Ps.-Martyrius are also in PG 47, xlii–lii; cf. *BHG* 871.

57 Ommeslaeghe, the pre-eminent authority on the text, calls it 'un ardent plaidoyer se présentant sous l'aspect d'un panégyrique funèbre' ('Le témoignage', p. 393). For the dating and significance of this important source

see also id., 'La valeur historique de la *Vie de S. Jean Chrysostome* attribuée à Martyrius d'Antioche (*BHG* 871)', *SP* 12 (1975), pp. 478–83; id., 'Jean Chrysostome et le peuple', pp. 329–49; id., 'Jean Chrysostome en conflit', pp. 131–59.

58 Ommeslaeghe, 'Le témoignage', pp. 393–4.

59 Martyr. P 481b, P 487a; contrary to Pall. *Dial.* 3.76–91.

60 Martyr. P 479a–481a; 483a–486b.

61 Martyr. P 486b–489b; for example, the fact that he was reconciled with the exiled monks shortly after the synod.

62 Ommeslaeghe, 'Le témoignage', pp. 405–7.

63 Martyr. P 491b–495b; 499a–b is the only source to stress the hostility aroused by John's intention to build a leper hospital in a fashionable suburb. Cf. M. Aubineau, 'Zôticos de Constantinople, nourricier des pauvres et serviteur des lépreux', *Analecta Bollandiana* 93 (1975), pp. 66–108.

64 Martyr. P 497a–499b. Ommeslaeghe, 'Le témoignage', pp. 409–11.

65 Martyr. P 481b. Ommeslaeghe, 'Le témoignage', p. 400. For magic accusations, Martyr. P 499b–500b; cf. Ommeslaeghe, 'Le témoignage', p. 411.

66 This letter has been preserved as part of Pall. *Dial.* 1.177ff. in the only complete manuscript of the *Dialogue*, the *Mediceus Laurentianus* IX, 14. It is, however, a later insertion and has an extensive independent ms. tradition, cf. Malingrey, SC 342, 47–66, for discussion. In the following it will be cited according to its separate edition, ibid., 47–95; tr. Meyer, *Dialogue*, pp. 17–24; Gregory, 'Zosimus 5, 23', pp. 64–5; Ommeslaeghe, 'Le témoignage', pp. 391–2. For a stylistic analysis, see A. Milazzo, 'Le epistole di Giovanni Crisostomo ad Innocenze I e le epistole 1–4 di Demostene', *Orpheus* 2 (1982), pp. 200–223.

67 The precise sequence of events during that Easter night as well as the parties responsible for setting fire to the church are difficult to reconstruct, since our primary sources (John, Palladius, Ps.-Martyrius, Socrates, Sozomen, Theodoret and Zosimus-Eunapius) all disagree with regard to the specifics. It appears, however, that the disturbances were caused by disaffected Constantinopolitans, some of them monks who had opposed John, and clashed with his supporters; Baur, *John Chrysostom*, vol. 2, p. 295; Dagron, *Naissance*, pp. 489–92; Gregory, 'Zosimus', pp. 61–83; Liebeschuetz, 'The Fall', 15–23; Ommeslaeghe, 'John Chrysostom et le peuple', pp. 340–45.

68 Ommeslaeghe, 'Le témoignage', p. 409.

69 For a detailed chronology of the interventions of John's supporters with Innocent cf. Pietri, *Roma Christiana*, pp. 1300–1310.

70 *Letter* 32–42. Soz. *HE* 8.17.2, and Soc. *HE* 6.15 state that Theophilus lodged instead in an imperial residence. For other instances of this 'old custom' see canons 9 and 10 of Sardica, and for example Ambr. *Ep.* 41 on his visits to Rome; Paul. *V. Amb.* 10.1, 28.1; for his habit of entertaining guests at table, ibid., 30.1; Sulp. Sev. *Dial.* 1.25.6; McLynn, *Ambrose*, pp. 256–7.

71 For the significance and role of the archdeacon, cf. Dagron, *Naissance*, p. 490.

72 John repeats this formula which refers to Theophilus' breaches of both ecclesiastic and civil procedure several times, in 11.61–2, 89 and 229–30.

73 This is an allusion to can. 6 of Constantinople stipulating that those who are themselves under accusation may not accuse others prior to having cleared themselves; Malingrey, SC 342 74, n. 4.

74 Constantinople being (in theory) a diocese in the province of Thrace. For the complicated relation between the two, cf. Dagron, *Naissance*, pp. 458–9.

75 *Letter* 128–38.

76 Cf. Innocent's letter to Theophilus, Pall. *Dial.* 3.22–33, referring to the admission to communion of excommunicated bishops as regulated in can. 5 of Nicaea, Hefele-Leclercq, *Histoire des concils*, vol. 1, pp. 548–9; J. Gaudemet, *L'église dans l'empire romain*, Paris, Beauchesne, 1958, p. 77, n. 3.

77 For the legal techniques used by bishops in heresy procedures see e.g. Syn. *Ep.* 105, addressed to Theophilus and the *scholastikoi* in Alexandria, men qualified in all stages of the law; *C.Th.* 16.10.19, issued by Honorius on 15 November 408; Ruf. *HE* 10.3; Augst. *Sermon 62 contra paganos*, ed. P. Dolbeau, *Recherches Augustiniennes* 26 (1992), pp. 90–141; id., *Ep.* 24*, 28* and 29*; id., *Serm.* 4.7 against Donatists. See esp. C. Humfress, 'Bishops as Forensic Advocates in the Formation of Christian Doctrine', paper given at the workshop on orthodoxy at the École Française de Rome, March 29–30, 1996 and her forthcoming Cambridge diss. on the same subject.

78 Already in 394 Epiph. *Ep. ad Johannem episc.* 9 = Jer. *Ep.* 51 warns against Palladius' Origenism.

79 For an overview of Theophilus' considerable (though fragmentary) writings see M. Richard, 'Les ecrits de Theophile d'Alexandrie', *Le Museon* 52 (1939), pp. 33–50, and Favale, 'Teofilo', pp. 224–7. New fragments can now be added, cf. Richard, 'Nouveaux fragments de Theophile d' Aléxandrie', *Nachrichten der Akademie der Wissenschaften Göttingen, Phil.-hist. Kl.*, Göttingen, Vandenhoeck & Ruprecht, 1975, pp. 57–65; and J. Declerck, 'Théophile d'Alexandrie contre Origène: Nouveaux fragments de l'*Epistula Synodalis Prima* (CPG 2595)', *Byzantion* 54 (1984), pp. 495–507.

80 Jerome translated Theophilus' *Festal Letters* 16 (AD 401) = Jer. *Ep.* 96; 17 (AD 402) = Jer. *Ep.* 98; 19 (AD 404) = Jer. *Ep.* 100. In addition, Jerome translated the second synodal letter of AD 400 (three fragments of the first are preserved by Justinian, *Lib. adv. Orig.* [PG 86 969–71]) = Jer. *Ep.* 92; one letter to Epiphanius = Jer. *Ep.* 90, and two addressed to Jerome himself, all from AD 400 = Jer. *Epp.* 87 and 89. For controversy regarding Jerome's translation of some of these letters cf. S. Rebenich, *Hieronymus und sein Kreis: Prosopographische und sozialgeschichtliche Untersuchungen*, Historia-Einzelschriften 72, Stuttgart, F. Steiner, 1992, pp. 200–201.

81 Writings reflecting Theophilus' broader development have fared even worse than those more specifically related to the synod. According to M. Richard ('Les écrits', p. 33): 'aujourd'hui, qui veut étudier cet auteur doit avoir à sa disposition toute une bibliothèque'. Much of his exegetical writings have to be culled from other collections. Cf. in addition to the above mentioned M. Aubineau, 'Membra disiecta d'un codex en majuscule, du IXe s. (Le Caire, Leipzig, Washington): Théophile d'Alexandrie, *In mysticam cenam'*, *Jahrbuch der Österreichischen Byzantinistik* 33 (1983), pp. 25–35; E. Drioton, 'La discussion d'un moine anthromorphite Audien avec le patriarche Théophile d' Alexandrie en l'année 399', *Revue de l'Orient Chrétien*, 2e ser., 10 (= 20) (1915–17), pp. 92–100, 113–28; P. Nautin, 'La lettre de Théophile d'Alexandrie a l'église de Jérusalem et la réponse de Jean de Jérusalem (juin–juillet 396)', *RHE* 69 (1974), pp. 365–94; T. Orlandi, 'Uno scritto di Teofilo di Alessandria sulla distruzione del *Serapeum?*', *La Parola del Passato* 23 (1968), pp. 295–304; M. Richard, 'Les fragments exégétiques de Théophile d'Alexandrie et Théophile d'Antioche', *Revue Biblique* 47 (1938), pp. 387–97; id., 'Une homélie de Théophile d'Alexandrie sur l'institution de l'Eucharistie', *RHE* 33 (1937), pp. 46–54. In the following, the reconstruction of Theophilus' doctrinal developments relies heavily on E. Clark's fundamental work, to my knowledge the

most comprehensive assessment available to date, *Origenist Controversy*, pp. 37–8, and especially 43–60, 105–21.

82 Primarily Palladius and the Church historians, who are despite their differing traditions nevertheless favourably disposed towards Chrysostom and the Constantinopolitan position, cf. above, n. 25.

83 Canon 5 stipulates that in cases of excommunication the local synod's vote has the force of law. It further prescribes that whosoever has been excommunicated in one province must not be accepted to communion in another. However, the excommunication has to be done for appropriate reasons; it must not be done out of personal hatred. See also canons 4 and 6, Hefele-Leclercq, *Histoire des concils*, vol. 1, pp. 539–69; Dagron, *Naissance*, p. 412. In other words, if Palladius wants to stress the illegitimacy of Theophilus' actions he needs to prove hatred as a motive, which he does, or at least attempts to do.

84 John's *Letter to Innocent* 46–52 also refers to can. 5 of Nicaea (Hefele-Leclercq, *Histoire des concils*, vol. 1, pp. 548–9), but now reverses the charge.

85 For Jerome's involvement in the Origenist controversy see Clark, *Origenist Controversy*, pp. 121–51. See Rebenich, *Hieronymus*, pp. 193–208 for Jerome's correspondence in Bethlehem and Rome during that period.

86 They can easily be identified as Ammonius, the Tall Brothers and perhaps Evagrius Ponticus, Palladius and John Cassian; Clark, *Origenist Controversy*, p. 107.

87 Jer. *Ep.* 92.2 and 4.

88 Apparently the examination centred on Origen's *On First Principle, On Prayer*, and *On the Resurrection*. For a detailed analysis of Theophilus' early criticism of Origen and the synod he convened see Clark, *Origenist Controversy*, pp. 108–11. Cf. also Theophilus' letters to Jerome, Jer. *Epp.* 87 and 88.

89 Jer. *Ep.* 92.3 (Volentes causam Isidori, quam nos propter verecundiam et Ecclesiae disciplinam episcoporum iudicio seruabamus, proferre in medium . . .).

90 Jer. *Ep.* 92.3.

91 Jer. *Ep.* 92.5 (Nihil eis nocuimus, nihil tulimus: una causa in nos odiorum est, quod usque ad mortem parati sumus fidem defendere).

92 Jer. *Ep.* 93. Bishop Dionysus of Lydda is the exception. He had been a monk from the region of Eleutheropolis, Epiphanius' monastery. Jer. *Ep.* 94. Clark, *Origenist Controversy*, p. 111.

93 Theophilus, *Letter to Epiphanius* = Jer. *Ep.* 90; Pall. *Dial.* 7.61–4.

94 Jer. *Ep.* 90; Soc. *HE* 6.10; Theophilus had already acted as a mediator between Epiphanius and John of Jerusalem in another conflict involving Origen's writings in 396. P. Nautin, 'La lettre de Théophile', pp. 365–94. For the development of Epiphanius' anti-Origenism, cf. Clark, *Origenist Controversy*, pp. 86–104 and Dechow, *Dogma and Mysticism*, pp. 243–403.

95 Theophilus had sent the monk Theodore to Rome, Jer. *Epp.* 86, 88, 89, 127.10. F. Cavallera, *Saint Jerome: Sa vie et son œuvre*, Louvain, 1922, vol. 1, p. 286; Hunt, 'Palladius', p. 473; Liebeschuetz, *Barbarians and Bishops*, p. 203–5; Rebenich, *Hieronymus*, pp. 106–8, 201–8.

96 *Ep. fest.* 401 = Jer. *Ep.* 96; Justinian, *Liber in Origenem* (PG 86 967); *CPG* 2.2602, 2603; Clark, *Origenist Controversy*, p. 105 and especially pp. 112–14 for new developments in Theophilus' thinking.

97 In particular the Gainas crisis and John's reorganization of the diocese of Asia. Pall. *Dial.* 13–16; Soc. *HE* 5.23 and 6.9; Soz. *HE* 7.17 and 8.13; Albert, *Goten*, pp. 151–62; Baur, *John Chrysostom*, vol. 2, p. 184; Cameron, 'Earthquake', pp. 349–50; Liebeschuetz, *Barbarians and Bishops*, pp. 118–20,

203–5. The exact chronology of the fate of the expelled monks in Constantinople, John's dealings with them and Theophilus' response is hard to reconstruct. Theophilus' own writings are not sufficient, and each of the other authors gives a slightly differing sequence and differing motives.

98 John's letter to Theophilus, Pal. *Dial.* 7.104–6 and passim; Soc. *HE* 6.9; Soz. *HE* 8.13.

99 Clark, *Origenist Controversy*, pp. 115–16.

100 Jer. *Ep.* 98.22–3; but no official summons is mentioned.

101 *Acts of the Synod*, acc. of Isaacius 2; Soc.*HE* 6.14; Soz. *HE* 8.14–15.

102 John's letter to Theophilus, Pall. *Dial.* 7.125–9; and Arcadius' summons via the *magister officium* charging him with calumny (cf. *C.Th.* 9.34), a serious offence, ibid., 8.18–22. According to Palladius a false report of John's acceptance of the monks prompted Theophilus' actions. Soc. implies the role of Eudoxia, *HE* 6.15. M. Clauss, *Der magister officiorum in der Spätantike (4.–6. Jahrhundert): Das Amt und sein Einfluß auf die kaiserliche Politik*, Vestigia 32, Munich, Beck, 1980, p. 126; Liebeschuetz, *Barbarians and Bishops*, pp. 204–7.

103 According to Palladius, Theophilus responded immediately to John's letter mentioning the monks' accusations against him (*Dial.* 7.125–9) with his own pointing to violation of canon 5 of Nicaea, *Dial.* 7.132–6; Hefele-Leclercq, *Histoire des concils*, vol. 1.1, pp. 548–9. See also Dagron, *Naissance*, p. 455.

104 Jer. *Ep.* 113, 1. of AD 405. The fragment of 404 preserved by Facundius, *Pro def.* 6 (PL 67 678), says that John's actions would have delighted Arians but does not call him a heretic or Origenist.

105 As confirmed by the exchange of letters between Theophilus, Chrysostom, Innocent, Honorius and Arcadius recorded in Palladius' *Dial.* chapters 3 and 7.

106 While in Constantinople in 403, Theophilus wrote to Atticus, the future bishop, the deacon Serapion, and to John Chrysostom explaining his grievances regarding Origen; Richard, 'Nouveaux fragments', pp. 57–65. His festal letter of 404 (= Jer. *Ep.* 100) also attests to a continuous involvement with issues raised by Origenist concerns; Clark, *Origenist Controversy*, pp. 117–18.

107 Liebeschuetz, *Barbarians and Bishops*, p. 204; Rebenich, *Hieronymus*, p. 108 and n. 531 with literature.

108 Liebeschuetz, 'Friends', p. 88, who notes that the charges nevertheless proved efficient.

109 See also V. Burrus' insightful remarks in *The Making of a Heretic: Gender, Authority, and the Priscillianist Controversy*, Berkeley, CA, University of California Press, 1995, pp. 1–24.

110 Through a juxtaposition of upper-class codes of conduct and anti-heretical labelling strategies I am seeking ways to form a synthesis between P. Brown's masterful analysis of the use of a rhetoric of power in *Power and Persuasion in Late Antiquity: Towards a Christian Roman Empire*, Madison WI, University of Wisconsin Press, 1992, as reflecting the interaction between the non-Christian and Christian elite and the *de facto* ruler, and E. Clark's analysis of an inner-Christian conflict in *Origenist Controversy*. Of course, as demonstrated by R. Lim, *Public Disputation*, anti-heretical labelling strategies are only one, and probably not even the most fruitful, avenue towards such a goal.

111 P. Brown, *Authority and the Sacred: Aspects of the Christianisation of the Roman World*, Cambridge, Cambridge University Press, 1995, p. 53.

6

GREGORY OF NYSSA

The force of identity

John Milbank

My excuse, as a systematic theologian, for addressing some issues in historical theology, is threefold. In the first place I am concerned with the way in which much recent treatment by systematic theologians of the Cappadocian position on the Trinity accords ill with the best and especially the most recent scholarship on Gregory of Nyssa. The implication of this scholarship is that many of the contrasts between Gregory and Augustine on the matter of the Trinity have been overdrawn, even as regards the yoking together of trinitarian with psychological concerns, as I shall later explain. In the second place I am concerned with the relevance of Gregory to contemporary debates concerning the relation of the philosophical category of being on the one hand, to the theological category of gift on the other. Thirdly, and most specifically, I am interested in Gregory's strong advocacy of *apatheia*, both as ontological norm and as ethical goal, which contrasts sharply with a tendency in recent theology either to reject or to qualify *apatheia* in both respects, in the belief that it represents a hellenic contamination of the biblical inheritance. In the face of this assumption I shall suggest that *in certain respects* Gregory stresses *apatheia* even more strongly than his pagan predecessors and near-contemporaries, precisely because he thinks this is demanded by the deliverancies of revelation and by categories of gift rather than being. This emphasis in his thought may seem, on the face of it, to accord ill with those aspects of his teaching which modern Christians have found congenial, namely his validation (or at least apparent validation) of relationality, communication and growth, distinct personal existence, emotions of certain kinds, generation and embodiment: in other words all that we might take to characterize the life of persons in material space and temporal duration. We take it that the positive valuation of the latter will be bound to include also a validation of the worth of the passions, and in this view we are, indeed, at one with much of ancient philosophy, although it made the correlation for opposite, negative reasons, being somewhat suspicious of the passions along with time, embodiment and spatial relation. From the point of view of both ancient and modern philosophy, it might be thought that Gregory is inconsistent in promoting a positive view of the latter three categories, and yet maintaining, even augmenting, *apatheia*.

However, I shall argue in this chapter that Gregory was not necessarily inconsistent, once one has grasped that instead of validating the passions he attempted the different task of redefining *activity* in such a fashion that it is no longer straightforwardly connected with notions of self-containment, self-sufficiency and autocracy normally taken to be the reverse of the passion-governed life. Instead, for Gregory, it is possible, at every ontological level, to be in the same instance both receptive *and* donating, *without* being in any sense subject to anything else that is not oneself, or in some way inhibits one's ideal reality. Here to receive is somehow *already* the movement of a counter-donation on the part of the will. I shall describe this conception, which will be further elaborated in due course, as active reception. For now one should note that if it redefines receptivity as action, it equally redefines action as receptivity. In my conclusion I shall suggest why the strategy of embracing active reception might be more radical and more defensible than the modern strategy of abandoning *apatheia*. But first of all I will outline this strategy of Gregory's under four headings: those of reputation, generation, growth and embodiment.

One of the key sites for the tyranny of the passions, according to Gregory, is that of *doxa*, or worldly glory, honour, credit or reputation. As with many of his pagan predecessors, a suspicion of worldly honour goes along with an apparent retreat from the social and political as such.[1] This sphere encourages us to believe in the realities of obscurity of birth or illustrious birth, or glory or splendour, or ancient renown, or present elevation, or power over others as Gregory puts it,[2] whereas such things have no real hold in Being. They are all rather a matter of human fictional imputation, and in *Against Eunomius* Gregory takes a fairly cynical view of human government: it being the case, he argues, that all humans are fundamentally equal as created, no human rule over other humans will ever be tolerated for long, and political history is bound to be a story of rise and fall.[3] In this sphere, prestige is a matter of reputation and reputation is *always* bloated, never adequately warranted. Thus Gregory shares the late antique tendency somewhat to devalue the political as a sphere of self-realization, in favour of the inner soul, as being more self-sufficient, less prey to the delusions or vagaries of repute and the degradations of time which tears from one every possession, whether of material goods or civic honour. He also augments this shift in so far as he advocates, at least for many, a withdrawal from the institution of marriage. The latter is viewed as peculiarly subject to the dominance of the passions, but not *especially*, and in fact, hardly at all, the sexual passion; much more as tied to the attempt to extend one's worldly glory beyond the present generation, to ensure that sons will preserve one's name along with their inherited possessions.[4] Also with a well-nigh inescapable *melancholia*: to embrace one's wife is always to embrace the one you know you will eventually have to mourn, or else will have to mourn you: therefore it is *already* an embrace of suffering, and a lure which engulfs the present in a perpetual reminiscence[5] (Gregory of Nyssa would not have liked *Shadowlands*). Marriage contains no remedy for these things within itself, although it can be used for the good, says Gregory, by those with sufficient gifts. For the weaker, however (presumably including himself), virginity is the safer course.[6]

Gregory's critique of marriage shows that he not only distrusts *present* civic glory, he also wishes to escape from all *traces* of human reputation left by time. Hence in *On the Christian Mode of Life* he exhorts us not to follow fashion, or seek truth in inherited opinions, but to turn inwards for the contemplation of abiding truth.[7] This sounds like a thoroughly Cartesian rejection of all inheritance and mere reception. However, Gregory builds his entire theology not round a defence of the inner citadel against the buffetings of illusory glory, but rather round *a different, and more abiding doxa*, which includes a more positive view of processes of historical transmission and public visibility. As to the first, one can mention the prologue to *On the Making of Man*, where Gregory wonders whether he should just praise his brother Basil's uncompleted *Hexamaeron* and not tarnish his reputation by producing an inferior conclusion, concerning man, since he regards himself as a far lesser thinker.[8] However, he justifies his enterprise by arguing that he will more reveal Basil's greatness if he shows that this can engender an equally great work in his disciple. In other words Basil's identity is no longer complete and bound up in his own works, and equally a praise of Basil is no longer just something conferred on him extrinsically, manifesting nothing new of his essential being. On the contrary, Basil's identity resides in the spirit of his writing, in a certain force which can communicate itself, and in praising Basil, Gregory is not just passively recording his greatness, but demonstrating it by *actively* appropriating it, so revealing its fecundity.

As to the second aspect of *doxa*, public visibility, one can mention Gregory's discussion of whether one should reveal one's good deeds in *On the Christian Mode of Life*.[9] Here, following the words of Jesus about not displaying one's piety, Gregory insists that good deeds performed for reputation will cease to be good deeds because they are being traded for a perishable, worldly good. However, he also has to confront texts about letting your light shine before men, which suggests that an entirely invisible good could scarcely be a good at all, since it would do no good, and certainly could not encourage in the good. Gregory resolves this *aporia* of virtue and visibility by requiring that we should give glory to God alone: that is to say, let shine in our deeds, God's deeds, since all good deeds are given from God.[10] Whereas for the world, virtuous deeds *result* in praise, for Gregory virtuous deeds are *only*, in themselves, the praise of another, attribution to God as their source, which is at the same time an offering of the deeds *back* to God as a return of gratitude. Inversely, in giving us the grace to become virtuous God is glorifying us, that is to say praising us not *for* our virtue, but that we can *be* virtuous. Virtue for Gregory is a power, *dynamis*, and a power that we must will, and yet this power, including our will, entirely begins before us as the Power of God. And though we receive it, we can *only* receive it actively (else it would not be our virtue) to the limit of our partici- pating capacity. Against Eunomius and his view that the Father's glory is essentially incommunicable Gregory calls attention to the fact that even human creatures, never mind the Son of God, can be glorified by the Father, without finite limit (that means for us, endlessly) with his glory, which is to say his active potential or *dynamis*.[11] The trinitarian context will offer a yet more radical twist; not only does God's dynamic praise of us precede and permit our virtue, this is even the case (though in an altered sense of precede which involves no temporal priority nor hierarchical supremacy) for the divine Logos who is fully and essentially God himself, since the Son is the glory and the *dynamis*, besides being the wisdom of the Father. And this means that the Father's own virtue consists in offering a previously unmer- ited praise to another, just as he essentially persists also in receiving back this praise.

We are now in a position to contrast Gregory's views of worldly and divine *doxa*. The former is empty, and here praise has a secret priority over what is praised. One would expect a contrast to this to be made in terms of an indication of stable identity, of what really belongs to things and to human beings. In other words, a rejection of the rhetorical world of persua- sion in favour of the dialectical realm or vision of abiding realities. Yet Gregory scorns dialectic as much as rhetoric: reality, as the infinite being of God, cannot be grasped under a category, nor can created realities be so grasped either, for they mirror this incomprehensibility and are in a state of constant flux.[12] How, then, can one identify Gregory's discourse, which one notes is marked by the piling up of persuasive arguments after the fashion of the second sophistic, and by the celebration of less ornate but thereby all the more sublime figures of speech which he takes to characterize biblical writing?[13] I suggest as a kind of *doxologic*, in which persuasion and encomium is not directed towards the possession of glory by oneself or another, but rather to the constant transmission of glory which is all the more one's own in so far as another person can receive it and repeat its force.[14] As with human glory, surprisingly, so also in the case of divine *doxa*, praise has priority over what is praised, yet this is no longer secret, but out in the open and with a different intent – not to hoard praise but to exchange it, such that praise is never simply of oneself or of another. Supremely, we know in praising God, in offering him glory which is his own, and not in seeing God, nor in manipulating men.

This 'doxologic' is followed by Gregory in *The Life of Moses*, where he defines virtue as perfection, as the infinitely active, unlimited, entirely dispassionate life. As such, it cannot be contained, and therefore, unlike

Plato and Aristotle, Gregory offers no *logos* of virtue.[15] Nor can he offer his own life, nor could anyone, as an example of virtue, since virtue as infinite cannot be attained.[16] All Gregory can do is exhort to virtue, and praise a virtue which is never present, but which nonetheless arrives through praise, since it is an offering of praise. For this reason Gregory can claim that though we do not know and cannot exemplify virtue, we can still have a part (*mesos*) in it, if we proceed from activity to activity, for activity only remains active if it does not seek to lay hold inwardly upon its activity but continuously receives more activity from the divine source. In this context a certain reception from the narrated memory of other human beings also is possible: one may praise Moses and offer him as a kind of example, since he was the sublime man who pointed absolutely beyond himself to God, and to the God-Man.[17] In imitating Moses, therefore, we are imitating a man who is paradoxically imitating – that is to say following behind the back of – a man who is yet to come: Christ, just as for us also the full body of Christ is yet to be realized, and we follow in its wake. Nonetheless Moses plays for us a slightly more positive role: his finished life is itself a *mesos*, a part, which has connotations of both role and inheritance (the double sense in English of a 'lot') just as Gregory insists that Moses played a part in the *politeia*, a political life, but a *polis* now more in time than space.[18] Moses is a more appropriate example than a present contemporary saint, since his life is over and therefore we are less tempted simply to copy it but see that it is to be taken further, extended differently and yet sustained as the same. In other texts Gregory suggests that properly speaking there is only one human being transmitted from person to person;[19] it follows that *epectasis* applies transgenerationally as well as internally, and Gregory does not exhort us to leave behind the Chaldeans and Egyptians in the sense of leave behind history, but in the sense of leave behind our passions, which they allegorically stand for, and pass, not from place and body to spirit, but in every place and every body from passivity to activity.[20]

My second heading is that of generation. I have already mentioned how Gregory treats an exchange of glory within the Trinity. The Son is the Father's *doxa*; without the Son the Father is without *doxa* and the glory of both is the Holy Spirit.[21] Here the Spirit is the bond of glory in *exactly* the way he is bond of love for Augustine. This giving of glory within God is dealt with by the Bible in terms of metaphors of generation, Father to Son. One of the main questions at issue with Eunomius was how this generation was possible without passion. Eunomius claimed that all generation necessarily involved passion, and therefore that the Son was subordinate to the Father, who is in himself utterly uninvolved in any such transitive activity. To this, Gregory responds that even in the case of human generation, children do not have a different or a lesser human essence than their parents. Even though human generation is passionate, it already gives the lie to Eunomius' assumption that cause and effect will diverge essentially, or that a beginning is a kind of pre-containing foundation.[22] (So much for the idea that all the Greek Fathers laid great store on the Father as *arche*, prior to relationality.) Furthermore, the *passionate* aspect of human generation is only an aspect of the post-fall emergency economy; humans were originally intended to self-propagate in a purely active mode. Such propagation was restored in the case of the Virgin birth, in which Mary's integrity was not cancelled but rather re-affirmed by her receiving of the Logos, when her body was entirely transparent to her active willed assent.[23] This assent involved a speaking of a word from her mind which Gregory presents as a further example of non-passive generation even amongst human beings: it is not that the word receives something from the mind, rather that it is the activity outgoing from the mental source. Therefore to defend generation without passivity in God, Gregory makes appeal to certain instances of causality within time to show that such a possibility exists even when generation involves movement and alteration. And, as Michel Barnes has shown, he is involved here in defending a certain account of the diversity of kinds of causality.[24] Gregory accuses Eunomius of assimilating all causality to the model of a voluntary, artisanal imposition of form on matter.[25] In so far as Eunomius speaks of *dynamis*, he thinks of it not as a power that is automatically self-communicating, but rather like the power of an emperor which can be exercised or not at will. No action or *energeia* for Eunomius belongs essentially to a nature but arises only for the occasion of producing a particular work (*ergon*) and is precisely adapted to just this *one* work and no other; whereas Gregory points out that many causes produce diverse effects in different receptacles, thus rain always moistens, but quickens myriads of diverse seeds, fire always heats, but heat hardens some things, melts others.[26] For Eunomius the Son is an *ergon* caused by an act of *energeia* of the Father precisely adapted to this one work (whereas for Gregory the same causal *dynamis* of the Father both generates the Son and creates the cosmos with all its diversity of effects), but the act of the Father is not in itself the Father, who as strictly the ungenerate does not of his essence enter even into causation.[27] Here it is worth noting that while Gregory attacks, on apophatic grounds, Eunomius' identifying of God with an essence for which we can give a word – ungenerate – there is another sense in which Eunomius' God is more ineffable than Gregory's in so far as it is totally non-participable.[28] Gregory defends not just God as incomprehensible *ousia*, but also God as incomprehensible *dynamis* – as inherently giving and effecting (and affecting).

According to Gregory, to grasp divine causality, one must employ analogically examples of all modes of created causality. The artisanal model applies somewhat to creation, but here it must be supplemented by, and in the case of trinitarian generation abandoned for, other causal models. Physical generation is one, the generation of mental power in the incorporeal word is another, yet equally crucial is the much more materialist instance of material efflux, or the self-propagation of a material power. Here the supreme example is fire – fire, like mind, is in ceaseless motion, inherently contagious – it exists to effect, and it cannot but heat. Again and again Gregory says that the Father is like this.[29] Barnes has shown how Gregory is here drawing on a key motif within Platonism itself.[30] From the Hippocratic tradition, Plato took over the notion of a power physics according to which the cosmos is composed of fundamental self-propagating elemental qualities usually arranged in pairs of opposites. Unlike the materialist philosophers, the more human scientists, the doctors, refused to treat the combination of those elements as merely epiphenomenal in relation to their corporeal components. This, however, suggested that the philosophy of material elements could not provide an adequate ontology, and that what arrives later cannot be explained as an aggregate of the earlier, but only in teleological terms as an arrival from a transcendent source. Hence in *Phaedo* (an important source for Gregory) Plato says that the number 2 is not to be explained as 1 plus 1, but as a participation in the form of Twoness.[31] However, the spiritual forms themselves are conceived on the model of power physics. Just as fire heats, so justice makes just and so forth. Despite the continued dominance of the artisanal model in Plato's account of the relation of ideal to matter – that is, ideas inform a substratum – the transposed power physics gives an idea of participation which the Neoplatonists can later develop into the notion of emanation.

Hence Gregory's insistence on *dynamis* represents a very Platonic moment in his thought. And the notion certainly lent itself to thoughts of threeness – for Plato in the *Sophist* there is a *dynamis* to affect and a *dynamis* to be affected. The combination of the two is a third reality.[32] However, in that dialogue Plato supposed that real being must be outside affecting and being affected, including being known, and if to the contrary it appears that being can somehow be known then true being must after all embrace both the unchanging and the changing.[33] Without truly solving the problem of the self-dissolution in Platonism which this suggests, the Neoplatonists insisted that what is truly and absolutely One does, nonetheless, communicate itself, just as the sun must pour forth its rays. Yet Gregory, of course, takes one step further: the source is now in no sense beyond its rays, and there is no way to return to the source by abandoning the rays as merely a mirrored reflection. The Father, Son and Spirit are one equal dynamic display of glory.

While at times Gregory treats the Son as especially the power of the Father, at other times he insists that power is common to all three persons in the way that *ousia* is also common. Here his usual mode of argument is from the experience of salvation. The Son saves, the Spirit saves, but only God can save, so all three persons display equally the saving *dynamis* of God.[34] In this case an economic trinitarian argument is also automatically an immanent one, and one notes that Gregory insists just as strongly as the West on one essence whose nature cannot possibly be in any way defined via personal relation, any more than the fact that I am born declares what I am.[35] However, Barnes's remarkable contribution has been to show that Gregory (although in this respect paralleled by Latin treatment of *virtus*) speaks more often of one *dynamis* than one *ousia*.[36] And this term provides something very like a trinitarian ontology which is in keeping with a doxological discourse, for it mediates between the *ousia* register and the *prosopon* (person) register. What is must affect, and for Gregory this affecting is identical with the being affected, since there is no receptable prior to this being affected, and therefore passivity in the usual sense is denied all ontological purchase. Yet generation remains, without suffering and without interval – but thereby, as all the more essential.

Gregory, therefore, charts a specifically trinitarian path beyond the self-dissolution of Platonism, not available to Neoplatonism. Whereas Stoicism construed the equality in Being of both the unaffecting/unaffected and the affecting/affected in terms of a priority of the cosmos which rendered Platonic ideas (the unaffecting/unaffected aspect) mere surface effects (incorporeals) of a material process in flux,[37] Gregory articulates a paradoxical identity of these two, of unaffecting/unaffected *ousia* and affecting/affected *dynamis* in the transcendent source itself. This paradox is exemplified in Gregory's boldest move against Eunomius when he claims that to deny generation in God actually limits God, precisely because this denial construes God as a beginning (or a foundation). Beginnings, says Gregory, imply also ends and therefore relational circumscription.[38] By declaring that there is some sort of causal transition in God, Gregory negates not only temporal and spatial interval (*diastasis*) but also an identification of *adiastasis* with an absolute beginning or absolute presence to self. God's incomprehensibility is not, for Gregory, just an epistemological matter, but is rather ontological and means that God literally does not comprehend himself. Therefore, although he fully knows himself, this knowing is not on the model of our knowing which is a grasping or manipulative effecting, the Stoic *katalepsis*.[39] And nor is it vision, which also grasps. Instead it is infinite bestowing and bestowing back again. And the same, doxological account of knowing extends even to the human creation – here also the earlier does not explain, and *katalepsis* is only for purposes of pragmatic technological benefit. There can be no grasp of essences, since the essence of the world is a mirroring of divine incomprehensibility.[40] The world does not comprehend itself, cannot be known within itself, but instead, as Gregory repeatedly insists, the *logos* about the world is bigger than the world itself because it accounts for it only as derived from a transcendent elsewhere and therefore as unfathomable even down to its smallest details. The identity of the world resides in a power from beyond the world that gives the world itself a power to go beyond what is previously given.

The third heading is growth. The other site for discussion of passion in Gregory is the soul. However, it is linked with the Trinity. In *On the Making of Man* Gregory declares that if the soul is in the image of God and the soul cannot be divided then this proves that the Trinity cannot be divided.[41] This is Gregory's development of an earlier argument for the unity of God as creator from the unity of the cosmos and the unity of the soul; just as the soul can originate man's diverse activities in the unified body, so God can do many different things in the unified creation.[42] Here, however, it is a question specifically of the three Aristotelian faculties of the soul: intellective, sensitive, nutritive. The difficulty is, can the soul be both threefold and unified, especially as sensitivity and nutrition are involved in passion. But here also, as with the Trinity, the solution is provided in terms of a kind of active receptivity, even if this is not so immediately apparent.

Commentators have divided concerning Gregory's account of the soul: for some he is essentially a Posidonian – all three faculties belong in some way to the soul, and the passions have a positive educational function. For others, Gregory insists on an absolute unity of the soul in accord with one strand of Platonism. What is quite clear is that Gregory, along with most of his immediate forebears, rejected the account of the soul given in Plato's *Republic*, according to which it has three parts: *nous, thumos, epithumia* – on the usual grounds that this suggested three different people (the homunculus problem).[43] However, Gregory assimilated the Platonic division of the soul to the Aristotelian one, and rejected both in the name of a united and active rational soul. The lower faculties are said to be improperly named souls and more properly called *hormai* (impulses).[44] Nonetheless, he persists in a faculties of soul language and insists that the presence of the rational soul is necessary to animate these powers – the mind in order to sense, and a kind of unconscious emanation from the brain to perform all other natural functions, including generation. So how are we to understand how the one, active soul everywhere animates, even when this appears to involve passions?

First of all, one needs to realize that *psyche* for Gregory's inheritance was a fundamental ontological category. In the cosmology which Gregory shared with Basil, the universe consisted not of informed matter but of essentially immaterial qualities – light, heat, motion etc. which have an abstract character and so can properly be thought to derive from mind (i.e. the mind of God). These elements are held together in harmonic and oppositional arrangements which often counter expectation: for example, light falls. Only our mind grasps these patterns (though it cannot comprehend them) and so knows that they have their origin in mind. The cosmos is therefore psychically bound together, just as our souls bind our bodies together. Rather, as much later for Spinoza, it seems that for Gregory body and mind never touch, yet are absolutely co-extensive. Now the implication of this cosmology is that Gregory believes he has followed rigorously the logic of creation *ex nihilo*: first there is no passive matter preceding creation and waiting to be informed, but second Gregory sees no need to posit created passive matter either (it is true he speaks sometimes of the aeons of time and space as containers, but they are not in any sense a *substratum*).[45] Thus Gregory has redefined bodies as essentially immaterial and active, since their entire being flows from the wholly active God. It is in this manner that Gregory's Christian outlook seems to give passion still less ontological purchase than for the Stoics or Neoplatonists. In *Against Eunomius* Gregory says that the break ups of bodies are not really passions of bodies, but *erga*, works of nature (again, the pre-echo of Spinoza is very strong here).[46] One can interpolate that these break ups are only passive from the perspective of the individual bodies, and that passivity here contributes nothing (as a *substratum* would). But only animal bodies would consciously have this illusory perspective, only they would undergo death as a passivity. Death, however, is for Gregory a result of the fall, and therefore the apparent passivity of even individual bodies is essentially unnatural (and here Gregory is able to transcend the dualism of perspective consequent upon Spinoza's monistic immanentism).

It is this consideration which helps us to understand how the one rational soul can be linked with apparently passive impulses. Their passionate character is part of the fallen economy – punitive, and yet merciful and delaying. For example, the fallen body can still receive being, by eating food, yet this causes him passively to experience repletion and later the passive need to eat again. Our fallen bodies now live for a merciful interval in which we can receive redemptive glory, but still get used up. However, these passionate aspects of the fallen body are not strictly to be called passions, according to Gregory in *Against Eunomius*: real passions involve sin, in other words the state in which the rational soul is dominated by such impulses – in which it identifies, for example, with our need to possess and appropriate food in order to live, and makes accumulation the goal of life[47] (the well-stocked fridge). The fallen *hormai* are neutral, and if we confine suffering to a material level this suffering purges sin by leading it to its result in death. In this way the *hormai* can be put to good use: self-preserving anger becomes anger at sin and so serves genuine self-preservation under grace, and fortitude in pursuing salvation.[48] Desire for things can generate desire for God, and Gregory can use the word *hedones* (feelings) in a perfectly positive active sense.[49] No passion does not mean no feeling. Rowan Williams rightly emphasizes the way in which the bodily energies of desiring and self-preservation can in Gregory be used to promote spiritual growth. However, he notes, with some concern, that Moses does seem to be presented as having left even such impulses behind.[50] By contrast, I think that this is not inconsistent because the *hormai* or bodily passions are only a hinge; they are not to remain and in this respect Gregory compares them to Paul's faith and hope, which will not remain at the *eschaton*.[51] Suffering, passive desire and self-preservation in the face of the enemy will pass away; since (even if neutral) they are merely the outworking of sin, the realization that we have been damaged, impaired in our being, which is to say, precisely, been rendered passive (and again there is an oddly Spinozistic fore-echo). However, an *eros* proper to the soul remains, and is never surpassed, just as the self-directing will, drive and self-preservation in the good also remain.[52]

The former, in particular, is fundamentally receptive and yet it remains, and has ceased to be regarded by Gregory as a passion. Neither *eros* nor will are for him any longer subordinate to reason – like the Platonic baser aspects, or Aristotelian lower faculties – nor are they parts or even faculties of the soul. They are one with reason, but reason is somehow also will and also *eros*. This strange mode of unity is presented in *The Life of Moses* and the *Commentary on the Song of Songs* as a temporal oscillation. Frequently we pass from what one might dub a Neoplatonic stage when reason mirrors God to either a sublime drive of the will to a God whom we realize we cannot exhaust (but only touch) or else a wounding of our tranquil contemplation of beauty by a sublime desire[53] (as it were beyond the pleasure principle).

In this oscillation the Spirit leads us to desire the Bridegroom (the Son) and moves us on to the Father as invisible source. However, it then moves us back in a circle to Son and to Spirit via the incarnation and the presence of Spirit in the Church.[54] These persons also are equally in the place of darkness and both equally belong to the face to face beyond the Pauline mirror, which direct vision means for Gregory, paradoxically, following the back of (so that full visibility realizes full invisibility). We follow Christ with the wings of the dove which is equally the Spirit's brooding or resting over the Church.[55] Via the flying/resting of the Church in the Spirit we are inducted into the trinitarian exchange of glory. But this movement of soul into God is also for Gregory a movement inside the soul – not from faculty to faculty, but from reason as reason into reason as desire and willing, since reasoning is no longer *katalepsis* but praise and loving and self-exceeding aspiration. So from this we can conclude, after the Mosaic example, that like Augustine Gregory can envisage the soul as modelled on the divine essence, realized through three persons. For he stresses that the same soul can adopt different characters (*prosopeia*) – so the soul is diversified without parts into reason, will and desire, just as earlier we saw many human individuals can be considered manifestations of one collective person. The soul is for Gregory relational and diverse, not in the sense of possessing parts or aspects but as a *dynamis* moving from relative stasis to relative *ecstasis*. Although there is little explicit development of a psychological analogue to the Trinity in Gregory as compared with Augustine, it is still there. And for this reason one must (in the wake of Rowan Williams and Lewis Ayres[56]) oppose the received wisdom which regards the psychological analogy in Augustine as a speculative substitute for a genuine existential experience of the Trinity in the East. This is a false contrast, for four further reasons: (1) it was natural at this time to associate ontological categories for the Trinity with psychological ones; (2) the experiential was by everyone placed in psychological categories; (3) the relation to God had to be conceived as a relation repeated within the soul since we do not really relate to God but participate in him, (4) to experience the economic is to experience the immanent Trinity and if God is essentially triune and we image God, then the soul must be in some sense triune.

These considerations, which tend to justify the psychological analogy, thoroughly accord with the notion of active reception whereby in receiving we actively become what we receive: the triune God. So, for example, in *The Commentary on the Song of Songs* the Bride first receives from the Spirit, then becomes a spirit, first receives food, then provides a banquet for the Bridegroom.[57] Gregory stresses that to go on receiving grace we must ourselves give back, and salvation for him means that (in the Spirit) we also, as receiving the life of all three divine persons, can glorify Father, Son and Spirit.

My fourth category is embodiment. I have already mentioned that for Gregory the body is by nature active. In *On the Soul and Resurrection* he claims that the resurrection is possible because the soul is essentially the bond (*sundrome*) between the disparate elements, and that after their dispersal, which constitutes death, the soul preserves memory-traces of them, just as they are in some way marked forever by the bond of that particular soul. Thus reassembly is possible. However, Gregory faces the question, which period in a body's life will return? His answer here is no age and no period, since these belong to the revolutions of passion and it is precisely by virtue of the purgation of passion that the body will return – as active[58] – but nonetheless via passion, the fully adequate passion of Christ. Here active reception takes the form of a clear doctrine of *communicatio idiomatum*.[59] The divine person in Christ is not the subject of sin, for he only enhypostasizes the human nature by way of an unlimited communication of his divine attributes, but he can nonetheless be the subject of tiredness and fear etc. which are the neutral outworkings of sin, and assumed as the redemptive hinge of fallen human nature (this does not necessarily mean that the divine person is conscious of these things).

A further relevant consideration regards Gregory's general account of the relation of God to the creation. Although, he says, the mind cannot comprehend the incomprehensible, the incomprehensible can incomprehensibly be mirrored in our mind. For were the incomprehensible to be simply outside the comprehensible, it would be limited by the comprehensible (or circumscribable) and would therefore no longer be incomprehensible (here Gregory is alert to what we should today think of as set paradox; this is an aspect of his superseding of philosophical dialectic).[60] In keeping with this transgressive thought, Gregory uses strong conjunction of opposites language with regard to the Incarnation, and also boldly conjectures that our vision of Christ in the body of Christ or the Church is the vision of incomprehensible Being realized inside the creaturely domain.[61]

Therefore one may surmise that, for Gregory, although God does not suffer, he nonetheless cannot be outside neutral, sinless suffering as it occurs in time, else he would suffer it as outside himself, as it occurs in time (of course he does not suffer the real suffering that is sin, since this is sheer non-being). Hence, in Christ's passion one has for Gregory nonetheless the supreme instance of active reception. And just as God as *logos* is subject of suffering and this, says Gregory, is the greatest of all communications of *dynamis*, as it is power manifest in its opposite, weakness,[62] which astonishes the heavenly powers with the force of an ontological revelation, so also the human body of Christ is entirely infused with Godhead, and in time transformed into an entirely active body – the passion is only a passage.

Here Gregory stresses the collectivity of Christ's body: Christ is the beginning and we take him as beginning in order to know what we should desire to be.[63] The world itself, as St John says, will not contain the book of Christ because this *dynamis* in the world which is Christ's body is the world beyond the world – the book that the world exists to become. And the Church as the new creation is precisely the world become self-exceeding, looking for itself beyond its seeming totality.[64] One can relate this world turned inside out, exceeding itself, to Gregory's idea in the *Commentary on the Song of Songs* that the psychic life can best be conceived in terms of nature turned against nature.[65] That is to say, instead of simply using the higher senses and especially sight as figures of the psychic life, Gregory follows the Neoplatonists and Origen[66] in using all senses as metaphors but intensifying them. The soul is now a distillation of sense such that one conceives its life as an inebriation that allows one to get more and more drunk, or as an orgasmic experience in which wanting only comes with fulfilment and fulfilment does not cancel wanting.[67] In other words an entirely active, and in no sense passive or lacking desire; but just for that reason all the more erotic. And the resurrected body will itself correspond to this active psychic norm.

Thus Gregory's mystical quest looks to the vision of God as mirrored in the always progressing Christ who is shown in the body of Christ which is the Church.[68] Only by receiving God eucharistically do we see him, and unconstrained activity now means primarily receive God inside your soul and body, and not primarily enjoy the vision of God. Here it is notable that the shape of our flight, of the Dove, is only given collectively and synchronically in the form of the Church. Hence there is an infinite progress not just temporally forwards – but also spatially outwards, and this tends to provide a form for the temporal *élan*. In both cases of *diastasis* one can make an assimilation to, yet also draw a contrast with, the thought of Plotinus. For the latter there is also a kind of *epectasis* and non-lacking *eros*, but one can pass beyond that to a direct communion of the centre of the soul with the centre of the One itself. This is, indeed, no mere monism, but nevertheless it is through our inner contradiction, our termination of relational tension, that we are at last alone with the alone.[69] For Gregory, to the contrary, the distance remains since it persists in God himself.

This same similarity and yet contrast is seen with respect to interpsychic relations in both thinkers. For Plotinus, the souls in the intellectual realm fully penetrate each other, so that greater interiority implies simultaneously a greater spatial *ecstasis*. In this sense Plotinus was not anti-political, and he speaks of the final choral dance of the souls around (although he stresses there is no real spatial distance) the one centre.[70] In the case of Gregory also, the social and synchronic remains in the *eschaton*, but because the co-ordination is here less of a pre-established harmony and more involves a direct distance of relation, it is shown also in the temporal here and now, in an external monastic social practice, in which for private possession is substituted an endless handing-on of glory. In this new *polis*, as in Plato's *Republic*, the superior in wisdom rule (else one has non-rule), but beyond Plato superiority is grasped as something which is only for time, and so for-a-time: it exists to be communicated to novices, who have the chance to become wise and just in their turn. And this restriction of subordination to a temporal economy is rigorously applied by Gregory also to the internal governance of the soul. Here, again, he outstrips Plotinus in distance from the classical vision: for the Neoplatonist the lower part of the soul is still an aspect of real being and nothing of real being perishes,[71] whereas for Gregory there is no ontologically lower part of the soul, destined to remain even in the final vision. Such things are rather emergency measures, temporary pedagogic devices.

The full significance of this contrast concerns different understandings of interiority. For the earlier antique thought of Plato and Aristotle, the intrapsychic space was constituted by the gap between the higher and lower aspect (whether conceived as part or faculty): it being the case that the lower soul could not touch the transcendent height above itself without mediation by the higher psychic element, while the higher soul required an inverse mediation to make contact with material reality. This conception renders the inwardness of the soul a mediating phenomenon which is interior to the degree that aspects of the soul are cut off from direct contact with external reality. Inwardness is also constituted by the hierarchic structure which it internalizes: mirroring the government of the cosmos, it must as the governance of a single whole by itself, or self-government, take the form of hierarchic rule, since within a whole constraint of one element by another must be construed as a permanent hierarchy, whereas if something is constrained by an external element (the other) this may be a temporary and reversible hierarchy. However, in the case of Neoplatonism, inwardness is construed differently, and the usual accounts of this philosophy (and then the Cappadocians and Augustine) as deepening an existing Socratic turn to interiority are oversimplified.[72] For Neoplatonism did not work with a metaphor of form shaping matter, as in the earlier period, which automatically invoked an interior space between two heterogeneous ontological modalities, and negotiated this incommensurability in necessarily hierarchical terms. Instead it adopted a metaphor of falling, reflected, light. What is interior is now the mirrored or speculative, and hence internal space is no longer that which is fenced off against the outside, constituted by the necessary mediation of the low by the high and vice versa, but is rather the direct, unmediated penetration of external light and its ecstatic return back upon itself. There is still hierarchy of course, of source over mirror, but formally speaking there is no limit to the receptiveness of the mirror, and nor does the hierarchy require to be repeated within the space of the mirror; government is now by the external, transcendent other, and is no longer in principle a matter of self-government of the cosmos over itself which is microcosmically reflected in the individual soul composed of heterogeneous and hierarchically ordered aspects. Now an access to the transcendent is indeed possible by a pure inward turn, precisely because the inner light is wholly from outside, and abides entirely in its ecstatic return to the external source. So whereas, for earlier antiquity, interiority was at the expense of exteriority, the more drastic interiority of later antiquity (often identified by commentators) was equally a more drastic externalizing of the soul (as they usually fail to realize).

However, this new logic of light is more perfectly realized by Gregory of Nyssa than by the Neoplatonists, because he fully abandons any notion of an ontologically persisting lower part of the soul, or any receptacle other to what is received, and which is thereby passionate over against the rays of actuality. Now the mirror truly is nothing but the apparent surface of light itself in its rebound. Thus we can see that, in Gregory, the perfecting of the late antique notion of an ecstatic and paradoxical interiority is precisely correlated with a more absolute doctrine of *apatheia*.

There are two prime aspects to this. First of all, by linking activity to relation and transmission Gregory has more completely detached the idea of activity from the notion of self-sufficiency. Precisely for this reason, *pathos* thereby loses its ontological space, since this was situated in a relational dependence deemed secondary and deficient compared with self-sufficiency (it is true that Gregory still speaks of a self-determining soul and a sovereign will; here Augustine's account of will and grace is required to complete the destruction of self-government).[73] Secondly, *pathos* is for Gregory destined to vanish, even in the cosmos, as there is no longer even the faintest vestige of underlying matter. Creation, since it is composed entirely of activity, is not a passive mirror of the soul caused by the soul's own act of reflection into which it can narcissistically fall, as for Plotinus.[74] In Gregory's writings, reflection involves no such inevitable establishment of a separate and lower reflecting surface apart from those self-rebounding rays of light themselves. Hence as we have seen, for Gregory not only can the soul be a pure mirror, also it is only thus as an aspect of the wider mirror which is the Church, the

Body of Christ, eschatologically co-terminous with the redeemed cosmos: 'in her [the Bride] they see more clearly that which is invisible. It is like men who are unable to look upon the sun, yet can see by its reflection in the water. So the friends of the Bridegroom see the Sun of Justice by looking upon the face of the Church as though it were a pure mirror, and thus He can be seen by His reflection.'[75]

This makes it possible to conclude that whereas earlier antiquity embraced the civic compromise of action governing passions, and Plotinus the apolitical retreat into a pure activity of the soul without windows, Gregory discovers the body and society as a site of pure activity, or of manifestation of the absolute, and even – in Christological terms – its full and unconcealed presence (the Hegelian echo is deliberate).

Finally, I think that Gregory was right. When we defend *pathos* we tend to make pity and suffering ontologically ultimate. Endless continued pity is an insult to the pitied, offers them no good gift and pretends to rob them of their own suffering. Likewise the prospect of endlessly continued suffering tends to make us construe virtue reactively, and to imagine a restricting response to a preceding evil as the highest virtue. This dethrones Charity, which presupposes nothing, much less evil, before its gratuitous giving (or at most the recipients of gifts with and as a primordial giving, as in the case of the Trinity).[76] In contrast with aspects of later Christianity, there is little that could be construed as a cult of weakness in Gregory, and he roundly declares that it is no more praiseworthy to be fearful than to be foolhardy, or to suffer than to enjoy merely temporary pleasure.[77] This robustly objective sense of sin is perhaps now more noticeable and appreciable for an intellectual climate informed by Spinoza and Nietzsche than it was for a certain sickly version of Christian Hegelianism, exalting pathos and dialectical negativity, which has persisted from the nineteenth century into the late twentieth.

NOTES

1 See Eric Alliez and Michel Feher, 'Reflections of a Soul', in M. Feher *et al.* (eds), *Fragments for a History of the Human Body*: Part Two (Zone 4), New York, Zone, 1989, pp. 47–84.

2 Gregory of Nyssa, *On Virginity*, tr. in V. W. Callahan (tr.), *Gregory of Nyssa: Ascetical Works*, Fathers of the Church 58, Washington, DC, Catholic University of America Press, 1967, pp. 343–71, here p. 349.

3 Gregory of Nyssa, *Against Eunomius* I.35. Tr. in NPNF 2nd series, vol. 5, p. 84: 'And human governments experience such quickly repeated revolutions for this very reason, that it is impracticable that those to whom nature has given equal rights should be excluded from power, but her impulse is instinct in all to make themselves equal with the dominant party, when all are of the same blood.'

4 *On Virginity*, IV, *Ascetical Works*, p. 349: 'A man must not be thought inferior to his forefathers, he must be deemed a great man by the generation to come by leaving his children historical records of himself.' And see Peter Brown, *The Body and Society*, London, Faber, 1988, pp. 285–305.

5 *On Virginity*, III, *Ascetical Works*, p. 346: 'Whenever he [a husband] is glad with gazing on her beauty, then he shudders most with the presentiment of mourning her loss.'

6 *On Virginity*, VIII, *Ascetical Works*, p. 352.

7 *On the Christian Mode of Life*, *Ascetical Works*, pp. 127–58.

8 *On the Making of Man*, tr. in NPNF, 2nd series, vol. 5, pp. 387–427, Foreword, p. 387.

9 *On the Christian Mode of Life*, *Ascetical Works*, pp. 134–5.

10 *On the Christian Mode of Life*, *Ascetical Works*, p. 134: 'He orders us to refer all glory and to direct all action to the will of that one with whom lies the reward of virtuous deeds.'

11 *Against Eunomius* II.10: 'For the very glory that was bestowed on the lawgiver (Moses) was the glory of none other but of God himself, which glory the Lord in the Gospel bids all to seek, when he blames those who value human glory highly and seek not the glory that cometh from God only. . . . For by the fact that he commandeth them to seek the glory that cometh from the only God he declared the possibility of their seeking what they sought. How then is the glory of the Almighty incommunicable . . . ?'

12 *On the Soul and the Resurrection*, tr. in NPNF, 2nd series, vol. 5, p. 439; *Answer to Eunomius' Second Book*, tr. in NPNF, 2nd series, vol. 5, pp. 250–314, here pp. 257–8, 262; *Against Eunomius* I.4–6; *On the Making of Man* X.14.

13 See Louis Mèridier, *L'influence de la seconde sophistique sur l'oeuvre de Grégoire de Nysse*, Paris, Hachette, 1906, p. 69, pp. 195–6.

14 I borrow this term from Jean-Luc Marion's characterization of the discourse of Pseudo-Dionysius. See Jean-Luc Marion, *L'idole et la distance*, 'Le discours de Louange', pp. 219–44. However, in Gregory, unlike Dionysius, there is no suggestion of a Good beyond Being, and therefore his doxologic remains entirely an ontologic, contrary to that which Marion advocates. For Gregory, God's supreme name is 'to be' as 'is' is included in all other names, and *also* because it is the most apophatic name: we do not know *what* God is (*Against Eunomius* VII.5, VIII.I). Hence, while Gregory's God is as much *dynamis* (and so a 'giving') as *ousia*, his *dynamis* is not 'before' Being. See John Milbank, 'Only Theology Overcomes Metaphysics', in *The Word Made Strange: Theology, Language, Culture*, Oxford and Cambridge, MA, Blackwell, 1997, pp. 36–52.

15 *The Life of Moses*, tr. in Abraham Malherbe and Everett Ferguson (trs), *Gregory of Nyssa: The Life of Moses*, Classics of Western Spirituality, New York, Paulist Press, 1978, Prologue, section 3. It is beyond Gregory's powers 'to encompass perfection in any treatise' as (5) perfection that is measurable is 'marked by certain definite boundaries', yet the perfection of *virtue* consists in its having no limit, according to St Paul at Phil. 3.13: 'never cease straining towards those things that are to come'. Hence (6): 'Stopping in the race of virtue marks the beginning of the race of evil' and concomitantly one cannot 'grasp perfection with reference to virtue', for 'what is marked off by boundaries is not virtue'. Therefore Gregory concludes, 'In effect whether it is a matter of encompassing by the *logos* what is perfection, or showing by one's life that which the *logos* has seen, I say that both the one and the other exceed our powers' (3).

16 *Life of Moses* 8: 'Perfection is not marked off by limits . . . it is therefore undoubtedly impossible to attain perfection . . . the one limit of virtue is the absence of a limit (*aoriston*).'

17 *Life of Moses* 9: 'Perfection is impossible, yet we are commanded to be perfect (Matt. 5.48).' Gregory construes this as 'taking part' in perfection or as being 'in proportion' (*pros meros*) to it. This part consists in 'growth in goodness' (10) and

cannot be defined except in narrative terms by pointing to a growing, virtuous life, to an *example* of *a whole course of a life*, in this case that of Moses (11). Instead of an unattainable *logos*, 'memory' acts as 'a beacon light' (13).

18 Gregory declares that, in the case of virtue, the epistemic exigency of narrative example may be 'the reason why the civil life (*politeia*) of those graced and elevated [ones] was narrated in such detail (*akribeias historeitai*)'.

19 *On Not Three Gods*, tr. in NPNF, 2nd series, vol. 5, p. 331; *On the Making of Man* XVI.1, p. 405. See also Hans Urs von Balthasar, *Présence et pensée: Essai sur la philosophie réligieuse de Grégoire de Nysse*, Paris, Beauchesne, 1947, p. 25.

20 *Life of Moses*, 1–15. The problem here is, how *can* we repeat the virtue of the patriarchs, since we are not Chaldeans like Abraham, nor were we nourished by the daughter of an Egyptian like Moses? Gregory then proceeds: 'We need some subtlety of understanding and pureness of vision to discern from the history how, by removing ourselves from *what sort of* Chaldeans and Egyptians and escaping from *what kind of* Babylonian captivity, we shall embark on the blessed life.' The phrases in italics translate *poios* and I have substituted them for the translation 'such' ('by removing ourselves from such Chaldeans' etc.) in the English version which seems false, and implies that the allegorical flight is from specific place and time as such (such attachment being construed as the essence of passion), as the solution to the problem of the universal exemplarity of Abraham and Moses. This would imply simply that morality is *indifferent* to space and time, whereas Gregory's allegorical flight is from the Chaldeans and Egyptians taken as passions, and so *his* solution is rather that *in every* place and time we may make a specific escape from the passions which are without true being and therefore unsituated. Since virtue for Gregory means nothing definable and universal, but only always specific growth, virtue must always be in a certain space and time, must always be 'different'. Hence, though he by no means truly attains to this insight, his solution to the problem, how *can* the different be exemplary? eschews an essentialist resolution (as implied by the English rendering) in favour of a Kierkegaardian 'non-identical repetition'. It is not that the literal movement out of Egypt points to a spiritual *stasis* of essence, but rather that the literal movement figures both spiritual departure from static nothingness *and* a movement for its own sake which will be virtuous and spiritual yet still 'placed' (in space and time) through all its displacements. These considerations are important, for they tend to establish that becoming dispassionate is not, for Gregory, equivalent to becoming without temporo-spatial bodily location.

21 *Commentary on the Song of Songs*, in H. Mursirillo (ed. and tr.), *From Glory to Glory*, London, John Murray, 1962, p. 286 (henceforth all references to the *Song of Songs* are given as page numbers from this collection): 'Now the bond of this unity [Father in Son, Son in Father] is glory'; *On the Holy Spirit*, tr. in NPNF, 2nd series, vol. 5, pp. 315–25, here p. 321. Here the Father is King, the Son King likewise, and the Holy Spirit is the Kingship: 'For the Son is King and his living, realized and personified Kingship is found in the Holy Spirit.' On the Son as the Father's glory, see *Against Eunomius* I.25: 'We have been taught by wisdom to contemplate the light in, and together with, the very everlastingness of that primal light, joining in one idea the brightness and its cause, and admitting no priority'; II.5: 'He who foretold of himself that he would appear in the glory of the Father, indicated by the identity of glory their community in nature.' Grounding this assertion in the metaphysics of light, Gregory declares at II.9: 'concurrently with the existence of the glory, there assuredly beams forth its brightness'. See also VIII.5: 'He who says that the ray "is not", signifies also

the extinction of that which gives light.' Under the figures of 'anointing' and 'sovereignty' (which concern respectively the bestowal or reputation of glory and the effulgence of glory) the Spirit is presented as the resultant and yet pre-enabling 'glorifying' involved in the Father's giving and the Son's receiving of *doxa*, and likewise as abstract wisdom, truth and power at II.2: 'Thus we conceive no gap between the anointed Christ and his anointing, between the King and his sovereignty, between wisdom and the Spirit of wisdom, between Truth and the Spirit of Truth, between Power and the Spirit of Power; but as there is contemplated from all eternity in the Father, the Son, who is Wisdom and Truth, and Counsel and Might and Knowledge and Understanding, and all else that the Spirit is called.'

22 *Against Eunomius* I.52: 'What disadvantage on the score of Being, as compared with Abraham, had David who lived fourteen generations later? . . . For it is not in the power of time to define for each one the measures of nature'; 32: 'Birth is one thing, the thing born is another: they are different ideas altogether.' And see II.11.

23 *Against Eunomius* II.7, IV.1.

24 Michel Barnes, *The Power of God: The Significance of Dynamis in the Development of Gregory of Nyssa's Polemic Against Eunomius of Cyzicus* (unpublished Toronto Ph.D. thesis: available on microfilm), pp. 4–18; 259–268.

25 *Against Eunomius* II.9.

26 *On the Soul and the Resurrection*, p. 433. See also Barnes, *The Power of God*, p. 363. For Eunomius' view that the same *energeiai* produce the same *erga*, see *Against Eunomius*, I.29. Gregory applies the point in a Christological context to argue that God's *dynamis* can touch suffering with its healing power without itself undergoing suffering, for this process involves an alteration of the cause in the effect: adapting the exercise of his healing *dynamis* in a manner corresponding to the suffering; *Against Eunomius* VI.3.

27 *Against Eunomius* I.17.

28 See Barnes, *The Power of God*, pp. 191–268.

29 *Against Eunomius* I.31; II.9, 15; VIII.2; *Answer to Eunomius' Second Book*, p. 273.

30 Barnes, *The Power of God*, pp. 81–191.

31 Plato, *Phaedo*, 960–88.

32 Plato, *Sophist*, 247C.

33 Plato, *Sophist*, 247D–E.

34 *Against Eunomius* I.31: 'Anyone who has gazed on the brightness of fire and experienced its power of warming, when he approaches another such brightness and another such warmth, will assuredly be led on to think of fire. . . . Just so when we perceive a similar and equal amount of providential power in the Father and the Son'; II.5: 'He who shines with the Father's glory and expresses in Himself the Father's person, has all things that the Father Himself has, and is possessor of all his *dynamis*'; II.15: 'In the Trinity the doctrine of the Church declares one *dynamis* and goodness and essence and glory and the like for if anything should perform the functions of fire, shining and warming in the same way, it is itself fire; so if the Spirit does the works of the Father, he must assuredly be acknowledged to be of the same nature with Him.' *On the Holy Spirit*, p. 320: 'We should be justified in calling all that nature which came into existence by creation a movement of will, an impulse of design, a transmission of *energeia*, beginning with the Father, advancing through the Son, completed in the Holy Spirit.' And see *On the Holy Trinity*, tr. in NPNF, 2nd series, vol. 5, pp. 326–30.

35 *Against Eunomius* I.31–2; II.7.

36 Barnes, *The Power of God*, pp. 346–452.
37 See A. A. Long and D. N. Sedley (eds), *The Hellenistic Philosophers*, Cambridge, Cambridge University Press, 1987, vol. 1, pp. 162–5, 196–7, 199–202, 240–41.
38 *Against Eunomius* I.42.
39 On divine incomprehensibility see *Against Eunomius* I.42: 'We find that we are drawn round uninterruptedly and evenly, and that we are always following a circumference where there is nothing to grasp; we find the divine life returning upon itself in an unbroken continuity, where no end and no parts can be recognized.' For Gregory's account of knowledge, see XII.2 and *Answer to Eunomius' Second Book* (see also the preceding editorial note on *epinoia* at p. 249). Also Balthasar, *Présence et pensée*, p. 63.
40 See *Answer to Eunomius' Second Book*.
41 *On the Making of Man* V, I–VI, 3, pp. 391–2.
42 *On the Soul and Resurrection*, p. 433: 'The soul is an essence created and living and intellectual, transmitting from itself to an organized and sentient body the *dynamis* of living and of grasping objects of sense'; '[God] penetrating each portion, combines these portions with the whole and completes the whole by the portions, and encompasses the universe with a single all-controlling *dynamis*, self-centred and self-contained, never ceasing from its motion, yet never altering the position which it holds.' There follows (p. 433) an account of man as microcosm and an inference to the soul from the unity yet diversity of the body as parallel to an inference to God from the equally mysterious unity of a diverse creation. The possibility of a *mechanistic* and reductive explanation of this mystery is refuted by Gregory by an appeal to our invention of mechanical artifices themselves: our ability for example to work out the abstract principles of sound emerging from a wind-pipe and then construct a musical instrument, implies 'an invisible thinking nature' (p. 435).
43 *On the Soul and the Resurrection*, pp. 439–40. See also Barnes, *The Power of God*, pp. 308–46.
44 *On the Soul and the Resurrection*, p. 442.
45 See David L. Balas, 'Eternity and Time in Gregory of Nyssa's *Contra Eunomius*', in Heinrich Dorrie *et al.* (eds), *Gregor von Nysse und die Philosophie*, Leiden, Brill, 1976, pp. 128–53, and Monique Alexandre, 'L'exégèse Gen. 1. 1–2a dans l'In Hexaemeron de Grégoire de Nysse: Deux approaches du problème de la matière', and comments of J.C.M. van Winden in M. Hart (ed.), *Écriture et culture philosophique dans la pensée de Grégoire de Nysse*, Leiden, Brill, 1971.
46 *Against Eunomius* VI.3: 'Nothing is truly "passion" which does not tend to sin, nor would one call strictly by the name of 'passion' the necessary routine of nature, regarding the composite nature as it goes on its course in a kind of order and sequence. For the mutual concurrence of heterogeneous elements in the formation of our body is a kind of combination harmoniously conjoined out of several similar elements, but when, at due time, the tie is loosed which bound together the concurrence of the elements, the combined nature is once more dissolved into the elements of which it was composed. This then is rather a *work* than a *passion* of nature.
47 *Against Eunomius* VI.3: What is 'truly passion' is 'a diseased condition of the will'.
48 *On the Soul and the Resurrection*, pp. 442–3.
49 *On Virginity* XI, p. 355: where the material elements do not form a ladder to intellectual beauty, there will be an 'absence, in souls faculties of *hedones*, of that exact training which would allow them to distinguish between true Beauty and

the reverse'. That is to say, feelings are intimately involved in the recognition of God, as much as in the lapse of such recognition.

50 Rowan Williams, 'Macrina's Deathbed Revisited: Gregory of Nyssa on Mind and Passion', in L. R. Wickham and C. P. Bammel (eds), *Christian Faith and Greek Philosophy in Late Antiquity*, Leiden, Brill, 1993, pp. 227–46; *On the Soul and the Resurrection*, p. 440; *The Life of Moses*, 157.

51 *On the Soul and the Resurrection*, p. 444: here Gregory reads Paul as also saying that every evil spirit will be annihilated along with every passion. Thus Gregory's universalism is profoundly linked with his doctrine of *apatheia* and refusal to give anything outside God and his active *dynamis* any ontological purchase.

52 *The Life of Moses*, 231: *eros* is a *pathein* which 'seems to me to belong to the soul which loves what is beautiful'; *Song of Songs*, p. 272 '*agape* that is strained to intensity is called *eros*' (section 237).

53 *Song of Songs*, pp. 178–9, 191, 200, 206, 263, 270, 272.

54 *Song of Songs*, p. 219: 'Perhaps if I may venture a rather bold conjecture, in seeing the beauty of the Bridegroom in the Bride they are really admiring the invisible and incomprehensible as it is in all creatures'; p. 272: 'He who sees the Church looks directly at Christ – Christ building and increasing by the addition of the elect. The Bride then puts the veil from her eyes and with pure vision sees the ineffable beauty of her Spouse.' There is a linking here of Christ's indwelling in the Church, his bride, with the beatific vision, which is to be construed in terms of the coincidence of that vision with the eschatological perfecting of the Church as an extension of the work of incarnation, p. 288: 'that day when all will look to the same end, when God will be all in all and all evil will be destroyed, and all men will be united together by their participation in the Good'. At this point the Church not only fully manifests Christ, but also fully manifests the Holy Spirit, spoken of in terms of a flying/resting maternal Dove which infuses the Church with its glory (pp. 286–8). We are able to contemplate the Spirit, because she was first received by the incarnate Christ and thence transmitted to the disciples, the beginning of the Church (pp. 187, 287).

55 *Song of Songs*, pp. 286–8.

56 See R. Williams, '*Sapientia* and the Trinity: Reflections on the *De trinitate*', in B. Bruning *et al.* (eds), *Collectanea Augustiniana: Mélanges T. J. Van Bavel*, 2 vols, Leuven, Leuven University Press, 1990, vol. 1, pp. 317–32 [= Augustiniana 40–41 (1990–91)]; L. Ayres, 'The Discipline of Self-Knowledge in Augustine's *De trinitate* Book X', in L. Ayres (ed.), *The Passionate Intellect: Essays on the Transformation of Classical Traditions*, Rutgers University Studies in Classical Humanities 7, New Brunswick, NJ, Transaction, 1995, pp. 261–96.

57 *Song of Songs*, p. 237: the *bride* calls the *bridegroom* to her feast: 'surpassing all bounds of generosity'. Nothing makes clearer the radicalism of deification in Gregory: the relation of Christ to the Church actually manifests the *reciprocity* of trinitarian gift-exchange. By grace, we return God's gift to God.

58 *On the Soul and the Resurrection*, pp. 462–3. Caroline Walker Bynum points out that Gregory combines the Origenist conception of the body continuing to evolve beyond death under the impulse of a seminal *eidos* with Methodius' anxious insistence on the return of the same body. Perhaps, as she thinks, the synthesis is contradictory, but it might be possible to read Gregory as stressing the discontinuity between the *diastasis* of time and the somehow remaining *diastasis* (which he *usually* affirms) of eternity. In the latter, *every* active moment of time returns, so that Gregory is more concerned with the resumption of our whole life in time than with the return of the 'same' elements of the body, whose

'marking' by the soul can only be through the course of their *flux*, and not in spite of it: Caroline Walker Bynum, *The Resurrection of the Body in Western Christianity 200–1336*, New York, Columbia University Press, 1995, pp. 81–6.

59 *Against Eunomius* VI.4: 'Even those names which are great and divine are properly applied to the humanity, while on the other hand the Godhead is spoken of by human names. For it is the *same Person* who both has the Name which is above every name, and is worshipped by all creation in the human name of Jesus.'

60 On mirrored incomprehensibility, see *On the Making of Man* XI.4, p.396. *Answer to Eunomius' Second Book*, p. 264. Regarding 'set paradox', see *Against Eunomius* VI.1.

61 *Against Eunomius* VI.4: 'that unspeakable mixture and conjunction of human littleness commingled with divine greatness'. For Gregory God also works more generally within the creation by fusion of opposites. See *On the Soul and the Resurrection*, p. 433. The cosmic and Christological aspects of this theme come together at *Song of Songs*, p. 218: 'That manifold quality of the divine wisdom which arises by the union of opposites, has only now been clearly revealed through the Church: now the word became flesh, life is mingled with death, in his bruises our wound is healed, the infirmity of the Cross brings down the power of the Adversary, the invisible is revealed in the flesh, the captives are ransomed, He Himself is both purchaser and price.'

62 *Against Eunomius* VI.2: 'we do not say, that one who touches a sick man to heal him is himself partaker of the infirmity, but we say that he does give the sick man the boon of a return to health'; 'the Father does these things [the crucifixion and resurrection] by his own *dynamis* by which he works all things'.

63 *Against Eunomius* VIII.2; *Life of Moses*, 147, 251. On the transformation of the human body see *Life of Moses*, 30: 'What is impossible by nature did not change into possible, but what is mutable and subject to passivity was transformed into impassibility by participation in the immutable.' That Gregory regards Christ's life as 'metahistorical' in the sense of showing and making possible again the nature of *every event, every passage* is shown at *Life of Moses*, p. 119 in his words regarding the cloudy pillar, a type of Christ: 'What we hear from the history to have happened then, contemplation of the divine word shows always to happen (*eisai ginesthou*).'

64 The Mallarmean echo is deliberate. See *Against Eunomius* VI.1: 'For verily the Godhead works the salvation of the world by means of *that body which encompassed it*, in such wise that the suffering was of the body, but the operation was of God' (my emphasis); *Answer to Eunomius' Second Book*, p.262: 'Holy Scripture omits all inquiry into substance. . . . For this reason John said the world could not contain the books of what Jesus did' and 'the whole creation cannot contain what might be said respecting itself'. In other words the essence of the world lies paradoxically beyond the world, and still more paradoxically, this 'beyond' once entered *into* the world. This idea links also to the Church as 'a re-creation of the world . . . a new firmament': *Song of Songs*, p. 273 .

65 *Song of Songs*, p. 154 (concerning the 'spiritual senses'): 'What could be more paradoxical than that nature itself should purify its own passions. For in words that seem to suggest passion it offers us precepts and instruction in purity.'

66 See Emilie zum Brunn, *St Augustine: Being and Nothingness*, New York, Paragon House, 1988, p.10: zum Brunn stresses that metaphors of food and fullness were already used by the Neoplatonists.

67 On spiritual sense as a distillation of the physical senses see *Song of Songs*, p. 224. On non-replete yet replete *eros* see p. 270: 'The veil of her [the Bride's] grief is

removed when she learns that the true satisfaction of her desire consists in constantly going on with her quest . . . seeing that every fulfilment of her desire continually generates a further desire for the transcendent', and p. 176, 'her thirst is not quenched even though a whole cup is brought into her mouth, but she asks to be brought into the very wine cellar, and have her mouth held right beneath the vats, bubbling over with sweet wine'.

68 *Song of Songs*, pp. 219 and 285, 286 for the flying/resting motif.

69 Plotinus, *Enn.* 6.9.8 and 6.9.10. And see J. M. Rist, *Plotinus: The Road to Reality*, Cambridge, Cambridge University Press, 1967, pp. 225, 230.

70 Plotinus, *Enn.* 6.9.8.

71 Plotinus, *Enn.* 4.7.14; 1.1.12; 6.4.16.

72 See for example Charles Taylor's version in his nonetheless exceptionally insightful *Sources of the Self*, Cambridge, Cambridge University Press, 1989, pp. 115–43.

73 *Against Eunomius* II.11: 'our soul is self-determining . . . with sovereignty over itself'; *On the Soul and the Resurrection*: 'Now liberty is the coming-up to a state which owns no master and is self-regulating (*autokrates*).'

74 See Alliez and Feher, 'Reflections of a Soul'. Also Julia Kristeva, 'Narcissus: The New Insanity', in *Tales of Love*, tr. Leon S. Rondiez, New York, Columbia University Press, 1987, pp. 103–22. On interiority and mirrors in Gregory see *Commentary on Ecclesiastes* in *From Glory to Glory*, p. 102: 'in gazing upon his own purity he [a Man] will see the archetype within the image'; *Song of Songs*, p. 164: 'For all the perfect virtue of God sends forth rays of sinlessness to illumine the lives of those who are pure, and these rays make the invisible visible, and allow us to comprehend the inaccessible by impressing an image of the sun upon the mirror of our souls'; *On Virginity*, XL, p. 356: 'the virgin soul is like a mirror beneath the purity of God'.

75 *Song of Songs*, p. 219. The final coinciding of the mystery of the Church with the mystery of all creatures is declared in a preceding passage (p. 218): 'Perhaps (if I may venture a rather bold conjecture), in seeing the beauty of the Bridegroom in the Bride they are really admiring the invisible and incomprehensible as it is in all creatures.'

76 See John Milbank, 'Can Morality Be Christian?', in *The Word made Strange*, pp. 219–32, and 'Can a Gift Be Given?', *Modern Theology* 11 (1995), pp. 119–61.

77 See *On Virginity* XVI, p. 362. Here Gregory enunciates an important critique of melancholia and resentment: whereas, he says, some are slaves to pleasure, 'others fall a ready prey to melancholia and irritation, and to brooding over injuries, and to everything that is the direct opposite of pleasurable feelings, from which they are very reluctant to extricate themselves. . . . But God is not pain any more than he is pleasure . . . but very wisdom and sanctification, truth and joy and peace and everything like that. . . . It matters not whether we miss virtue in this way or in that.' And see *Against Eunomius* VII.2 for a critique of *sym-patheia* in the passage already cited above (n. 59).

7

CONSTANTINE, NICAEA AND THE 'FALL' OF THE CHURCH[1]

Daniel H. Williams

> Men and women of Christendom, I am your mother the
> Church. I was born in a poor fisherman's hut; but our Lord
> nourished and brought me up to be the bride of the Trinity.
> While yet He sojourned in the world, He bade me learn the
> government of purse and sword, and made me the keeper of
> the Keys of Heaven . . .
>
> Dorothy Sayers, *The Emperor Constantine*

No one will dispute that the accession and thirty-one-year reign of the emperor Constantine was one of the most significant turning points in the story of the Church. The fourth century saw that moment in ecclesiastical history when the context and community of Christian faith was radically changed once a Roman emperor adopted its beliefs and lived long enough to enforce politically its way of expressing those beliefs. In her imaginative play *The Emperor Constantine*, Dorothy Sayers presents what has been the common-place rendering of the emperor; that it was Constantine who called for a council to meet in Nicaea, sat among the bishops as Christ's appointed regent and suggested the insertion of the famous (or infamous) word 'consubstantial' (*homoousios*) into the creed subsequently produced by that council. Of course such a rendering is no more than an exaggerated carica-ture of actual events. Nevertheless, Sayers is not shy about propounding a historical thesis, namely, that it was inevitable for Christianity to cease from being a minority cult, if not by Constantine then by some other means, such that 'the power of the purse and sword' must come into Christian hands.[2]

This issue of inevitability is not without importance for the interpretation of Church history. For most of those denominational groups which compose the Protestant tradition, called the Believers' or Free Church,[3] the impact of the Constantinian era was not at all unavoidable or desirable in the develop-ment of the early Church. The famous John Wesley was most insistent upon this point in his sermon 'The Mystery of Iniquity':

The grand blow was struck in the fourth century by Constantine the Great, when he called himself a Christian . . . [j]ust so, when the fear of persecution was removed, and wealth and honour attended the Christian profession, the Christians did not gradually sink, but rushed headlong into all manner of vices. Then the mystery of iniquity was no more hid, but stalked abroad in the face of the sun. Then, not the golden, but the iron age of the Church commenced.[4]

While contemporary theologians, such as Mennonite John Yoder or Methodist Stanley Hauerwas, have generally construed the Constantinian downfall in terms of its effect upon political and ethical theology, their assessments have also implicated the doctrinal development of the fourth century, particularly that of the Nicene creed and the subsequent production of confessions. Once the driving forces of the Christian Roman empire became transformed into the politics of power, the formulation of Christian doctrine would swiftly mirror its environment. For Yoder this means that the definitions of faith or the creeds were no longer established in accordance with the assembly of believers as its base. 'As a result, therefore, the eyes of those looking for the church had to turn to the clergy, especially to the epis- copacy, and henceforth, "the church" meant the hierarchy more than the people.'[5] Such expressed views are neither new nor isolated, evidenced by a general suspiciousness or even irrelevance with which Free Church attitudes have regarded the creeds and doctrinal developments of the fourth century. Among the many issues generated by the 'Constantinian fall' thesis, here I want to deal with this particular problem – a problem exacerbated by the fact that texts and concepts from the patristic era are utilized as 'evidence' in support of modern syntheses without due regard for the historical location of such texts. It is necessary therefore to place the 'fall' thesis under the bright lights of patristic historiography and see how it holds together. But first let us briefly review the origins and animus of this thesis.

I

The concept of the 'fall' of the Church has long been perceived as axiomatic for the Protestant identity. Opinions vary as to the moment when the decline began in the post-apostolic Church given increasing episcopalization and sacramentalization of ecclesiastical polity. For some Radical Reformers such as Thomas Müntzer, the Christian congregation lost its virginity and became an adulteress soon after the death of the apostles because of corrupt leadership,[6] that is, the predominance of a rich and powerful clergy; whereas early manifestations of deterioration for Menno Simons were indicated before the apostles' deaths by the growing practice of infant baptism.[7] Not surprisingly, the stated abuses attributed to the practices of the ancient Church have a striking resemblance to the hierarchical and sacramental system of medieval Catholicism with which these men contested.

For most of the later Middle Ages, however, the critical transformation of the Church as an institution occurred with the Constantinian era thus effecting a breach with earliest Christianity. Already by the time of Wycliffe (ca. 1325–84) and Hus (1369–1415) the Church's welcome embrace of Constantine's patronage was perceived as the beginning of its corruption and a degeneration from its original apostolic character to a position of temporal supremacy, necessarily involving the accretion of unbiblical practices and misalignment of the true faith. This meant that one could not think of the Christian past in continuity with the present, but as a chronicle of mounting apostasy in which the Church was in need of radical revision or restitution.[8]

To my knowledge, no one has attempted to trace specifically the historical roots of the concept of the 'Constantinian fall', with the exception of Seeburg earlier this century.[9] The topic is complicated by the fact that the idea of a Christianity compromised after Constantine was hardly unique to Protestant reformers, having taken less divisive forms already in the preaching of Francis of Assisi or Jean Gerson. Moreover, it was fuelled in large part by the pervasive influence of that infamous forgery, the 'Donation of Constantine'.[10] Deeply embedded in the dynamics of Church and State, everyone in the Middle Ages accepted this pernicious eighth-century decretal as genuine. Supposedly issued by the emperor Constantine to Pope Sylvester of Rome as a reward for healing him from leprosy and baptizing him,[11] it granted the pontiff and his successors the imperial Lateran palace in Rome, rule over the provinces and cities of Italy and the West, and supremacy over the 'patriarchates' of Antioch, Alexandria, Jerusalem and Constantinople. More amazingly still, the Council of Nicaea is said to have given its approval to the Roman pope's preeminence. So Wycliffe, in his *De ecclesia*, repudiates papal authority and the entire papal system on the grounds of having been founded by Constantine and not Christ.[12] Indeed, any distinction in rank among the clergy or elevation of bishops above priests is traceable to the Constantinian endowment. Even strong papal supporters as early as the twelfth century, including Bernard of Clairvaux, acknowledged that the moral decadence afflicting Christianity should be traced back to the 'Donatio'.[13] Four centuries later we hear Luther fulminating that '[i]t must have been by virtue of a special plague sent by God that so many knowledgeable people let themselves be talked into believing falsehoods'.[14]

Despite the fact that the forgery had been exposed as such by Lorenzo Valla in 1440,[15] its symbolic role as an ancient document legitimatizing papal domination over the increasing independence of Europe's kings continued to be defended and repudiated.[16] Late medieval popes insisted that the role of the temporal ruler was one of *adjutor* to the Roman pontiff because the 'sword' which the king claimed over his dominion had in fact been given him to serve the *societas Christiana* by the authority of the Pope – a leading implication of the *Donatio* and of Roman papal theory that governing the empire rests with the head of the Church.[17] Important for this chapter is how those bloated images of papal and conciliar authority defended by medieval Catholicism were being 'read back' into the early Church with telling effect on the apprehension of patristic ecclesiology. These were critical images for sustaining the theology in which movements such as Waldensians, Hussites and the later 'Radical' Reformers had invested themselves; namely, that they were restoring the primitive Church which they valued precisely because it represented the pre-Constantinian age.[18]

Indigenous to Free Church ideas about a 'fall' of the Church is the glorification of the pre-Constantinian or apostolic period as a kind of 'golden age' of the faith. It is not simply that the earlier years are foundational for establishing the Christian identity and so act as a guiding norm for all future development. There is rather a tendency towards primitivism,[19] in which the original condition is symbolic of all that was spiritually vital and organizationally simple, unsullied by the trappings of institutional secularism before Christ's mystical body became a privileged corporation. This pristine period is characterized by a Christianity when it was still a minority religion of the Roman empire, often suffering for the faith, able to boast of many martyrs. Anabaptist traditions especially stressed the early Church's repudiation of power and violence, and therefore its own vulnerability, since it had borne the brunt of the power of the edict and the sword. When Melchior Hoffmann propounded his view of Church history using the letters to the seven churches of Revelation 2–3 as an eschatological map, he interpreted the second church of Smyrna as representing the 'church of the martyrs'.[20] This was the time of persecution for the Church prior to the rise of the papacy. It was also a time that existed in continuity with the first age of the Church, that of Ephesus, which was the Church of the apostles and symbolized true teaching of the faith. In stark contrast, Hoffmann saw the third church of Pergamon (Rev. 2.12–17) emblematic of the reprobate Church, when divine truth became polluted by human wisdom and moral compromise was generally accepted. In his account, the great fall of the Church followed hard on the heels of the age of martyrs, that is, roughly located in the period of Constantine (and his Donation) whereby 'the pope and antichrist were very pleased to accept the same power, authority and strength of worldly rule'.[21]

A critical attitude towards the Church as having deviated from the true ideals of apostolic Christianity does not rule out historical continuity as a hopeless conception. Yoder has stressed the necessity of developing a truly historical perspective as the first step for developing a critique of the institutional Church and proposing a revisionist alternative.[22] More generally, however, the restitutionist ideal is the preservation and succession of the true or invisible Church from the apostolic age to the present, which means a different kind of historical continuity is envisioned. In the words of one modern theorist, 'The Free Church has had an unbroken existence in Christendom from the first Christian Church in Jerusalem, AD 30, to the present day.'[23] There is an obvious attraction between the attempts at articulating a Free Church identity and those patristic or medieval religious movements that rejected the institutional form of Christianity for a more Spirit mediated existence, such as the Montanists – 'outstanding advocates of the free church idea' (according to Murch) – or the Waldensians who are thought to have maintained the priesthood of all believers against the Constantinian endowed Church – *ecclesia spiritualis in ecclesia deformandis*. As creeds, liturgies, dogmas and ecclesiastical offices became the antitheses of Christian freedom, the external or Catholic Church no longer guaranteed, and instead obscured, the means by which the apostolic faith was transmitted to succeeding generations of believers. Nevertheless, faithful Christians throughout the ages in various forms – remnant pockets of pristine spirituality – survived until the time of the Protestant Reformation. At least since the seventeenth century, Free Church chronicles, such as the *Martyrs' Mirror*,[24] or John Smythe's proto-Baptist ecclesiology,[25] have located their antecedents not chiefly in their organizational roots, but within a spiritual successionism that can be traced back to the day of Pentecost in Acts 2. The thread that unites their history of the Church is one that transcends the external institution, finding it rather in a catena of disparate movements which bear little relation to each other and which are utilized as historical witnesses with little, if any, regard to their historical context.

Having glanced at some of the historical precedents, I want to consider several implications which the Free Church paradigm of the 'fall' of Catholicism in general and of the fourth century in particular has had on contemporary Protestant perspectives of doctrinal development. Despite the longstanding, and often unquestioned, dependency on this notion, I will show what kind of problems occur when we test it for historical validity.

II

It goes almost without saying that a view of Church history as one of increasing degeneration has served to devalue theological formation between the age of the apostles and the Reformation. Patristic tradition becomes suspect of superimposing alien interpretations on the simple biblical revelation, replacing the straightforward narrative of Jesus' life and death with credal formulae that define Christ in ontological categories, thereby losing sight of New Testament Christianity.[26] The result is that the Christological and Trinitarian formulations which became orthodoxy are thought to reflect the power structures and understanding of the Constantinian Church instead of a Christian one. What is sought for is some way of reading the Bible without passing through the interpretive grid of the Constantinian Church. It is not at all clear how such a 'reading' could be made possible, although such an uncontaminated reading would allegedly yield a Christology more in harmony with scriptural language and images.

Of course this perspective makes the common but erroneous assumption that a particular period of Church history, namely, the apostolic, can be appropriated in a pure, unmediated way, free of social, political and economic factors. Yet such factors, precisely because theology is fashioned in human communities, must inevitably influence each phase of doctrinal, ecclesial and canonical construction. Spokespersons for denominations within the Free Church are quick to define post-Constantinian Christianity in a way reminiscent of Sohm or von Harnack, that is, as an era so circumscribed by mundane pressures that its theological constructions have limited, if any, value outside its own context, whereas the earliest stages of Christianity are free from such distorting affectations. The same kind of perspective is taken with how the 'true' or 'invisible Church' maintained its unpretentious spirituality throughout the ages; within the ecclesiastical institution, encumbered with the weight of its own worldly attachments, is the life of the spirit, freed from all dissimulating influences. An unwillingness to accept such an idealistic view of doctrinal history does not mean one must detract from the normative authority of Jesus and the apostles. On the contrary, one may propose to take the incarnational principles which are so central to Free Church Christologies and apply them more consistently by embodying the apostolic age in its full historical context. Just as the Church is a historically developing organism whose life is the incarnated extension of Christ's incarnate life, so the orthodox or 'true' faith of any age is itself a construction within a particular context. It is a historical process that cannot be written in abstraction from the vicissitudes of 'ordinary' history.[27]

An overall problem that the 'fall' paradigm shares with many modern theological paradigms is a tendency to create theological categories and distinctions based on artificial presuppositions about the early Church. These presuppositions are derived more from a governing hermeneutic about how doctrinal development allegedly occurred than from critical analyses of the primary sources *in extenso*.[28] J. Denny Weaver's argument that Christians in the post-Constantinian Church believed it was more important to preserve the empire than to live by the teachings of Jesus[29] is a fantastic generalization which could only be perpetuated without having read the sermons of Augustine on I John about the emulation of Christ's love, or Chrysostom's moral discourses against compromising Christians in Constantinople who were attending the circus instead of church. Not untypically, Weaver's interaction with patristic materials is centred solely on the ecumenical creeds from which he extrapolates a general assessment of doctrinal or ecclesiastical development. Contemporary characterizations about Constantinian Christianity and the delineation of the 'true' Church often betray a greater familiarity with versions of early Church dynamics that have been filtered through post-Reformational syntheses. Without pretending to offer an exhaustive survey of such syntheses, one can look to the *Chronica* of Sebastian Franck,[30] which had a formative role in the shaping of Anabaptist historiography,[31] in that citations and usages of early texts are carefully selected in accordance with Franck's drastic ideas about the character of the fallen Church. Like Hus, Hubmaier or Schwenckfeld, Franck knew firsthand the writings of the 'doctors of the Roman Church' but (unlike his contemporaries) he utterly scorned them. Referring to them as 'wolves' and 'antichrists', Franck claimed that the works of Clement, Irenaeus, Tertullian, Cyprian, Origen, Chrysostom, Hilary, Ambrose, Augustine, etc. were still available (to whoever read Latin) and were quite unlike the spirit of the apostles, that is, 'filled with commandments, laws, sacramental elements and all kinds of human inventions'.[32] The inference from Franck's work is that there is no reason whatsoever for a faithful Christian to become familiar with this literature. As the 'doctors' of the Church are swept into the category of 'fallen' Christianity as its principal participants and architects, a caricature of their unfortunate writings is produced, implicitly teaching future generations to ignore the substance of their views. One can also point to comparable Church historical models published in the seventeenth century such as the *Martyrs' Mirror*, from which the Free Church historian Ludwig Keller developed his successionist interpretation of the Reformation,[33] and which in turn inspired Ernst Troeltsch to take up a similar theme in his magisterial *Social Teaching of the Christian Churches* (1911). In an earlier century there was produced the massive synthesis by the pietist Gottfried Arnold, *Impartial History of the Church and Heretics*.[34] This carefully documented work wielded a considerable degree of influence on subsequent Protestant ideas about ecclesiastical and doctrinal formation which has not been sufficiently recognized.[35] Its thesis is that true Christianity, once it had fallen with the poisonous embrace of Constantine, had been preserved over the centuries, not by powerful prelates and conciliar decrees, but by the despised dissenters, sometimes labelled as the heretics of the age. Arnold's method of employing primitive Christianity as a *regula* for identifying the earmarks of the true and ongoing Church, in contrast to its corrupted Constantinian form represented by the rise of the episcopal lust for power and manifested in issuing dogmatic formulae to enforce orthodoxy, continues to be operative in contemporary analyses of Church history. The result is that the complexities and nuances of the patristic era have been both obscured and systematized for the purposes of easy discreditation.

III

In order to test the historical validity of the Constantinian 'fall' thesis, we want to learn if the radical changes in the Church's status effected a near or complete loss of theological identity as the paradigm suggests. There is the corollary concern in this thesis that the role of the worshipping congregation and normative concerns of Scripture were marginalized to such an extent that doctrinal formation became the domain of councils and episcopal power plays. Some of these issues have been addressed in the recently published essays entitled *Faith to Creed: Ecumenical Perspectives on the Affirmation of the Apostolic Faith in the Fourth Century*.[36] What is at stake in these interdenominational dialogues is the question whether the Nicene creed should or could still act as an authoritative expression of the Church's faith today. If so, what does it mean that Nicaea became the platform of the new imperial Church, and thus the *symbolum* of a new ecclesiastical establishment? Both E. Glenn Hinson (Baptist) and A. James Reimer (Mennonite) have argued positively that there were impulses from within the Church that formalized and recognized this creed; impulses which were generated by a primary concern for faithfulness to Scripture and towards maintaining the confessional heritage of the churches.

I should like to extend these discussions by observing that the 'fall' thesis operates on the basis that episcopal or imperial power was the driving force of the fourth century with only nominal concern for the preservation of orthodoxy. In other words, there is the tendency to reduce what was a self-conscious search for a Christian doctrine of God in the age of Constantine to a phenomenon of ecclesial-political manoeuvres. Such an approach has been largely shaped by a view of Church history which accepts the veracity of the Eusebian portrayal of emperor, empire and Church in the *Life of Constantine*. Under Eusebius' pen, Constantine is installed as an integral part of God's salvation history, 'as a general bishop constituted by God'.[37] Because he is divinely appointed, Constantine is central to the welfare of both the affairs of humanity and Church,[38] thus an alliance between Christianity and empire is forged. Scholars still debate the historical value of the *Life*, for it is noteworthy both for what it says and what it omits.[39] To say that it speaks for the general aspirations of the Church or of the Church's actual relations with Constantine must be squared with the fact that the work is an unabashed panegyric, celebrating 'in every way the praises of this truly blessed prince' (I.11) and what he has brought to the once persecuted Church. The picture which emerges here may be confidently said to represent Eusebius' own ideal of the new Christian empire, and only approximates historical actualities. The same can be said of Eusebius' *Oratio* in which Constantine is called the 'friend and interpreter of the Word', whose aims are to recall the whole human race to the knowledge of God.[40] The response of the Church is no less idealized than the portrait of its emperor.

Admittedly, a critical interpretation of Eusebius does not completely nullify the institutional intersection which occurred at points between Church and State in the later fourth century. Certain political components of the 'Constantinian thesis' are undeniably true, although most of the political events which established the Church in a position of secular power are more rightfully attributed to the imperium of Theodosius (378–95) and his sons rather than to Constantine.[41] It was, for example, a telling moment for the relationship between Christian Church and Roman society when in 395 Ambrose, bishop of Milan, invited the new emperor, Honorius, to stand with him at the side of the altar before the congregation as a means of confirming his succession from the recently deceased Theodosius.[42] Nevertheless, an interpretation of 'power politics' is hardly sufficient to describe the interdependence of, and sometimes opposition between, doctrinal formulation and imperial politics that characterized the fourth century.

I want rather to direct our focus to the use of the Nicene creed by churches in the fourth and early fifth centuries since it is this conciliar statement which has been the most scrutinized as emblematic of 'Constantinian' Christianity. A careful examination of those sources which delineate the reception and diffusion of the creed after 325 reveal that its acceptance as a uniquely authoritative symbol of faith was a much more fragmented and gradual affair than the 'fall' paradigm allows. The modern version of the paradigm tends to invest Nicaea with such dominating influence over ecclesiastical identity as a mandatory statement of Constantinian dogmatics that it fails to recognize its practical limitations as a conciliar document. For although Nicaea became the official norm of orthodoxy, the Nicene creed never excluded the use of local creeds and doctrinal formulae which were proper to individual churches. Throughout the fourth and fifth centuries such creeds continued to operate in churches, whether catechetically or liturgically, no less as authoritative standards of faith. Where we know of such creeds functioning in particular churches, we discover that Nicaea (or Constantinople) served as a theological hermeneutic for defining orthodoxy and heresy, but it by no means usurped the traditional language with which the congregation worshipped or baptized its members.[43] We will return to how Nicaea was incorporated in this limited fashion.

Before we do so I want to look briefly at a methodological issue which contemporary versions of the 'fall' paradigm do not take into account. Part of the focus upon Nicaea as a political and theological extension of Constantinianism is based upon the supposition of its imperial character and thus its centrality for introducing a uniformity of doctrine: 'one Church, one empire, one faith, one truth'.[44] But how central was Nicaea for defining Christianity after 325? It is commonly recognized among patristic scholars that the Nicene creed, and its controversial term *homoousios*, registered almost no notice at all in the theological disputations for over a quarter of a century after the council. This is largely because the creed did not solve the trinitarian or Christological disputes which were dividing Eastern bishops at the time since its language was controversial and, for many, seemed to endorse a form of modalism. Athanasius, who is usually credited with being Nicaea's most vociferous proponent, in fact exhibits no inclination to use *homoousios* until ca. 352/3 when he defended its validity as scriptural in principle.[45] Whatever ecclesial unity Nicaea was supposed to achieve had not been working. This is dramatically underscored by Constantine himself who was present at a small synod in Nicomedia (327/8) and agreed with the decision to grant the presbyter Arius re-admission to the Alexandrian clergy on the basis of a formula that made no allusion to Nicaea.[46] Not surprisingly, the event is ignored or distorted by later ancient Church historians.

In the West it was no different. Not until the 350s do we begin to see the Nicene creed mentioned in local synods as the sole standard of orthodoxy. Hilary of Poitiers's personal admission in 356, 'I never heard the Nicene faith recited until I was about to go into exile,' could have been echoed by a large number of bishops. At councils in Arles (353), Milan (355) and especially Ariminum (359), the Nicene creed was put forward only to be rejected by a vocal minority who substituted another creed and cowed the majority of Western bishops into endorsing their opinion.[47] While Nicaea was certainly acknowledged as an authoritative statement by 359, this acknowledgement seems to have just begun to enter the ecclesial consciousness of the West. De Halleux makes the plausible argument that the Nicene creed did not become a part of the Church's 'web of tradition' until the Alexandrian synod (362). It was then that Eastern and a few Western bishops jointly confessed the *Nicaenum* as an exclusive canon of orthodoxy by which every confession should conform.[48] Whereas the size and influence of the synod was itself unremarkable, its decisions were symptomatic and confirmatory of a Nicene hegemony.

This Neo-Nicene era, in which there was a widespread identification of bishops and churches with one theology, was not propelled by the conviction that the creed acted as a symbolization of the unity of the empire, or that it provided an avenue for domination over one's opponents. To allow polemics only to tell the story of doctrinal development is too one-dimensional. Fidelity to the sense of the Scriptures and to the ancient tradition of the Church, however loosely this may have been handled in practice, occupies the concern for most bishops in the age of Constantine. The ecclesiastical-political theory of 'one Church, one empire, one faith' is more the product of later Church historiographers such as Orosius and Sozomen who organized their accounts in accordance with the conviction that the triumph of an orthodox faith was what enabled the Christianization of the Roman empire. Influence of the Eusebian model of empire and Church is readily discernible.

IV

Once the 'Neo-Nicene' period had commenced, we need still to consider how the Nicene creed was integrated by the Church. As a conciliar formula and thus a new phenomenon in the production of creeds, I would suggest that it had a limited function among the churches which, apart from any doctrinal considerations intrinsic to its language, also explains its gradual assimilation. It should be remembered that prior to the fourth century, all confessions and summaries of the Christian faith were local in character. It was taken for granted that these enshrined the universally accepted Catholic faith handed down from the apostles. 'But', as J. N. D. Kelly once observed, 'they owed their immediate authority, no less than their individual stamp, to the liturgy of the local church in which they had emerged.'[49] Creeds propounded in conclaves of bishops purely for the establishment of determining orthodoxy and heresy represented a dramatic turn from the way in which statements of faith had always evolved and been deemed authoritative. Perhaps the difference between the two kinds of creeds should not be overemphasized since the motive behind both was to obtain assurance about the nature of belief, and the use of credal formulae artificially constructed as a test for ascertaining orthodoxy had happened at least twice before Nicaea.[50] It is nevertheless true that the difference is significant for evaluating the 'fall' paradigm which construes Nicaea as an essential feature of the Constantinian impact on fourth-century theology, asserting that conciliar productions had replaced the voice of the worshipping communities in the development of doctrine. Three concrete examples will show to what degree this paradigm has been built on mistaken assumptions.

The first is Ambrose's *Explanatio symboli ad initiandos*[51] which, as the title implies, was an address explaining to candidates for baptism (*competentes*) the meaning of the creed. Once Ambrose delivered (*tradere*) the creed, they were to memorize it and then 'give it back' (*reddere*) on the day of their baptism (12). The *symbolum* here of course is the creed of Milan, which can be reconstructed from Ambrose's address, as well as from three sermons of Augustine, who was baptized in Milan and learned this very creed.[52] Ambrose declares twice that this symbol is that which the Roman church holds (7; 10); a comment which is not so much about the similarity of wording between the two church's creeds, as a perception of the creed's apostolic origins. It was a given that the creed of Milan and Rome had descended directly from the apostles themselves, and especially through Peter's agency at Rome, 'the common understanding (*sententia*) was brought forth'. All of this served Ambrose to stress in his homily the inviolability of the Milanese symbol and his hearers' need to preserve it as such just as those believers before them had done.

When we look more closely at this document, it is clear that a pro-Nicene theology is the governing *explanatio* of the creed.[53] In fact Ambrose claims that the wording of the creed, which was adequate for addressing past heretical notions, is not completely sufficient for meeting the 'species of calumny contrived by the Arians' (7). In the creed, the Father only is said to be 'omnipotent', and thus invisible and impassible, implying that the Son is visible and passible, and therefore, they say, not of the same *divinitas* (Godhead) as the Father (7). Thus Ambrose defends the creed's statement about Christ's birth, death, burial and resurrection to mean 'that in no way could the flesh cause any detriment to the glory of the Godhead' – an argument that occupies all of chapter 8 and manifests the same kind of anti-'Arian' exegesis the bishop employed in *De fide* III and *De incarnatione*.

Augustine, our second example, will offer the same argument as Ambrose about the relationship between the creed and the faith in *De fide et symbolo*, but with greater clarity:

> The exposition of the faith (*fides*) serves to fortify the creed (*symbolum*), not that it is to be committed to memory or repeated instead of the creed. . . . But it guards the things contained in the creed against the wiles of heretics with full catholic authority and with a stronger defence.[54]

Here, as in sermon 215, a version of the North African creed is being interpreted by using Nicene terminology and doctrine.[55] Augustine begins an exposition of the creed, 'we believe in his Son Jesus Christ our Lord', immediately followed by the Nicene qualifier, 'true God from true God' (*Sermo* 215.3). The standard Nicene distinction of the Son's existence and his human birth is also applied to this second article of the creed: 'Jesus Christ our Lord, *Only-begotten of the Father*'. After a careful discussion about the meaning of 'begotten', Augustine explains in *De fide et symbolo* that the Word was not made out of nothing or out of ready-made materials (ii.4). Rather, the Son by nature 'was born uniquely of the substance of the Father, being what the Father is, God of God, Light of Light' (iv.6).[56] It is apparent then that the Nicene faith acted as a commentary for the creed, but the two were consciously kept distinct; the conciliar was not confused with the congregational, nor was there an intention to replace the latter with the former.

Finally, when Rufinus of Aquileia responded to a certain bishop's request that he would write 'an essay on the faith (*de fide*) based on the contents and rationale of the creed (*symbolum*)', he wrote not on the Nicene creed but on the creed to which he pledged himself in baptism at the church of Aquileia.[57] His *Commentary of the Apostles' Creed* provides the most extensive credal exposition in patristic literature, and from which is supplied chief testimony for the reconstruction of the Roman and Aquileian creeds. Rufinus was very aware that the two were related, but more importantly, that they were witnesses to the apostles' own *symbolum* from which they were derived, investing these local creeds with a unique authority for the preservation of Christian doctrine. However, in his introduction he states that recent heretics, such as Photinus, have so twisted straightforward orthodox statements so as to support their contentions that Rufinus is obliged in his exposition 'to restore and emphasize the plain, simple meaning of the apostles' words, and at the same time, to fill in the gaps left by my predecessors'.[58] In other words, the traditional wording, susceptible to false interpretation, must be translated in terms of orthodox thought which, for Rufinus, is according to Nicene-Constantinopolitan theology. Unlike Ambrose or Augustine, Rufinus makes no citations or specific allusions to a conciliar creed, but he recognizes that the doctrinal extremes of modalism or 'Arianism' are refuted by explicating the proper meaning of the creed, namely, that the Son was begotten before the ages of the Father's very substance ('non ex ipsa Patris substantia natum'), and that the Holy Spirit is in no less a category of being than the Son.[59]

Rufinus also acknowledges a certain fluidity exists in the wording of the Church creeds made necessary by Marcellan/Photinian distortions. For example, in the first article about God the Father Almighty, he defends the Aquileian addition of 'invisible and impassible' (which is not in the Roman creed) so as to avoid any suggestion that it was the Father who became incarnate and suffered. It was the Son alone who became flesh and was made visible and passible. Keeping in common with the anti-'Arian' exegesis of the day, however, Rufinus is quick to point out that the Son's incarnation does not mean he was visible and passible according to his *divinitas*: 'as concerns the immortal substance of the Godhead, which the Son shares equally and identically with the Father, neither the Father nor the Son nor the Holy Spirit is visible or passible'.[60] Similarly the article about the Son's birth 'by the Holy Spirit from the Virgin Mary' is carefully clarified to mean an act of divine condescension, not the transmutation of the Son's divine substance (8). While the word *homoousios* never appears in the text, Rufinus abundantly uses substance language to define Father and Son relations, implying the same to the Holy Spirit.

In sum, the formulations of the three church confessions considered above varied in small details from one another in accordance with the practical and doctrinal agenda peculiar to each setting. This was a common feature. Minor differences can be detected in the forty-four identified and anonymous Latin *expositiones*.[61] The authority attributed to these creeds was grounded on their venerable connection to the apostolic faith, and on the practice of *traditio* and *redditio*, which engaged the congregation in preserving the essentials of the Christian *fides*. *Symbola* from Nicaea and Constantinople are distinguished as having another origin which provided an interpretive mechanism for defining contemporary parameters of orthodoxy and heresy. They were not meant to replace the baptismal confessions still regarded as the sacramental *regulae* of the Christian faith. This explains why Hilary, at the end of his twelve-volume *De trinitate*, after providing a detailed defence of pro-Nicene trinitarian theology, concludes with the prayer:

Keep, I pray Thee, this my pious faith undefiled, and even until my
spirit departs, grant that this may be the utterance of my convic-
tions, so that I may ever hold fast that which I professed in the
creed of my regeneration when I was baptized in the Father, and the
Son, and the Holy Spirit.[62]

We can discover little to underwrite the notion that post-Constantinian,
Nicene 'orthodoxy' is best understood as a functional part of imperial polity
and therefore a drastic departure from the Christianity of earlier centuries.
On the contrary, churches and bishops tended to be suspicious of the Nicene
creed, especially in the East, long after the council. And when its usefulness
resurfaced in the 350s, many bishops discovered that the reigning emperor,
Constantius II, supported initiatives to introduce other, seemingly less divisive, creeds that could achieve ecclesiastical unity. Without a doubt
Constantius' chief aim was more political than theological, but it does an
injustice to attribute the same motivation to most of the bishops. People
like Athanasius or Ambrose were only too willing to receive promotion of
their ecclesiastical platform by orthodox emperors. At the same time they
rejected the notion that the affairs of doctrine and Church should be legis-
lated single-handedly by imperial policy. Hilary articulates a view that was
the norm:

I forbear to mention that although the highest regard is due to the
emperor – for kingship is from God – yet his judgements should
not be admitted without reservation into the deliberations of the
bishops: to Caesar should be rendered what is Caesar's, to God what
is God's.[63]

The relationship between Church and State in the fourth century was one of
interdependence; each being defined by the other without collapsing into
the kind of unity discerned and proscribed by the 'fall' thesis. Conciliar and
local church creeds acted upon each other in the same way.

In the above response to the 'fall' paradigm of the Free Church, I suppose
I have been asking 'how far'? For most groups of the Free Church, the
answer is based upon a perception of radical discontinuity within Church
history, which is itself based on certain models of appropriating the Church's
past. My concern has been with determining the usefulness of those models
by testing them against those sources about which they purport to speak.
The Church's tendency in every age toward secularism and forsaking its
scriptural and traditional identity is not being debated here. Any good
Protestant will annex the idea of human depravity to the life of the Church.
At issue is how the 'fall' model has exaggerated, to the point of distortion,
the ecclesiastical and doctrinal forces which composed the fourth century in
order to supply a stronger case for the Church's need of radical restitution.

Central to this distortion is how the conception of 'Constantinianism' has operated to reduce the development of the early Church's doctrine to an epiphenomenon of fourth-century ecclesiastical politics.

It may have been inevitable, as Sayers suggests, for a Constantine to arise and propagate Christianity with the result that his patronage caused significant changes in the Christians' view of the empire and of themselves in it. But the essential formulation and construction of the Christian identity was something that the fourth century *received* and then expanded upon through its biblical exegesis and liturgical life as reflected in the credal traditions. In other words, I have postulated that the continuity between the post-apostolic period and the kind of Christianity articulated in the fourth and fifth centuries was more complicated and durable than Free Church typologies of ecclesiastical history has been willing to allow. That there were linguistic or conceptual innovations to the original kerygma of Jesus was a necessary outcome, as theologians in the fourth century discovered, of redefining the parameters of orthodoxy in their age. The very controversies that gave rise to various formulae and doctrines demonstrated that there was a need to move beyond older categories of thought and the repetition of biblical terminology. At the same time, the resulting constructions of these debates were formulated and then read within the shadow of the worshipping experience of the churches. As we saw from the evidence above, these formal and local expressions of theological faithfulness were understood in a dynamic relationship of complimentarity which was not circumvented by the political and social benefits provided by Constantine and his successors for the Church. On the contrary, as Rowan Williams put it,

> What the Church discovered in the painful years after Nicaea was that its own inner tensions could not after all be solved by a *deus ex machina* on the imperial throne; and that its relationship with the empire intensified rather than solved the question of its own distinctive identity and mission. It was unable to avoid reflection on its defining conditions, unable to avoid a conscious and critical reworking of its heritage, unable, in short, to avoid theology.[64]

There are immediate and practical ramifications for a modification of the 'fall' model. If Free Church Protestants are ever to recognize that tradition is not the automatic antithesis of the Bible, and that Church history between the New Testament and the Ninety-Five Theses is an essential part of *their* history, they will have to see that there were indeed forces of theological integrity and spirituality in the post-Constantinian Church. At the very least, this should bring the emperor down to his proper, historical size.

NOTES

1 I am grateful to my colleague Dr Dennis Martin for his criticisms and biblio-
graphic suggestions on an early draft of this chapter. My thanks also go to Dr
Peter Erb of Wilfrid Laurier University for his unselfish advice on historio-
graphic matters.

2 *The Emperor Constantine: A Chronicle*, New York, Doubleday, 1951, p. 5.

3 That family of diverse churches which descends (directly and indirectly) from
the sixteenth-century 'Radical Reformation' (or Anabaptist heritage) and shares
the general characteristics of attributing its origins to no one founder (except
Jesus and the apostles), never identifying with or accepting assistance from the
State to organize churches, looking to the Bible alone as the sole authority for
Christian faith and practice, with voluntary membership of only those who
confess the lordship of Christ, emphasizing discipleship as the primary means of
exhibiting an authentic Christian lifestyle, and with exception of American-
originated groups, an experience of persecution in their early history. It was Max
Weber who spoke of the 'Believers' Church' as that which no longer looked
upon the religious community or visible church 'as a sort of trust foundation for
supernatural ends', but as a community of personal believers of the regenerate,
and only these; *The Protestant Ethic and the Spirit of Capitalism*, tr. T. Parsons,
New York, Scribner's, 1958, pp. 144–5.

The following broadly labelled denominations/traditions are commonly
included under the designation of 'Free Church': Anabaptist, Mennonite,
Brethren, Baptist, Methodist, Quaker, Congregationalist, Pentecostal, Pietist,
Disciples of Christ (Church of Christ) and Evangelical Free. This is of course not
an exhaustive list. See F. H. Littell, *The Free Church*, Boston, MA, Starr King
Press, 1957, pp. 86–90; A. Rasmusson, *The Church as Polis*, Notre Dame, IN,
Notre Dame University Press, 1995, pp. 17f. D. F. Durnbaugh, *The Believers'
Church*, New York, Macmillan, 1968, pp. 8–22, classifies 'Free Church' into
three 'schools of thought': sectarian, Puritan and the Anabaptist (although it
might be argued that by nature all ecclesial groups which stem from the Free
Church are sectarian).

4 *Sermon* 61.27, A. C. Outler (ed.), *The Works of John Wesley*, Nashville, TN,
Abingdon, 1985, vol. 2, p. 463.

5 *The Priestly Kingdom: Social Ethics as Gospel*, Notre Dame, IN, Notre Dame
University Press, 1984, p. 136.

6 'Sermon Before the Princes' (Allstedt, 13 July 1524), in G. H. Williams (ed.),
Spiritual and Anabaptist Writers, Library of Christian Classics 15, Philadelphia,
PA, Westminster Press, 1957, p. 51.

7 *Complete Writings of Menno Simons c. 1496–1561*, tr. L. Verduin, Scottsdale, PA,
Mennonite Publishing House, 1956, pp. 279–80, 724, 775. Sebastian Franck,
among the Spiritualist Reformers, railed against the idea that the Antichrist
broke into the Church not until the advent of Constantine and his sons. He
firmly believed that the 'outward church of Christ was wasted and destroyed
right after the apostles' since the early Church Fathers (who he calls 'wolves')
and all the popes used the Old Testament to justify war, power of magistracy,
tithes, the priesthood, etc.; *Spiritual and Anabaptist Writers*, pp. 151–2.

8 Dennis Martin describes the restitutionist motif as the key organizing principle
for interpreting Anabaptist-Mennonite history; 'Nothing New Under the Sun?
Mennonites and History', *Conrad Grebel Review* 5 (1987), p. 2. Cf. F. H. Littell,
The Origins of Sectarian Protestantism, New York, Macmillan, 1964, pp. 48f.

9 See note 35 below.

10 'Edictum domini Constantini imperatoris' (PL 130 245A–252B). The forgery seems to have composed no later than the middle of the eighth century and is itself an elaboration of an earlier product, the *Legenda sancti Silvestri*, a romantic version of Constantine's conversion and according to which the Christian emperor conferred on the Roman church the role of being head of all priests in the Roman world just as the king was head of all rulers. W. Ullmann, *The Growth of Papal Government in the Middle Ages*, London, Methuen, 1965, pp. 75ff.

11 Of course Constantine never had leprosy and was baptized in Nicomedia by the bishop of that city, Eusebius. The fact that the baptism was performed by an 'Arian' bishop was unnoticed, or more likely, repressed, by ancient historians until the later fifth century. As a means of completely circumventing such a scandal, the fragmentary history of Gelasius of Cyzicus reports that the emperor was baptized by an orthodox priest (E. J. Yarnold, 'The Baptism of Constantine', *SP* 26 [1993], p. 96), and it is not a far step for the *Liber ponticalis* to claim that Constantine received the sacrament at the hands of Silvester.

12 Of his 'Forty-Five Articles' (condemned on 10 July 1412), article 33 reads: 'Silvester papa et Constantinus imperator erraverunt ecclesiam dotando.' Cf. M. Spinka, *John Hus' Concept of the Church*, Princeton, Princeton University Press, 1966, pp. 22f.

13 M. D. Chenu, *La théologie au douzième siècle*, Paris, J. Vrin, 1957, p. 81.

14 'An Appeal to the Ruling Class' 9 (J. Dillenberger [ed.], *Martin Luther: Selections from his Writings*, New York, Doubleday, 1961, p. 440).

15 For the history and evolution of the text, see C. B. Coleman, *The Treatise of Lorenzo Valla on the Donation of Constantine*, New Haven, CT, Yale University Press, 1922.

16 Valla's work was edited by Ulrich von Hutten (1520) whose German edition was the basis of Luther's own version. That Luther felt the need to produce this attack on the *Donatio* indicates it was still being used to exonerate papal claims of sovereignty. Augustinus Steuchus, bishop of Chisamo, attempted to refute Valla with his *Contra Laurentium Vallam, de falsa donatione Constantini* (Lugdunum, 1547), which was in turn criticized by Calvin (*Institutes* IV.11.12) and Johannes Sleiden's history of the church and its corruptions by the Roman papacy.

17 Ullmann, *The Treatise of Lorenzo Valla*, pp. 416–17. Thus, both 'swords' (that of the 'sword of God' and the 'physical sword') are the Pope's.

18 A. Molnar, *A Challenge to Constantinianism: The Waldensian Theology in the Middle Ages*, Geneva, WSCF, 1976, p. 54.

19 See G. Boas, *Essays on Primitivism and Related Ideas in the Middle Ages*, Baltimore, MD, Johns Hopkins Press, 1948; Littell, *The Free Church*, pp. 58f. A primitivistic ideal is also operational in monastic literature of the late patristic period. Cassian's *Conference* tells how the system of coenobitism arose during the days of the apostles: 'The whole church, I assert, lived then as coenobites live, now so few that it is difficult to find them. But after the death of the apostles, crowds of strangers and men of different races flowed into the church . . . so that the faith of the whole Christian body began to grow cold' (XVIII.5; O. Chadwick [ed.], *Western Asceticism*, Library of Christian Classics, Philadelphia, PA, Westminster, 1958, p. 266). The purpose of the writer, however, does not seem to be to offer an assessment of Church history as much as to defend the apostolic origins and thus a justification of the coenobitic lifestyle.

20 Hoffmann appears to have been borrowing directly from Olivi's principles of a heightened spiritual understanding of the Bible from which he developed a theory of ecclesiology based on the seven churches. W. O. Packull, 'A

Reinterpretation of Melchior Hoffmann's Exposition against the Background of Spiritualist Franciscan Eschatology with Special Reference to Peter John Olivi', in I. B. Horst (ed.), *The Dutch Dissenters: A Critical Companion to Their History and Ideas*, Leiden, Brill, 1986, pp. 49–50.

21 Hoffmann, *Auslegung der Offenbarung*, p. P vii recto, quoted from 'A Reinterpretation', p. 54. Packull notes that for Olivi, the period of Constantine and Pope Sylvester marked a triumph in Church history, whereas Hoffmann saw the Constantinian legacy as the cause of spiritual decline (p. 53). On the Franciscan idea of reform, see G. Leff, 'The Making of the Myth of a True Church in the later Middle Ages', *Catholic Historical Review* 68 (1968), pp. 1–11.

22 *The Priestly Kingdom*, pp. 127ff.

23 J. D. Murch, *The Free Church: A Treatise on Church Polity with Special Relevance to Doctrine and Practice in Christian Churches and Churches of Christ*, Louisville, KY, Restoration Press, 1966, p. 36.

24 Thieleman J. van Braght, *The Bloody Theater or Martyrs' Mirror of the Defenseless Christians Who Baptized Only Upon Confession of Faith, and Who Suffered and Died for the Testimony of Jesus, Their Saviour, From the Time of Christ to the Year A.D. 1660*, tr. J. F. Sohm, Scottsdale, PA, Mennonite Publishing House, 1938. It is van Braght's contention that a remnant of 'Anabaptists', or those who maintain such a confession as they do, have existed through every century, from the days of Christ to the present time'. This view is directed as a polemic against those who have contemptuously declared that the Anabaptists have but recently sprung from the Munsterites.

25 W. M. Patterson, *Baptist Successionism: A Critical View*, Valley Forge, PA, Judson Press, 1969, p. 15. Smythe repeatedly denied belief in an outward succession, i.e. popes, bishops, etc., claiming, 'there is no succession in the outward church, but that all succession is from heaven'. The practice of finding a remnant of true believers in each age of the Church has been particularly favoured by Baptist and Disciples of Christ historians. See D. F. Durnbaugh, 'Theories of Free Church Origins', *The Mennonite Quarterly Review* 41 (1968), pp. 85f.

26 J. Denny Weaver, 'Christology in Historical Perspective', in *Jesus Christ and the Mission of the Church: Contemporary Anabaptist Perspectives*, Elkhart, IN, General Conference Mennonite Church, 1989, pp. 89–91.

27 See Rowan Williams's remarks in R. Williams (ed.), *The Making of Orthodoxy: Essays in Honour of Henry Chadwick*, Cambridge, Cambridge University Press, 1989, pp. viii–ix.

28 As persuasively demonstrated by M. Barnes in 'Augustine in Contemporary Trinitarian Theology', *TS* 56 (1995), pp. 237–50.

29 'Christology in Historical Perspective', p. 96.

30 *Chronica: Zeitbuch vnnd Geschichtbibell von anbegyn bisz in diss gegenwertig* (Stuttgart, 1536).

31 It is already mentioned in 1560 by Obbe Philips as a reference work for the teachings of Anabaptism.

32 *Letter to Campanus* 2 (G. Williams, 142).

33 *Die Reformation und die älteren Reformparteien* (Leipzig, 1885). Keller did not use the expression 'Free Church' but Old Evangelical Brotherhood or Alliance.

34 *Unparteiische Kirchen- und Ketzer Historie vom Anfang des Neuen Testaments bis auf das Jahr Christi 1688* (Frankfurt am Main, 1699/1700).

35 E. Seeburg, *Gottfried Arnold: Die Wissenschaft und Die Mystik seiner Zeit*, Darmstadt, Wissenschaftliche Buchgesellschaft, 1923, repr. 1964; Peter C. Erb, *Pietists, Protestants, and Mysticism: The Use of Late Medieval Spiritual Texts in the Work of Gottfried Arnold (1666–1714)*, Metuchen, NJ, Scarecrow Press, 1989.

36 E. Glenn Hinson, 'The Nicene Creed Viewed from the Standpoint of the Evangelization of the Roman Empire', and A. James Reimer, 'Trinitarian Orthodoxy, Constantinianism, and Theology from a Radical Protestant Perspective', both in *Faith to Creed: Ecumenical Perspectives of the Affirmation of the Apostolic Faith in the Fourth Century*, Grand Rapids, MI, Eerdmann, 1991.

37 *Vita Const.* II.44.

38 *Vita Const.* II.28; IV.24; esp. I.8 where the extension of Constantine's rule to other countries is tantamount to Christian missions.

39 T. D. Barnes, *Constantine and Eusebius*, Cambridge, MA, Harvard University Press, 1981, pp. 265–71.

40 *Oratio* II.4.

41 C. Pietri, 'La politique de Constance II', in *L'église et l'empire au IVe siècle* (*Entretiens sur l'antiquité classique* 34), Vandoeuvres, 1989, p. 115.

42 *De obit. Theodosii* 3.

43 Not until the sixth century do we find the Nicaeo-Constantinopolitan creed progressively supplanting the particular confessions of churches as the sole baptismal creed. See J. N. D. Kelly, *Early Christian Creeds*, 3rd edn, London, Longman, 1972, pp. 345f.

44 E. Hoornaert, 'The Nicene Creed and the Unity of Christians', in *Faith to Creed*, p. 113. 'The unity and even uniformity of the faith proclaimed symbolizes, and in a very concrete way realizes, the unity of the empire. Constantine foresaw this, with perspicacity.'

45 In *De decretis*.

46 Athanasius, *Ad episcopos Aegypti* 18; *Ad Serapionem* 2.

47 D. H. Williams, *Ambrose of Milan and the End of the Nicene-Arian Conflicts*, Oxford, Clarendon Press, 1995, pp. 16f.

48 'Toward a Common Confession of the Faith According to the Spirit of the Fathers', in *Faith to Creed*, p. 29.

49 Kelly, *Creeds*, p. 205.

50 At Antioch in 268 for the examination of Paul of Samosata (A. Hahn and G. Hahn [eds], *Bibliothek der Symbole und Glaubensregeln der Alten Kirche*, Breslau, 1897, no. 151), and in the same city just several months before the convening at Nicaea (R. P. C. Hanson, *The Search for the Christian Doctrine of God*, Edinburgh, T. & T. Clark, 1988, pp. 146–51).

51 The authenticity of this work had been disputed by Caspari, but it has been recently and generally deemed genuine. See *Patrology* IV.170–71; R. H. Connolly, *The 'Explanatio Symboli ad Initiandos': A Work of Saint Ambrose*, Cambridge, Cambridge Uuniversity Press, 1952.

52 Sermons 212–14 given in Hippo on different occasions. Kelly offers a comparative reconstruction of Ambrose's and Augustine's versions, *Creeds*, p. 173.

53 The dating of the work is very problematic. One of the only internal indicators is found in chapter 10 where he refers to Christ as 'omnipotent' according to the exegesis of Rev. 1.8. This has a parallel to the arguments in *De fide* II.35 and *De incarnatione* 114 which would place the *Explanatio* in the period of his anti-'Arian' polemics, pp. 378–81.

54 *De fide et symbolo* i.2, CSEL 41 4.

55 It is not certain that the formula commented upon in the sermon and the one in Augustine's address to the bishops gathered for a council at Hippo (393) are identical. I think both have features that make them sufficiently distinct from the old Roman, contra Meijering, *Augustine: De fide et symbolo*, Amsterdam, J.C. Gieben, 1987.

56 Cf. *Sermo* 215.4: 'Just reflect, O man, what your God undertook for you, your creator for a creature; that God abiding in God, the eternal living with the eternal, the Son equal to the Father, did not disdain . . . the form of a servant' (tr. E. Hill, *The Works of Saint Augustine: Sermons III/6*, New York, New City Press, 1993, p. 162).

57 *Commentarius in symbolum apostolorum* 1; 3 (CCSL 20 133; 136).

58 *Comm.* 1 (tr. J. N. D. Kelly, *Rufinus: A Commentary on the Apostles' Creed*, Ancient Christian Writers 20, New York, Newman Press, 1955, p. 29).

59 *Comm.* 37 (CCSL 20 171–2) (Kelly, *Rufinus*, ch. 39).

60 *Comm.* 5 (Kelly, *Rufinus*, pp. 37–8). Cf. chs 9; 17.

61 See the study of L. H. Westra, 'Enigma Variations in Latin Patristics: Fourteen Anonymous Sermons *de symbolo* and the Original Form of the Apostles' Creed', in the forthcoming volume of *SP* from the 1991 Oxford Conference.

62 *De trin.* XII.57 (NPNF, 2nd series, vol. 9, p. 233).

63 *Collectanea Antiariana Parisina*, B.1 (5) (CSEL 65). It is important to note that Hilary said this before his declared rejection of Constantius' legitimacy as emperor (in *In Constantium*).

64 *Arius: Heresy and Tradition*, London, DLT, 1987, pp. 236–7.

Part III

CHRISTIAN ORIGINS AND THE WESTERN TRADITION

8

DENYS AND AQUINAS

Antimodern cold and postmodern hot

Wayne Hankey

Scholars need to have a greater sense of irony about themselves. This reflection arises out of an examination of the connection between movements in philosophy and theology, on the one hand, and what we make of our history, on the other.[1] Led by the theologians, for more than three centuries, we have been replacing metaphysics with what we call history.[2] Now we need a sense of irony, both to avoid cynicism and self-delusion. For theologians, biblical studies, patristics and Church history and, more recently, liturgical scholarship are probably the first places we would look in order to observe characteristically modern interpenetrations of 'critical' history and theology. Biblical scholars have advanced far down that road; they have become so self-aware as to have given up more than exploring diverse ways of reading. Worshippers suffer in hope, waiting for the liturgists to do the same. For me, contemplating the valuation of Platonism in general, and the valuation of the thought of the pseudo-Dionysius in particular, among Thomists during the last 130 years has been instructive.

Those who work where historical, philosophical and theological studies meet are used to twists and turns. But, looking at the judgement of the role and worth of Neoplatonism and Denys from within the perspectives of the nineteenth and twentieth century revival of the thought of Thomas Aquinas, we find complete reversals. No doubt this is partly because of the institutional interest in Thomism, but we cannot simply blame it on the bishops. They are not involved in what I will call the postmodern retrieval of Christian Neoplatonism. Nonetheless, a comparable logic seems at work, a logic imposed by the negative relation to modernity common to both retrievals. But here we have come to a conclusion, prematurely, and must turn to our argument.

POSTMODERN RELATIONS TO THE PAST

I have been attending to philosophical and theological thinkers, mostly French, who find, in ancient and medieval Neoplatonism, something of the future for Christians about to cross the border of a millennium. In a very general way, these thinkers are 'postmodern', if by that we mean, among other things, those who turn again to the premodern to find what they judge modernity has forgotten. Graham Ward recently described Professor Jean-Luc Marion's work on Descartes thus: 'It is in grasping the roots of modernity that Marion's postmodern thinking sees the possibility of returning to the premodern world which de Lubac, Daniélou and Gilson had reintroduced into early twentieth century French Catholicism.'[3] Professor Marion's kind of relation to the premodern, as thus described, is an example of the postmodern, so far as my purposes are concerned. However, we shall not examine Professor Marion's Cartesian studies, but rather his writing on the Pseudo-Denys and Thomas Aquinas.

Before that, let us consider, in a preliminary and general way, the problematic I hope to explore. We note the dependence of this movement into the future on what is found in the past, and thus on an understanding of it. Most of the thinkers we call postmodern, in the sense just given, are disciplined students of intellectual history. One thinks immediately of those distinguished contributions to Cartesian scholarship by Jean-Luc Marion as well as of the scholars who recover the texts and thought of ancient and medieval Neoplatonism. However, there is another side. Part of what they want to escape in the modern is what they perceive as its objectification of our past, an alienation by which what is human becomes inhuman. The double-mindedness of their position, and of his own relation to himself, is present in their grandfather, the Professor of Classical Philology, Friedrich Nietzsche. We find harsh and angry criticism of scientific history in a work he rightly called *The Genealogy of Morals*,[4] though the work depends on recovering what is prior to the moral opposition of good and evil.

These thinkers have an essential relation to the past, because there one hopes to find what is dimly recollected as forgotten, or experienced as lack. Their deeply ambiguous relation to history is not just due to the objectification belonging to methods of the historical sciences. There is also an endeavour to get free from the necessities imposed by the thinking that generates modern metanarrative and from the particular metanarratives dominating contemporary philosophy. Increasingly critical engagement with Martin Heidegger's account of the history of Being is almost universal. With this double-mindedness in view, I use the story of the relation of Thomas and Denys over the last century in order to consider how much some postmodern thinkers who are engaged in a retrieval of elements of Neoplatonism are likely to find what they seek in the past.

CONTEMPORARY EVALUATIONS OF PLATONISM: THOMISM AND NEOPLATONISM

French Neoplatonic scholarship

I discovered the context of the extensive contemporary French interest in Neoplatonism as I was trying to unearth the continuity, if any, between the *summae* of St Thomas Aquinas and the systems of Greek Neoplatonism especially as they acquire explicit form in Proclus. Undertaking such a study in Oxford, I became aware of a difference between the relation of philosophical work and historical study in England and France. Étienne Gilson noted about philosophy in English speaking America that philosophers' ignorance of the history of their discipline was intentional, regarded as necessary to creativity.[5] My arrival at Oxford had been immediately preceded by the folding up of the Readership in Medieval Philosophy. Moreover, for centuries, theology's field had been defined there by ignoring a millennium of its history – that between the end of the patristic period in the sixth century and the Reformation in the sixteenth.

Happily, I was taken in hand by a wandering French mendicant, the *doyen* of Thomistic studies, Père Louis Bataillon, o.p., of the Leonine Commission. He told me to go to Paris and sit at the door of St Thomas's old convent, St Jacques, and beseech the assistance of one of his brothers, Henri-Dominic Saffrey. Père Saffrey had produced – in 1954! – the first strictly correct critical edition of a text of St Thomas, the circumstances of the Leonine Commission having prevented for seventy years its edition of Aquinas being properly done.[6] He edited the *Commentary on the Liber de causis*, that Arabic mixing of Plotinus with a dominating Proclus.[7] This late, extremely important, commentary involved a comparison by Thomas of the text of this work, until then thought by him to be the theology of Aristotle, with the newly translated *Elements of Theology* of Proclus – which he discerned as one of its sources – and with the *De divinis nominibus* of Denys, on which Thomas had commented at the beginning of his career and which he found to have a doctrine like that of the *Liber*.

Père Saffrey then went to Oxford where he began his now complete (in 1987) edition of the *Platonic Theology* of Proclus[8] as a D.Phil. thesis for E. R. Dodds, whose programme as Regius Professor of Greek remains controversial to this day. Dodds laid an indispensable foundation for the last sixty years of intense Neoplatonic scholarship by his canonical 1933 edition of the *Elements of Theology*.[9] Henri Saffrey's edition of Thomas's commentary on the *Liber de causis* was to have been a beginning of an attempt to map the extent of the Procline influence in Western theology and to indicate the consequences for theology of that discovery, but, mostly, he stayed with ancient Neoplatonism. Nonetheless, by important studies of objective connections between Proclus and the Pseudo-Denys, he further assisted those who undertook to carry forward his initial project.[10]

The Thomist side of our consideration requires mentioning the Parisian scholar of whom Saffrey is heir and of whose memory he is a custodian,[11] A. M. J. Festugière. A Dominican, Père Festugière's most important work was originally moved by the hope of finding in Neoplatonism the medium by which Aristotle could be adapted to Christian purposes. The intended result was to have been that the Philosopher, identified by the Fathers as a veritable font of heresy, could become instead one foundation of Aquinas's thought.[12] Instead, Père Festugière preceded Saffrey in publishing primarily about Plato and pagan Neoplatonism after a Thomistic beginning. In 1944, he started publishing an edition of *La Révélation d'Hermes Trismégisté*[13] – which came out in the series Études bibliques (!) and which is essential to the Iamblichan–Procline tradition in Neoplatonism.

In 1966, the Jesuit Édouard des Places published an edition and translation of Iamblichus, *Les mystères d'Égypte*.[14] In 1971 and 1989, the same Société d'édition brought out his Greek text and French translation of the *Oracles Chaldaïques* and of the *Protrepticus* of Iamblichus. So, between the Jesuit and the Dominican, the picture of the oracular and theurgic aspects of Neoplatonic spirituality in late antiquity was filled out. The Sulpician priest Jean Trouillard had significantly developed Plotinian studies with his *La procession plotinienne*, published in Paris in 1955, and went on to Proclus, for example *L'un et l'âme selon Proclus* in 1972 and *La mystagogie de Proclus* in 1982.[15]

Of the French scholars mentioned so far, Père Trouillard was the first to harvest the fruit from the Neoplatonic tree in order to undertake a philosophical and theological revolution. He became the advocate of a Neoplatonic henology which he wished to substitute for Aristotelian and Thomistic ontology as the logic of Christian thought. In the 1960s he and Henry Duméry developed with the Passionist priest Stanislas Breton and Joseph Combès a 'radicalisme néoplatonicien'.[16] Père Breton, in an informal intellectual and religious autobiography, *De Rome à Paris: Itinéraire philosophique*, described Jean Trouillard, Henry Duméry and Joseph Combès as 'la triade néo-platonicienne de France, qui n'était pas sans écho à celle de jadis'.[17] The significance of this is summed up in the words of Breton:

> Ce qu'ils ont inauguré, sous les apparences d'un retour au passé, c'est bel et bien une manière neuve de voir le monde et d'y intervenir, de pratiquer la philosophie, de comprendre le fait religieux, en sa forme chrétienne comme en son excès mystique; puis, et j'ai hâte de l'ajouter, de relier le vieil occident à son au-delà extrême-oriental.[18]

His move – and that of French Catholicism – from Rome to Paris corresponded to a move from a Roman 'philosophie aristotélico-thomiste' as the basis of theology, to a Neoplatonic thinking and spirituality in a Parisian Athens where he could be open to the thought of his lay compatriots. He became one of the most creative philosopher theologians working out the implications of this shift, one bound up with the consequences of the Second Vatican Council.

Neothomism

Why anti-Platonic

The French Neoplatonic scholars mentioned so far are mostly Catholic priests, members of religious orders. In the twentieth-century circumstances of French Catholic intellectual life, they came to their studies out of a relation to a revived Thomism. Our present, and very recent, appreciation of the importance of Neoplatonism, in general, and of Denys, in particular, for the thought of St Thomas, is bound up with overcoming the Neothomism of the late nineteenth-century Leonine revival, an overcoming largely carried out from within.[19] That Neothomism is a primary form of contemporary anti-modern thought.

From the perspective of the Neothomists, Neoplatonism appeared as an ally of modernity, the predecessor and support of its idealisms. The positive present interest in Neoplatonism depends on a reversal of this judgement. In the last third of the twentieth century, the dead Neothomism and Neoscholasticism of the nineteenth-century revival, appears, instead of Neoplatonism, as having been thoroughly infected with modern objectifying rationalism. At its heart is discerned the ontotheologism identified by Martin Heidegger through which the West has forgotten Being. Most ironically, it may have been Heidegger's own neo-scholastic background which partly caused him to read medieval theology as ontotheology.[20] Neoplatonism, in contrast, especially the Procline and Dionysian variety, and medieval thought so far as it is thus Neoplatonic, is conceived as a way back beyond modernity, become manipulative technocracy. But it was not so in the beginning.

Erected against what it conceived as modern idealisms, like the condemned 'ontologism', Neothomist anti-modern suspicion extended even to the Neoplatonism of Augustine.[21] No Platonism served its various purposes. No Platonism, neither ancient, nor medieval, nor modern, encouraged the separation of philosophy, nature and state from sacred doctrine, grace and Church to which Pope Leo would subordinate them.[22] Still less does Neoplatonism reduce theology to a deductive science of concepts, true thought to realism, or nature to empirically comprehended objectivity. It was no kindness to Aristotle that these characteristics of the Leonine Thomas were attributed to his logic.[23] His Aristotelianism was supposed to be so total that Leonine Neothomists who exposed the magnitude of Thomas's citation of Denys maintained also that nothing characteristic of his Neoplatonic mentality had penetrated Thomas's mind.[24]

Let us note ironic results of the Leonine revival. It had set out to oppose what it conceived to be the totalitarian rationalism founded in bad philosophy, above all that of Descartes and of his successors, which it supposed underlay the all engulfing advance of the modern secular state. But the Thomism it erected against this enemy acquired, in accord with the iron laws of dialectic, the characteristics of the mentality against which it wrestled. So far as the Leonine Thomism has continuing protagonists among us, they are in some measure the disciples of one or another of the baroque Thomistic schools, and they still advance a doctrinal tradition. Now, however, they have been freed from their former service as institutionally enlisted warriors. The result is astonishing. One of them recently treated Thomas as if the poles of his thought were Augustine and Denys and maintained in the course of his argument 'la doctrine de l'analogie occupe en réalité peu de place dans la pensée de saint Thomas'.[25] Nothing was said of Aristotle! Here Thomists and recent historical scholarship can meet. Both are now conscious that Aristotle is not best opposed to these Christian Neoplatonists in the Neoscholastic manner.

An English Dominican scholar Edward Booth has put this case strongly in the last fifteen years.[26] As Father Booth represents it, the reasoning *mens*, through which Augustine flattened the Plotinian hypostases in order to arrive at the trinitarian God, and its human image, recuperates the Aristotelian *nous*. Equally, an Aristotelian sense for the priority of individual material substance is not to be set against a Dionysian idealistic realism. Rather, insofar as Denys understands the act of creation through a Procline logic which sees the similar formlessness of the top and bottom of the cosmos, the One and pure matter, and which also understands the One as the cause of substance at every level of the universe, Denys assists the recovery of the kind of Aristotelian ontology we associate with Aquinas. It is at least as true to say that Thomas interprets Aristotle through Denys as the contrary. Moreover, it is surely the quasi-apostolic authority of Denys which enabled Aquinas to give so much weight to Aristotle. He did find them mostly in agreement and this was not only because for most of his life he thought Aristotle to be the author of the *Liber de causis*.[27]

Transcendental Thomism

The Neoscholastic Thomism which Pope Leo revived was gradually replaced by that of the Thomistic philosophical historians and of the Transcendental School. The latter was primarily a Jesuit phenomenon and its first centres were in Belgium and Germany.

The purposes of the Leonine revival distorted the pattern of Thomas's thought just where he was close to Denys. The Transcendental Thomism, though sharing the general distortion, had more sympathy for some of the Dionysian aspects of Thomas's thought than did the historians. This was because the Transcendental school was more open to modernity than were the historians. Because the school was not so dogmatically and narrowly realist in its epistemology, nor so determined to establish being outside the self, the Transcendental Thomists shared something of the Dionysian assumption that the hierarchy of intellectual forms and the hierarchy of being were the same.

Karl Rahner took into the centre of his Thomism the equation from the *Liber de causis* between the perfection of being and intellect's complete self-return.[28] We shall see that this Procline idealist and essentialist equation is at the heart of Thomas's treatment of God and enables him to connect the fundamentals of his theology. Gerald McCool, s.j., pressing the Transcendental cause, which he thinks to be Platonic, Thomistic and contemporary all at once, wrote:

> Rahner's metaphysics of being's self-expression in its other is much closer to Neo-Platonism than St Thomas's metaphysics is usually thought to be . . . Thomas's metaphysics of *esse*, at least in Gilson's understanding of it, is considered to be distinct from and incompatible with the Neo-Platonic metaphysics of the good.[29]

François-Xavier Putallaz, Ruedi Imbach, Rudi A. te Velde, Swiss and Dutch lay scholars, and the American Jesuits W. Norris Clarke and J. M. McDermott, are among those writing about this at present. Because, like the Neoplatonists, they came to being through the self, and, with the Neoplatonists, unified the cosmos in accord with the structure of the self, the Transcendental Thomists did not deny that the *summae* were systems. Contemplating the compact and tightly ordered Dionysian *corpus*, with its explicit references to the inner connection of its own elements, and meditating upon its hierarchies and concepts also stimulated medieval systematizing in theology. Here, among the Jesuits, antiquity, the Middle Ages, baroque Thomism, nineteenth-century idealism and the present met. They saw their Transcendental thought as continuing the interpretation of Thomas by the sixteenth-century Jesuit Suarez. The Thomas who emerges out of such a consideration may be positively compared to Hegel.[30]

The Transcendental thinkers preferred to find the way to God through the structure which the self exposed in its quests rather than through objective conceptual knowledge. This opened them to what in Thomas's assimilation of Denys would most interest the second half of the twentieth century, namely his negative theology. In their opposition to positive conceptual knowledge as appropriate to philosophical theology, we touch the point where the Transcendental Thomists are one with Étienne Gilson.

The Thomas of the philosophical historians. Étienne Gilson

The most important of the Thomist philosophical historians had no sympathy for the Transcendental school, but, in his views that essence was always finite, and that *esse* was not knowable conceptually, we have the place where Gilson's opposition to modern idealism meets the Transcendentalist movement toward the postmodern.[31] This is the point where the turn towards Denys among Thomists is one with their uncritical relation to Heidegger.

The twentieth-century Thomism which regarded itself as recuperating for us the historical thought of Thomas as against the initial tendency of the Leonine revival to assimilate his teaching both to a common scholasticism and to the traditions of the baroque Thomistic commentators, was less able to recognize essential features of Thomas's thought than were some of those who approached Thomas with their own philosophical projects more directly in view. This irony helps to show that philosophy and the study of its history are not separable, though it was certainly not the case that Étienne Gilson wished ultimately to separate them. His endeavour to find something metaphysically distinctive in Thomas, combined with his confidence that what made Thomas distinct would best serve the anti-modern aims of the Leonine revival as well as coincide with the postmodern in our own world, was Étienne Gilson's undoing.

Within the French intellectual world Gilson is a transitional figure. Professor Marion, and many others, learned important aspects of their history of philosophy from him, including their suspicion of the Scotistic Thomism of Suarez as corrupting modern thought,[32] as well as a way of thinking which habitually opposes the modern and the premodern. But they have discovered that Gilson's views on Heidegger's relation to Aquinas were false. In consequence, they judged first that his Thomas of *ipsum esse subsistens* was every bit as much a problem as Gilson thought it the once and final solution. Now, again very lately, they have recovered Thomas for themselves, but only by finding in him that Dionysian Neoplatonism which was for Professor Gilson the worst essentialism.

Gilson identified in Aquinas an existential metaphysic which he supposed to be the true Christian philosophy, though Thomas, by Gilson's account, taught this metaphysic in opposition to his contemporaries. Equally, almost all his commentators not only missed the crucial point, but even assimilated his distinctive position to its opposite. For Gilson, and equally for Jacques Maritain, Thomas's existential metaphysic of Exodus rose out of a return to a sense for Being against all the ancient and medieval idealisms. In Gilson's history, Thomas's sense for Being conformed to Heidegger's most profound reflection, enabled authentic Thomistic ontology to escape the Heideggerian criticism of ontotheology, and stood resolutely against the false subjectivism of modernity.[33] This existential Thomism was opposed to all essentialisms, both ancient and modern. Neoplatonism was its ancient foe.

Denys was the main conduit of the Neoplatonism which was essentialism's most pernicious invasion of Christian metaphysics. Clearly, then, according to Gilson, Thomas used Dionysian thought only to transform it completely into its opposite, though Denys's apophatic side could be used to squeeze all conceptualization out of the act of being. Thus Denys's contribution assisted Aquinas to preserve the ontological difference between the Divine Being and beings. Beyond this use within an existential ontology to which Denys was at heart opposed, he contributed nothing to Thomas's metaphysics.[34] It is now clear, in contrast, that Thomas's metaphysic of being is both formed in a positive relation to Neoplatonism and retains fundamental elements of Neoplatonic logic.[35]

Professor Gilson's Thomism is past, being sustainable neither historically nor philosophically.[36] In France, both the historical study of Greek Neoplatonism and its tradition in Latin patristic and medieval thought and Heidegger's understanding of how Being was forgotten in Western philosophy were turned against Gilson's own treatments of these matters.[37] His way of representing Thomas historically and philosophically was succeeded for many by the work of Cornelio Fabro.

The Thomas of the philosophical historians: Cornelio Fabro

Cornelio Fabro was one of the first Thomists of the Leonine revival to give positive attention to the role of a Neoplatonic pattern of participation in the thought of St Thomas. Although he also paid great attention to developing a Thomistic ontology and to working out the exact relation between essence and existence in it, and although he saw this as part of the war against 'idealismus',[38] he was critical of Gilson. In general, Fabro was more careful than Gilson about how the construction of that ontology stood to philosophy both in Thomas's time and in our own. Fabro realized that Heidegger made no exception for Thomas in his history of ontotheology, and that this was not caused by a simple ignorance of Thomas's doctrine. Defending Thomas required a criticism of Heidegger even if there were also convergences between them. Further, he was clear that the genuine engagement with contemporary philosophy, both positively and negatively, which is necessary for the construction and defence of Thomism in our time, required that the result be more than the representation of a past historical position.

What was true for our time was equally the case for the thirteenth century. The philosophic logic Thomas gave the metaphysic of Exodus 3.13 could not come out of Scripture itself. Fabro did not hold with Gilson that Scripture revealed a philosophical metaphysic which was privileged as the true Christian philosophy, and was, therefore, protected against dissolution in the movement of rational reflection. Thomas's ontology was a philosophical construction related to his situation in history. Its particular matrix was Neoplatonic and decisively Dionysian. Because of this recognition, Fabro's Thomism has not been rendered untenable by the historians' discovery that Thomas's ontology does not stand against the so-called 'essentialism' of earlier pagan, Islamic and Christian Neoplatonists, but rather is anticipated by their developments and is dependent on them.

With its more sophisticated relation both to contemporary, and to medieval, philosophy, Fabro's Thomistic ontology is not altogether anti-Platonic, the identity of *esse* and *essentia* in the Divine simplicity is not interpreted, as in Gilson, as if essence had been squeezed out. Nonetheless, his formulation of the hierarchy of being in terms of 'intensity' is intended to meet something of the Heideggerian criticism of ontotheology as well as to avoid idealism.[39] Fr. Fabro's interpretation of Aquinas remains too existential. It still carries too much of the anti-modern (always anti-idealist) mentality of the Leonine revival. His representation of how causal participation is understood by Aquinas has been criticized strongly and effectively in a recent treatment of the Thomas–Denys connection, *Participation and Substantiality in Thomas Aquinas*, by Rudi te Velde. Both Fabro and Gilson are shown to have fatally misconstrued the essence–existence relation in Aquinas.[40]

Fr. Fabro does not simply think from within Heidegger's judgements. Decisively, for him, negation, even Denys's negative theology, stands within ontology, not against it.[41] This is crucial because the most recent developments in the discovery of a Dionysian Thomas are by that postmodernism whose relation to the history of philosophy remains determined by Heidegger, even if there is a growing freedom from the Heideggerian categories of judgement. For example, John Milbank thinks that Professor Marion's attempt to get beyond Heidegger, by substituting love for being, too much mirrors the logic of what he opposes.

For Cornelio Fabro, the negative way is used to modify the forms of conceptually knowable being. The negative way is not rather, as in the subsequent developments, placed against all philosophical theology. Negation and affirmation are ontological and epistemological means for constructing and moving within a hierarchy. That this is true both for Thomas himself, and for Fabro's construction of Thomism, is, at our moment in philosophy, the central point in determining their relation to Denys.

The remains

In France, all that remains of doctrinal, baroque or Neoscholastic Thomism is more or less assimilated to the position of Fabro. These Thomists tend to be associated with the Dominican École de Théologie at Toulouse, or work at the Catholic, but state supported, Faculty of Theology at Strasbourg, or they are French working at the predominantly Dominican University at Fribourg in Switzerland. A few names to list are S.-T. Bonino, o.p.,[42] Y. Labbé, T.-D. Humbrecht, o.p., and Gilles Emery, o.p.[43] They are sharply to be distinguished from the Dominican scholars at the Couvent St Jacques in Paris – H.-D. Saffrey's base – where the most theologically active Dominican medieval scholar is É.-H. Wéber.[44] His work in understanding the Neoplatonism of Thomas, Bonaventure, Eckhart, Duns Scotus and others may usefully be compared to that of the secular scholars Émilie Zum Brunn (who works mostly on Augustine), Olivier Boulnois (who specializes in the study of Duns Scotus)[45] and Alain de Libera (who has produced important studies of Albert the Great and the Rhenish theologians). The latter is about the same age as Jean-Luc Marion and, as the dominating spirit in the study of medieval philosophy and theology at the École Pratique des Hautes Études at the Sorbonne, represents those whose commitment to medieval philosophy is too open to the whole historical and philosophical problematic of contemporary French scholarship to permit assigning them to a school.[46]

Thomism and Neoplatonism

The Neoplatonic theology of Père Jean Trouillard

Beyond Fabro's Thomism, two further stages have emerged. There are those who looking, on one side, to the priority of the negative way in Denys, and, on the other, to Heidegger's criticism of ontotheology, demand a radical transformation of our understanding of Thomas's system. These keep something of the form of Thomistic philosophical theology but deny that what is *said* can be *thought*. The predications made of God by Thomas have no proper positive significance. They do not intend being conceptually or positively grasped. As in Denys, predicative thought and affirmative knowledge belong to and indeed constitute the realm of creatures. But there is no continuous ontic hierarchy for thought, no ontology, by which we may move from speech about creatures to significant speech about God. This stage in the development of contemporary Thomism[47] roughly corresponds to the Neoplatonic theology of Père Jean Trouillard.

Père Trouillard found in Proclus not only the basis for a henology, an ordering of all things relative to the One, rather than to being, but also the notion of the self-constituted. This enabled breaking the continuity of the chain which, in the old ontological systems, too closely bound heaven and earth. On the Thomist side, since this position leaves Thomas's theology an empty shell, speech not only without significance but properly opposed by thought, it gives way to the second of these last stages. Seen within a more general consideration of the relations of philosophy and theology, theology, in this penultimate position, remains too dependent upon philosophy.

Philosophy is still here, to use David Tracy's categories, 'correlational', 'correlating reason and revelation'.[48] Some sophisticated French theologians, imbued with the instincts of a Thomism which, as a system, they had largely abandoned, maintained a commitment to philosophy by such a strategy. Père G. Lafont, o.s.b.,[49] is an example. But this unstable compromise was not radical enough for the moving spirits.

The postmoderns: Denys against philosophy and against Thomas

Theologians with a more radical freedom perceived that for Westerners to get beyond the spiritual malaise which Heidegger identified, they had to know the power and reality of revelation before and independent of philosophy. There must be for us divine revelation which cannot be contained, reduced, entrapped by conceptualizing and objectifying reason. So a position emerges of which the nearest likeness in our century is the neo-orthodoxy of Karl Barth.[50] The French thinker best articulating it is Jean-Luc Marion. As an historian of philosophy, he is, as we noted, a most important student of Descartes. In his creative philosophical writing, he is a contributor to the phenomenological tradition. As a lay theologian, he is the sign of the passing of the old structures of French ecclesiastical life and of the relation between theology and philosophy in them. As theologian, he explicates Denys and has developed a theology sans être.[51] In contrast, Professor Gilson maintained theology to be beyond him; he was an historian and a philosopher. Crucially, the authoritative decisions of the Roman Church were decisive for his philosophical judgements. Gilson placed great value on the choice of Thomism as the official Christian philosophy by the Roman magisterium; indeed, he spoke as if this choice belonged to its infallible teaching. It was impossible both that the Church of Rome was the true Church and also that it had made an error about the thinker it had chosen to be its 'common doctor'.[52]

In Professor Marion's position, the Dionysian negative theology is taken to be the negation of philosophical or conceptual theology. The Dionysian writings are not the medium of Neoplatonic philosophy, but its overcoming by the Christian religion. Thomas was fatally wrong, not only in making Denys an authority contributing to a system in which Being was God's highest name, a system where God was identified with a form of Being in an ontologically understood cosmic hierarchy, where there were positive proper predications of God, where negation was a means within philosophical theology for constructing the hierarchically ordered modes of being and moving between them, but also, and most fundamentally, Thomas misunderstood and betrayed Denys by treating his writings as contributions to the tradition of philosophical theology. Rather they are directions for religious acts, hymns of praise and guides to union. Denys's statements are not propositions conveying a conceptually graspable philosophical and theological content.

When Denys is understood against Aquinas as theologically negating philosophy, rather than as providing theology with a tool, he is seen as doing in the ancient world what Heidegger attempts in ours. The God of the Hebrews has been freed from fatal entanglement with the philosophy of the Greeks and their fateful ontology.[53] We can and must substitute a theology built on the Good, not as concept, but as divine name, not to be understood, but to be praised. With God we have to do not with being, but, rather, with love.

This development completes a circle. It began with the Neoscholastic Thomism of the Leonine revival. As at that beginning, Thomas and Denys are now again completely opposed to one another, and Thomas is judged to have misconceived what he had in common with his highly revered authority.

The postmoderns: Denys and Thomas, Neoplatonists both

This point is, however, a place from which movement may begin again. In March, 1995, I sent to Professor Marion a paper on St Thomas and Denys which I had delivered at a conference in Paris in September 1994.[54] Professor Marion was to have participated in the conference but could not. The paper described his position in the way just outlined. He replied that I must read his article appearing in the next issue of the *Revue Thomiste*. I discovered there a formal retraction.[55] Professor Marion had decided that Thomas's philosophical theology is fundamentally Neoplatonic and is not *onto-théo-logie*, imprisoning God beyond the power of revelation within our conceptualization of being, but rather *théo-onto-logie*, revelation which determines the concept of being. This moves Thomas toward Denys. But now Thomas is evaluated from the perspective of Denys, either Denys against philosophy or Denys the Neoplatonist. This last twist in the relations of Thomas to Denys places us in a position to question our approach to our philosophical and theological past.

The French study of old Greek Neoplatonism, pagan and Christian, is, finally, an attempt to remain with theology, while getting beyond metaphysics, and perhaps philosophy. And that is an attempt to get beyond modernity – or, at least, what has been taken to be central to modernity. For, to quote John Milbank, 'It is arguable that recent researches suggest that "modernity fulfills metaphysics" should be radicalized as "modernity invented metaphysics".'[56] In making this judgement, he is drawing on his extensive, deep and critical engagement with Marion's work and that of other French thinkers, many of whom we have mentioned. These French scholars have devoted such a quantity of effort to understanding antique Neoplatonism in order to help contemporary thought and life escape, transform or reappropriate modernity. For Marion and Milbank, getting beyond secularizing modernity requires reducing or eliminating the autonomy of philosophy. Certainly, it requires that the Cartesian ego not be taken as adequate philosophical foundation.[57] Here, the anti-modern Leonine Thomist and postmodern Christian Dionysian or Neoplatonist meet. At this meeting point the problems arise.

We can articulate the problem in our deeply ambiguous relation to history more clearly. There is a problem with history itself. We need to find, and do find, a radical discontinuity between the modern and the premodern. But, equally, history is governed by a logic which we discern as if from the point of its completed working out. The discernment of this logic brings with it a freedom, which may become arbitrary, at least in the obvious sense of depending on a choosing will.[58] Certainly, the retrieval of elements from the past outside of that logic's dominating necessity requires there to be a choice between elements tied together within the historical actuality and its existent intellectual systems. But, if the choosing will and its choices have no other basis than an opposition to an assumed modernity and a wish to escape it, the *liberum arbitrium* will be arbitrary in a more negative sense. The question of this arbitrariness we need to explore further. In my view, it does arise in respect to the particular history to which this paper attends. Here it is a consequence of our misunderstanding of the relations of religion, philosophy and theology in Denys and in the late Neoplatonists whom he follows. This misunderstanding is required by the purposes with which we approach Denys. If we could get beyond these to a freer and more contemplative, a less manipulative, relation to him, the continuities and discontinuities between Denys and Aquinas, and between them and us, would become clearer. We would come at the same time to a different understanding of the logic by which our history is governed and to a different freedom in relation to it.

NEOPLATONISM AND MODERNITY: THE PROBLEM OF PHILOSOPHICAL REASON

Is Denys a Neoplatonist?

During the present revival of enthusiasm for what may be discovered in the Dionysian text, diverse, even opposed things are found there. Despite linguistic, philological and historical learning and extraordinary critical self-awareness, we share this with our predecessors, who likewise found opposed things in those mysterious depths, and often hated one another heartily on that account. There is, however, also something common to the Dionysian *corpus*, to our new Dionysians, to his older readers in East and West, and, indeed, to the late pagan Neoplatonic schools in relation to which his doctrine was developed. What is common is the high value they all place on the religious integration of the diverse features of life.

The whole Dionysian *corpus* is a spiritual anagogy whose goal is the union to which *The Mystical Theology* is dedicated. That this treatise, and the *henosis* it describes, is the sum and reason for the whole is made clear by its references to the rest of the *corpus*. All Denys's reasoning, both that which is clearly traceable to pagan philosophical sources, and his meditation on and theological reflection about sacred Scripture, as well as the moral purification and prayer necessary for all ascent, are directed to one end. Reason, purification and prayer are integrated with activities, theophanic, angelic and ecclesiastical, which are hierarchical, communal, liturgical and sacramental. All lead to the soul's union with God. On this there is accord. But with, and after, that agreement, the trouble starts.

The answers to a fundamental question differ strongly. What is the place of the philosophical reasoning in the anagogy? Since Christians tend to designate what paganism contributes to their theological reasonings as philosophy, the question about the place of philosophy in Denys arises sharply in respect to the character of Denys's relation to pagan Neoplatonism. Why are the place of philosophy, and thus, the relation to Neoplatonism, such big questions for us?

To understand the new enthusiasm for Denys in terms of a religious reaction against the disintegration of the elements of life in contemporary society, is also to see it as part of the contemporary reaction against modern or Enlightenment reason, at least as that reason is now characterized. The autonomy and abstractly self-related subjectivity of that reason are displayed in Descartes's new beginning for philosophy in a rational self-certainty. This new beginning, which Descartes said he found in Augustine,[59] is now, among us, perceived as loss rather than gain. What was forgotten in the apparent clarity of the new beginning, now comes again to remembrance. The deceptions of objective and objectifying reason are, it seems, more evident to us than they were to those in the midst of modernity. For these deceptions lead, by way of the division between intellect and will, itself following on the division of mind and body, to that manipulative relation to the world, animate and inanimate, human and even divine, in which our technocratic freedom seems entrapped.

In these very generally post- or anti-modern relations to the premodern, many of our diverse and opposed interpretations of Denys occur. These diverse interpretations have a polemical opposition precisely on account of the negative relation to modernity which they share. The trouble is that Denys, at least as he was appropriated by the West, did not stand outside or against that which has made us what we are.

A consequence of Thomas's submission to the authority of Denys is that he is essential to constructing Latin intellectual and political systems. Doubtless, Denys is transmuted in the systems of intellectual and institutional power he enables. But ironically, this is precisely because the logic he conveys is more inclusively dialectical than those Aristotle or Augustine provided Aquinas. Though he represents the Greek theological tradition, but carries from it a logic of such synthetic power, because of its embedded Iamblichan–Procline Neoplatonism, Denys has been essential to making Latin Christendom the most potent tradition. Whether that power is only the power for the greatest of self-overcomings or has another fate is also profoundly a question of what the Dionysian *corpus* really is about. Above all it is a question of the difference between what Denys said and what Aquinas heard, together with the questions as to whether we are either more profound, or more accurate, listeners than Thomas was. The trouble is that we shall be able to answer none of these pressing and difficult questions about the discontinuities if we do not recognize the continuities.[60]

When we try to read Denys against ourselves, who are postmodern only because we were and are first modern, we make his thought almost completely incomprehensible to ourselves, *in principle*. When we *begin* by opposition to what our history has made us, we must read Denys against our own inherited traditions of reading, but that is also precisely the work of historical critical scholarship as developed in modern times. Its aim is to distinguish history and tradition.[61] Getting behind the reading of Denys in our Western tradition to what is premodern is a work made possible by the critical modern spirit from which we would also escape. Thinking within this paradox unresolved tends to produce arbitrariness in our reading.

Jean-Luc Marion and John Milbank

John Milbank

Let me give a recent example of choosing made within a postmodern way of thinking, as Graham Ward defined it. So far as this choice involves selecting some elements, united within a Neoplatonic systematic thinking, without showing how what is selected can exist outside that thinking, the choosing is logically arbitrary. Dr John Milbank seeks in 'Christian Neoplatonism':

> notions . . . [which] remain essential for a Christian theological ontology: these are those of transcendence, participation, analogy, hierarchy, teleology (these two in modified forms) and the absolute reality of the 'the Good' in roughly the Platonic sense. The strategy, therefore, which the theologian should adopt, is that of showing that the critique of presence, substance, the idea, the subject, causality, thought-before-expression and realist representation do not necessarily entail the critique of transcendence, participation, analogy, hierarchy, teleology and the Platonic Good, reinterpreted by Christianity as identical with Being.[62]

To be left behind are precisely those notions which would found an autonomous philosophical reason enabling secular reason to 'position' theology instead of being 'positioned' by it. Dr. Milbank's choice of elements from Neoplatonic systems is not, however, for the sake of a 'restoration of a pre-modern Christian position'.[63] Nor is he uncritical of patristic and medieval thought which 'was unable to overcome entirely the ontology of substance'.[64] Yet, by a theology which makes such choices, Dr Milbank hopes to help us get beyond the secular reason central to modernity.

An examination of the actual forms in which patristic and medieval Christian Neoplatonism occurred will discover not only that the desired and the rejected elements are found bound together, but also that their union and development are more Christian than pagan. The Christians united traditions divided against one another in pagan Neoplatonism and combined extremes beyond those contained within the thought of their pagan predecessors. Partly, Dr Milbank recognizes this; indeed, it is essential to his criticism of Professor Marion. We may ask whether to select some elements from the historically existent *summae* of Christian Neoplatonism is either to revert to earlier pagan forms or to renounce the logic of theology become systematic for something more arbitrary.

Jean-Luc Marion: the question of the Dionysian hierarchy

We return to Jean-Luc Marion for another example of our treatment of Christian Neoplatonism. Professor Marion has erected Denys as a model for theology. In an early book, *L'idole et la distance: Cinq études*, Professor Marion interprets hierarchy, the term Denys invented, so as to set Denys's representation of it against hierarchy, as it actually developed in our historical institutions.[65]

Professor Marion, rightly, sees hierarchy as solving the problem at the heart of the Dionysian theology, the problem of how to reconcile the absolute distinction between creature and creator, on the one hand, with the creation's reversion to the creator, *henosis*, on the other. This problem is related to, though not identical with, another problem. How are we to reconcile the hierarchical relation to God which is a mediation, to its goal, mystical union, which is immediate? This second problem has bedevilled the tradition of Dionysian spirituality at least in the Latin Church from the later Middle Ages.[66]

Professor Marion represents the contrast as follows. In the political model of hierarchy, each superior level possesses something, an ontic content, which gives it authority over its inferiors, and which must be protected for the hierarchy to survive. The First for Marion's Denys, in contrast, renders itself sacred not to hide itself as origin, but because that origin is also to be the goal of every level of the hierarchy. The goal is possible because the creator defines himself, not by a content, but by an ecstasy. So Christ defines himself by giving himself away as gift to the hierarchy. The process, ours in his, is charity and ecstasy all at once. This ecstasy reconciles mediation with immediacy and creates a hierarchy which is not ontological. Since the Principle defines itself as action, rather than as a content, the continued giving of the gift involves immediate communion with the action and, thus, the mediation of a new giver. This mediated immediacy allows the return of creation to its creator in what would destroy the political model of hierarchy, but fulfils the sacred order of Denys.

Here we encounter the gravest problem for Marion's account. In the Procline–Dionysian tradition, and especially in its reception, development and transformation within the Aristotelian Neoplatonism of Aquinas, the fundamental gift of the Creator is the substantial or self-sufficient being of the creature. But if there is, in fact, real gift and real reception, then each who receives in the hierarchy receives something of its own, indeed receives its own substantial power of existence. So far as John Milbank's criticism of Marion's 'extra-ontological gift' shows that the demand is for *another ontology*', it involves the same principle.[67]

This comes out when Thomas transforms Denys's hierarchical thinking in following it. At the root of that thinking is the *lex divinitatis*, the divine ordering law, the law of mediation. Denys derived it through the Platonic tradition from Iamblichus. For Aquinas it is the Dionysian principle that between extremes a mediating third always intervenes.[68] Looking at celestial, ecclesiastical, social and salvific orders through such a logic transmutes them. The influence that Denys has on the mind of Aquinas grows throughout his life, and is strengthened by his late reading of a translation of the *Elements of Theology* of Proclus. The discovered coherence of Denys, the *Liber de causis* and of Proclus did not unnerve Thomas. Rather it enabled him to give more completeness and subtlety to his choice of mediating hierarchy as his fundamental model of good, indeed, divine order.

Denys, and the Neoplatonism which derives from Iamblichus, are responsible for the principles governing celestial hierarchy in Aquinas, for the enormous role it plays in his system, for the distinctions of its forms and ranks and for their names. However, Thomas conforms it to his ontology which gives greater weight to creation of substantial being as the work of the First Cause. Thomas insists rigorously on a distinction between the donation of substantial being, which is the creative act, and all other subsequent donations. The higher angels confer knowledge but not, as in Denys, being, grace and glory on the lower spirits. Moreover, the equality of humans as compared to angels prevents hierarchical communication in the celestial order being the model for that communication in the Church. This modelling is fundamental to Denys's purpose.[69]

There is an analogous difference in respect to the ecclesiastical hierarchy. Evidently, Thomas does not derive its population from Denys. It and the characteristic powers of its members are given in the evolution of ecclesiastical and political institutions. Denys contributes the principle that the more eminent in the hierarchy contains what derives from it, and the indispensable necessity of hierarchical mediation for the reception of divine knowledge. Here again Thomas's strong distinction between the substantial creation of creatures, on the one hand, and their operations, on the other, applies.

Because what is given in the spiritual hierarchy cannot, for Aquinas, totally constitute the being or character of any of its members, a fall into spiritual ignorance or pollution does not destroy the underlying sacral character of the members of the hierarchy, nor prevent them from remaining vehicles of grace and exercising the functions of their offices.[70] So, despite the authority of Denys for him, Aquinas contributes to the particular emphasis of Western ecclesiology on sacramental character and formal validity.

Hierarchy is understood by Thomas politically. It is the medium of divine government. The celestial hierarchy governs the cosmos; the ecclesiastical governs the Christian republic. In a move Denys did not take, and would not have taken, Aquinas follows a hermeneutic tradition which identifies the principal ecclesiastical hierarch with the Roman pontiff. This tradition specifically associates the papal mediation between the spiritual and earthly realms with the pope's possession of the highest and most perfect *potestas* in virtue of his possession of both swords. Aquinas, the Aristotelian, absolutizes this *potestas* by making the pope, as head of the Christian republic, heir to the prerogatives of the governor of the *polis*. The hierarchy whose laws derive from Denys has now altogether another character than that in his *Ecclesiastical Hierarchy*.[71]

Metaphysically, ecclesiastically and politically, the West has followed the direction in which Aquinas and his Latin predecessors developed the Iamblichan–Procline tradition largely received through Denys. Substantial being grounds political power in Western hierarchies. Each who receives in the hierarchy, receives in virtue of having something of its own, indeed, receives in virtue of having its own substantial power of existence.

Milbank and Marion, Thomas and Denys

For all their efforts to get around this conclusion, so as to avoid giving any basis to the substantiality of the modern self-related subject, the thinkers at whom we are looking cannot manage it. In fact, Dr Milbank has effectively recognized this in his 'Can a Gift be Given? Prolegomena to a Future Trinitarian Metaphysic', which is based in a critique of Derrida and Marion. Here, from the mutual recognition inherent to giving, Milbank shows the need for 'another ontology' which is 'another philosophy' and 'another metaphysics'.[72] Were he to fully work out the implications, he should bring back substance, as well as being, which he already embraces, as a category within the Christian Neoplatonism he desires. This belongs to St Thomas's development of the doctrine of Denys.[73]

This difficulty for Dr Milbank is parallel to the problem for Professor Marion since his recantation. If Thomas's identification of God and *ipsum esse* is acceptable, because Thomas is a Neoplatonist, does not Denys also become a philosophical theologian? Thus, Denys will be doing theology as science, like the Neoplatonists to whose thought he gave quasi-apostolic authority. But this Professor Marion has denied, and continues to deny. Marion has moved Thomas towards Denys, but not Denys towards Thomas.

Does, and can, Neoplatonism exist as a School of Spiritual Life apart from philosophical systematizing in the way that Marion represents Denys? If not, must we not move Denys towards Thomas, at the same time as Thomas is moved towards Denys? Does not the Dionysian *corpus*, in its appropriation of philosophy by Christian theology, do, with Proclus, what Augustine had done earlier with Plotinus? Is this Neoplatonic theology as science not essential to Christianity? These are disputed points. They are historical as well as theological and philosophical questions.

H.-D. Saffrey's inaugural lecture for the Twelfth International Conference on Patristic Studies is relevant. Entitled 'Theology as Science (3rd–6th centuries)',[74] it represents the pseudo-Denys as the heir of the movement by which Christian theology became philosophically scientific. For Saffrey, this development reached its highest point in the great thirteenth-century *summae*. As against such a view, the perspectives and positions from which Professor Marion and Dr Milbank make their choices from Neoplatonic theologies seem external. The result is a movement back and forth between what are, in fact, necessarily united aspects of determined wholes. Consider the problem of being in Christian Neoplatonism.

There is a lot in common between the contentless Dionysian Principle, as Professor Marion represents it, and the Neoplatonic One. The One is not, precisely because it is no thing. Being appears in such a view as limitation, a particular content.[75] Professor Marion wants to find a way to a Christian God who is not subject to Heidegger's critique of ontotheology. For this reason, he wants to separate God and being.

According to Heidegger, Christian philosophical theology confuses Being with beings, and turns God into a super being. God becomes comprehensible within a particular conception of being. From the divine perspective, we have a rational hold on the world. Here, we are also related to being from the side of the Creator's will. This relation reduces the cosmos to manipulable things.[76] For Marion, the way around this critique is found via Denys's God, whose first name is not 'being' but 'self-diffusive good'. So, in *Dieu sans être: Hors texte*, published in 1982, Professor Marion developed the notion of God, not as being, but as love. There also he criticized theologians like Aquinas who spoke of God as *esse*, because his most proper name was being.

158

In contrast, Dr Milbank, when he published his *Theology as Social Theory: Beyond Secular Reason* in 1990, was laying down, as a desirable characteristic of Christian Neoplatonism, 'the Platonic Good, reinterpreted by Christianity as identical with Being'.[77] In subsequent articles Dr Milbank has continued this, developing his description of God as being within a Neoplatonic logic, working out aspects of his position within a critique of Professor Marion. He detects that Marion's theology of love is too closely dependent on the Heidegger it would answer. But, in fact, their positions increasingly converge as Marion moves towards Aquinas and as Milbank sketches his other ontology.

Their opposition has mostly to do with the question of philosophy in theology. Given their common view of its late medieval and modern history, both are suspicious of philosophy with any inherent reason or content under-ived from revelation. John Milbank carries his opposition to independent or autonomous philosophical reason further than does Marion. He is able to bring back ontology and the God Who Is, both because his departure from Heidegger is at a different point than is Marion's and because, negating philosophy in relation to revelation even more completely than Marion does, he is able to restore elements of a traditional metaphysics of being more completely. All of which brings us back to our question as to how to read the Dionysian *corpus*. Its answer depends on how we understand the place of philosophical reason in theology.

Philosophy in theology

In agreement with Professor Marion, Dr Milbank wishes a reduction of philosophy relative to religion. And although there is little room for philos-ophy in Professor Marion's theology, Dr Milbank finds that Marion's phenomenology of donation still concedes philosophy too much. So he writes, criticizing Marion:

> An independent phenomenology must be given up, along with the claim, which would have seemed so bizarre to the Fathers, to be doing philosophy *as well as* theology. Philosophy as spiritual disci-pline, oriented to (an always in any case implicit) abstract reflection on the 'context' of our ascent, can indeed be embraced and consum-mated in a Christian version by theology. In this sense theology can still have recourse to *theoria* and *logos*, and if the latter constitute 'metaphysics', then talk of its overcoming is absurd. But philosophy as autonomous, as 'about' anything independently of its creaturely status is metaphysics or ontology in the most precisely technical sense. Philosophy in fact *began* as a secularizing immanentism, an attempt to regard a *cosmos* independently of a performed reception of the poetic word. The pre-Socratics forgot both Being and the Gift,

while (*contra* Heidegger) the later Plato made some attempt to recover the extra-cosmic vatic *logos*. Theology has always resumed this inheritance, along with that of the Bible, and if it wishes to think again God's love, then it must entirely evacuate philosophy, which is metaphysics, leaving it nothing (outside imaginary worlds, logical implications or the isolation of *aporias*) to either do or see, which is not manifestly, – I judge – malicious.[78]

Even if we allow for Dr Milbank's other philosophy, ontology, or metaphysics, Aquinas does not think like this. For Thomas, theology as *sacra doctrina* does not need to evacuate philosophy which is metaphysics. When Professor Marion wanted to make peace with Aquinas, an essential consideration was the question of the subject of theology in Aquinas and the relations between its scripturally revealed side, on the one hand, and that side of it which Aquinas says is one of the philosophical sciences, on the other. John Milbank identifies this consideration as 'the absolute crux of this matter, and the turning point in the destiny of the West'.[79] When Marion drew closer to Aquinas, he also reduced the difference in principle between himself and Milbank, but neither can embrace philosophical reason in the way Aquinas does.

By 1991, when *Dieu sans être: Hors texte* was translated into English, Professor Marion was already reconsidering his view of Aquinas. In his formal 'recantation', he discerned that, in Thomas Aquinas, and in Neoplatonic Christian theologians generally, God is not determined according to comprehensible being, from below. The Neoplatonic God is not imprisoned within the horizon of our understanding of being and without power to reveal himself. When Aquinas, and Neoplatonic Christian theologians generally, do *théo-onto-logie*, revelation determines how we understand God, and God, ecstatically good beyond being, gives being from above even to Himself. It is in this giving that being receives its logic.

Despite the recantation, there is a fundamental continuity as well as a shift in Marion's thought. His recantation is more a revision of his view of the place of Aquinas within his abiding judgements about how being must stand to the divine, than it is a revision of his theological principles. When he allows that Thomas's philosophical theology is fundamentally Neoplatonic, Thomas is moved towards Denys. But has his view of philosophy shifted? How are religion, theology and philosophy related? These are questions within Neoplatonic philosophy where reason has a positive relation to myth and religion.

Historically, Neoplatonic philosophy's embrace of these allowed a reciprocal Christian embrace of philosophy. Dr Milbank sets out a good part of such an argument thus:

Yet faith remains possible, as *another* logos, another knowledge and desire, which we should not hesitate to describe as 'another philosophy' (another metaphysics, another ontology) since the Church fathers themselves did not hesitate to do so and Platonic/Neoplatonic philosophy *already* pressed against any philosophical subordination of *mythos*, *cultus* and community.[80]

This goes a way towards such reciprocity, but it remains a one-sided representation of the relations between philosophical reason and religion in Platonism and Neoplatonism, pagan and Christian. In both, philosophical reason recognizes its need for *mythos*, *cultus* and community, but it does not evacuate its content or surrender its proper autonomy and integrity. Because the continued independent substantiality of philosophical reason even in such religiously oriented systems is not recognized or understood, confusion and arbitrariness appear. Relative to a diminution of philosophic reason, for one theologian, the key to Christian thought is to identify the Platonic Good with being, for the other, the opposite. For one theologian, Christian Neoplatonism saves us from autonomous philosophy; for the other, the Neoplatonic beginning beyond being brings with it into theology a systematic science which must still be resisted.

In the end, we are dealing here with two one-sided relations to Denys, and certainly to the Dionysian Aquinas. And we are confronted with the problems inherent to perspectives on Denys and Aquinas which do not share the sense Denys and Aquinas had of the singleness of the enterprise of theology, whether pagan or Christian, its historical continuity, nor their sense of the unity of the divided aspects of life when they are seen religiously. This whole view included for Denys a sense that there was something indispensable to the life of the Christian Church in the Platonic tradition. Why else would he have enwrapped his baptized Procline theology in the mantle of Paul's convert on the Areopagus whom Père Saffrey judges may have been his predecessor as Bishop of Athens? In self-hiding identification with the Areopagite, Denys wrote. Even in this pseudo-anonymous identification, he was likely following examples established in the Neoplatonic schools.[81]

The errors about older forms of Christianity we observe result from projecting our sense of the irreconcilable dividedness of life, including the exclusive division between philosophy and theology, pagan and Christian, backwards on to earlier thinkers for whom division was united in the actual Principle. Overcoming this will require seeing Denys in the light of Thomas's integration of the two aspects of theology, just as it will involve seeing Thomas as a Neoplatonist. Our most immediately demanding question arising within this necessary perspective is as to the relation of revelation, or the theology which comes from above, to philosophy, or the theology which ascends towards God from below, within the total theological system.

AQUINAS, BOETHIUS AND DENYS: THE
RELATIONS OF PHILOSOPHY AND THEOLOGY
IN CHRISTIAN NEOPLATONISM

In the context of our discussion, Aquinas' treatment of the relations between *sacra doctrina* and *quaedam pars philosophiae dicitur theologiae* – which has as its subject one of the kinds of being[82] – are astonishing. His *Summa theologiae* begins by assuming philosophy within the power of human reason which treats every form of being. Justifying *sacra doctrina* requires inquiring whether beyond philosophy another knowledge is needed! Its necessity is found in our orientation to an end beyond our natural powers. Another science develops in relation to that necessity which assumes, mirrors, imitates, opposes, judges, stands above and contains philosophy and especially metaphysics, philosophical theology or first philosophy. There are two total discourses and they do not exclude one another. We cannot elaborate here Thomas's complex arguments on the subject or subjects of theology in its two aspects.[83] But it is significant that Thomas develops his thinking on this completely and definitively in his commentary on the *De trinitate* of Boethius. There, as elsewhere, the two sides of theology are primarily distinguished by the direction thought takes in them. It is also crucial that for him the upward moving theology, which he regards as a part of philosophy, meets the downward moving theology, which proceeds from God's revelation recorded in the canonical books of Sacred Scripture. Aquinas uses, in this context, the old dictum of Heraclitus, the way up is the way down.[84]

When Thomas read *The Consolation of Philosophy* of this philosopher and theologian, who was an explicit disciple of Plato, and probably a near contemporary of Denys, he would have seen Lady Philosophy described by Boethius. She wears a dress whose alphabetical symbols indicate her embrace of the practical and theoretical sciences.[85] Of her Boethius writes:

> It was difficult to be sure of her height, for sometimes she was of average human size, while at other times she seemed to touch the very sky with the top of her head, and when she lifted herself even higher, she pierced it and was lost to human sight.[86]

It is revealing about the relations of philosophy and theology for Christian intellectuals when this was written, that Lady Philosophy leads the prisoner, to whom she comes, upward along a saving *itinerarium mentis in deum*. About to be martyred, Boethius, fallen, as he was, from social and political heights, into disgrace and prison on the way to torture and death, wrote about what consoled him. Like the prisoner in Plato's cave, Lady Philosophy's therapeutic art raised him up, turned him around and gave him the power of motion again.[87] Though the work of this Christian facing death became a Christian devotional classic, it contained not a single explicit reference to the Christian Scriptures.[88] Lady Philosophy prays, and for her prayer she invokes the authority of Plato in the *Timaeus*.[89] In his dialogues, philosophy both needs and uses myth and prayer and criticizes, from the perspective of thought, representation, generally, and many of the particular poetic representations of the gods. Socrates in the *Republic* urges what Boethius does: the expulsion of bad poetry and the writing of philosophically sound verse.[90] The *religio mentis* of *The Consolation of Philosophy* was one aspect of a Platonism common to cultivated pagans and Christians living at the limit of antiquity.[91] Without surrendering her judicial authority and autonomy, philosophy persuaded and comforted, and would persuade and comfort, Christians, even *in extremis*, for a millennium and a half.

Boethius, like Denys, knew the works of Porphyry, and at least the mentality of the Procline *corpus* where theology is all inclusive system.[92] Viewed within this particular Neoplatonic context, *The Divine Names* of Denys becomes the correlative of *The Consolation of Philosophy* and, thus seen, becomes more intelligible.[93] Together 'Eadem via ascensus et discensus': *The Divine Names* descend from beyond the heavens so as to be the *prohodos* of an anagogy directed to mystical *henosis*, Lady Philosophy stands at full height to reach through the heavens and draws the fallen soul above. She actually leads an individual soul on a saving *itinerarium mentis* to the simplicity of God which only prayer can reach. Philosophy's work is the work of religion.

A central puzzle about *The Divine Names* is illuminated if we see it within a Neoplatonic logic where theology includes philosophy, indeed where philosophical and revealed theology have an equality as different directions of mind in regard to the same divine reality. Though Denys makes biblical revelation the absolutely necessary condition for the activity of naming God, and though he claims that the Bible is the source of the particular names ascribed to the deity, he clearly both derives many names from Proclus, and also orders the whole treatise according to a Neoplatonic logic primarily, though not exclusively, Procline. What is presented as Christian and biblical is, in logic and content, also a continuation of pagan Neoplatonism. *The Divine Names* is the side of that thinking developed in the *Platonic Theology* of Proclus. That first treatise on the names of the divine has two mutually necessary aspects. The divine manifestations raise the soul to thought towards union, and the mythic and cultic are rendered conceptual. Denys and Aquinas can imitate Proclus in order to proceed in theology from what is revealed because the pagan gods have been conceptualized.[94] This imitation and assimilation of what belongs to pagan myth and *cultus* is no less puzzling than the consolation of a Christian martyr in his death cell by Lady Philosophy. But, if we put the two puzzles together, and see them from the earlier perspective of Proclus and the later perspective of Aquinas, we move towards what makes both intelligible.

We will go further in understanding Denys when we see him in continuity with Thomas, than if we look at him from within an opposition between Christian theology and philosophy. I propose that we look at Denys in continuity with Procline Neoplatonism, on the one hand, and Aquinas, on the other, in respect to two problems we encounter when interpreting Denys. On one of them we have already touched indirectly, the problem of being as a name of God. The other is implied in the problem of the relation of philosophy and theology (or, better put, the problem of the relation of philosophical and revealed theology). This is the question of the structure of the treatise *De deo*, the question of the relation of the treatise *De deo uno* to the treatise *De deo trino*. But before these considerations, we need to reflect on the place of reason in the Neoplatonic tradition of which Denys and Aquinas are joint heirs.

PHILOSOPHICAL REASON IN IAMBLICHAN–PROCLINE NEOPLATONISM: THE *LEX DIVINITATIS*

In the Iamblichan–Procline tradition, the cause of substantial being at every level,[95] the formless henadic fullness, is mirrored in the opposed formless material emptiness at the extreme other end of reality. The divine *eros* connects all, pulling it into a triadic structure by which each thing exists because it remains within, proceeds from and returns relatively or absolutely with respect to the One.[96] Here, we encounter the *lex divinitatis*, the Divine Law of total mediation to which grace and nature both will be submitted by theologians at least up to the seventeenth century.[97] All extremes are mediated, there is no movement from bottom to top or from top to bottom except through a middle term. This mediation, to which theurgy belongs, is required to draw back to the simple Good, the soul completely descended into *genesis*.[98]

In this context, for Proclus and Denys, religious oracles and ritual acts become essential to philosophy's way of salvation, its work to restore the soul to union with its principle. The divine moves towards us in speech and act to raise us up. On the other side are Porphyry and Boethius, with their more Plotinian accounts of the place of the soul. For them philosophical reason includes poetry, myth and prayer, in order to reach the simple good. Philosophy herself is able to do, and piously does, the work of religion. The Greek *Divine Names* and the Latin *Consolation* show these two faces of Neoplatonic philosophical theology when it became Christian at the beginning of the sixth century. They can both be Christian because reason, also pagan, with its own self-certifying necessities, is common to both. It is illumining that the Iamblichan law of mediation is firstly mathematical, the form of thinking appropriate to the soul intermediate between intellect and matter.

Philosophy with its own norms and certainties continues within Christian Neoplatonism. Half a millennium after Boethius and Denys, Anselm finds that the doctrines of the Christian religion may be deduced by *rationes neces-sariae*. For Eriugena, true philosophy, by which the highest and first principles are investigated, is true religion, and conversely true religion is true philosophy without which no one enters heaven.[99] In him, Plotinus and Porphyry, imbuing Augustine's mentality, will be juxtaposed to Iamblichus and Proclus carried by Denys,[100] but only because philosophy has her reasons.

According to Aquinas, the highest vision granted to those *in via*, the primitive Church and philosophy were in accord. They agreed not on the order of nature which could be overruled by the higher order of grace. Rather, what St Paul, the early Church and philosophy understood in common was the higher order, the order of grace, which admits of no exceptions. Its law was the Iamblichan law of mediation, become for Latin Christendom the *lex divinitatis* which prescribes even for God.[101] In this judgement, Aquinas speaks for a tradition which, beginning with Denys, includes at least Eriugena, Hugh of St Victor, Alexander of Hales, Albert the Great and Bonaventure up to his own time. It has a future which can be traced at least to the seventeenth century. So it determines ontology, soteriology, the structure, activities and interconnection of the celestial and ecclesiastical hierarchies, and the interpretation of Scripture.

In the interpretation of Scripture, its prescribing strength can be seen. From Denys himself to John Colet and beyond, among those under the influence of the Dionysian teaching, Isaiah 6.6, asserting that a Seraph flew to Isaiah and touched his lips with a burning coal, will be explained so as not to break the law of mediation.[102] The top of the angelic hierarchy could not and did not leave the immediate divine presence to fly so low. It is impossible, in such a systematic view, that a Seraph should leap abruptly over the eight intermediate angelic ranks to fly on a mission to a human. While earlier medievals tried to avoid agreeing with Denys, the later more thorough builders of systems, like Alexander, Albert, Aquinas and Bonaventure, followed him. In this they were successors of Eriugena. It is a witness to continuity that the tensions between reason and revelation, between philosophy and *mythos*, which may seem to belong to seventeenth-century scientific rationalisms, were present from the beginning.

DENYS WITHIN THE NEOPLATONIC TRADITION

So we locate Denys within the Neoplatonic tradition, and in this tradition we set him with St Thomas, not against him. We can make some progress on vexing questions in Thomistic and Dionysian scholarship by using this hermeneutical perspective rather than those resulting from anti-modern stances dividing religion, theology and philosophy. I propose to experiment with the problems of being, unity and trinity in the two theologians. This requires some words about Denys largely borrowed from Werner Beierwaltes in a recent issue of *Hermathena*.

The inseparability of thought from the life of the religious community, which is so appealing in Denys, is a consequence for him of the ordering of life to union. The perfection or completion of everything is union, and we are directed and drawn to union with the divine in which we pass beyond rational objectivity. Here we recognize philosophical categories of Neoplatonism, and it is indeed here, at the heart of what attracts us to Denys, that such categories enter.

Henosis, beyond all being and knowing, though sought with the divine *Trias*,[103] comes with the domination of the simplicity of the divine unity. Unity as goal is present in the actual *proodos* of the *corpus*, *The Divine Names*. There is another beginning for the descent from the divine unity. Of this treatise Denys tells us, but we do not have it, perhaps because he never wrote it. Whether he wrote it, or only needed to pretend he had, matters little for our purposes. Evidently, Denys tells us about *The Theological Representations*, which should precede *The Divine Names*, and about *The Symbolic Theology*, which should follow it,[104] in order to show that he has a complete system for the movement from unity to multiplicity, from the intelligible to the sensible. He thus demonstrates his fidelity to *The Elements of Theology*, ascribed to his Christian teacher Hierotheus who is here a mask for the divine Proclus.[105] The demands of Neoplatonic logic clearly occupied him.

The Divine Names begins in several ways with unity, just as it ends with Perfect and One:[106] 'all these Scriptural utterances celebrate the supreme Deity by describing it as a monad or henad, because of its supernatural simplicity and indivisible unity'.[107] Just as the initial unity is not opposed by Denys's description in *The Mystical Theology* of the goal of the return as Trinity, no more is it contradicted by the next passage in *The Divine Names* which speaks of God as Three, *triada*.

Werner Beierwaltes writes:

> Dionysius' concept of the divine one-ness is philosophically determined by the essentially distinct concepts of the absolute *non*-being One and the *Being*-One as developed in Proclus' *Parmenides Commentary*.[108]

Here we recognize a paradoxical unification of the fundamental oppositions, a telescoping which scholarship has taught us to see in Porphyry,[109] who directly, and by way of Victorinus, certainly influenced the trinitarian theology of Augustine. In fact, the result in both Christians is like, though not identical. Both understand the First Principle as triadic unity and unified triad, perfectly simple, completely internally distinguished.[110]

The divine unity is *nonetheless trinitarian*, the Trinity "derived" from the unity, or the unity as an internally relational Trinity'. 'Dionysius conceives the absolute unity (the [!] One) also as an internally *relational* tri-une oneness.'[111] Crucially, trinitarian unity is possible because the Dionysian Principle is self-related. I quote more of Werner Beierwaltes: '[The Plotinian] form of immanently relational Thought, thinking Itself and yet reflecting towards its Origin, is the *philosophical* model for the Christian Unity in Tri-Unity: the Trinity.'[112] As Denys puts it:

> the differentiations within the Godhead have to do with the benign processions and revelations of God. . . . [T]here are certain specific unities and differentiations within the unity and differentiation. . . . Thus, regarding the divine unity beyond being, they [those fully initiated into our tradition and following sacred scripture] assert that the indivisible Trinity holds within a shared undifferentiated unity its supra-essential subsistence . . . its oneness beyond the source of oneness, its ineffability, its many names, its unknowability, its wholly belonging to the conceptual realm . . . and finally . . . the abiding and foundation of the divine persons who are the source of oneness as a unity which is totally undifferentiated and transcendent.[113]

On this Beierwaltes writes, 'This formula emphasizes the unity of the three within the trinity: unified through difference and differentiated through unity.'[114] The language of Holy Scripture about the Father, Son and Spirit require this drawing together of the unity and division, negation and affirmation more completely and more paradoxically than in Plotinus:

> [I]t entails the attribution of *both* negativity and positivity to *one* and the *same* object. In accordance with the first hypothesis of Plato's *Parmenides* the eminent (first) One is absolutely *transcendent* . . . pure, superessential eternally relationless Simplicity. The *second* form of unity, which arises from the absolute One and in self-knowledge turns back to the One, is . . . *differentiated* within itself. . . . This allows it to receive those relational predicates which are denied the superessential One. . . . The putting together of these dimensions must be considered as intending to abolish or lessen the realm of *difference* between both these two forms of unity, insofar as God with *all* his predicates must be thought of as pure unity.[115]

Porphyry's anticipation of this paradoxical unification was judged by pagan Platonists to have moved so much beyond Plotinus as to place him outside the true tradition.

In this way God is being for Denys. By the same logic that the gods and separated hypostases of Proclus become predicates and divine names, and to the degree that this is actually accomplished, triadic unity becomes self-related thought and love, and is, therefore, also being. These three elements, unity, the divine hypostases, and being, move inseparably together, as they have since Parmenides was modified by Plato. Considering unity and division as these appear in the relation of the treatment of God as one and God as three, we remain with what Thomas finds in the *Divine Names* and look at the formal structure in which his thinking about the divine being occurs.

THE RELATION OF THE TREATISE *DE DEO UNO* TO THE TREATISE *DE DEO TRINO* IN THEOLOGY

The major division of Thomas's treatise *De deo* (*Summa Theologiae* I, qq. 2–43) originates in the Dionysian mediations of Procline Neoplatonism. This is the distinction of the *De deo uno* (qq. 3–26) from the *De deo trino* (qq. 27–43). Thomas is said to be the originator of this fundamental structural determinant of the *De deo* of his *Summa Theologiae*. Further, it is maintained that the Augustinian tradition underlies his division of the treatise between the treatment of the names common to the unity of essence, on the one hand, and those names proper to the distinct persons, on the other, and beginning theology from the unity. In doing so, Thomas is accused of reducing the proper Christian understanding of God to the naturally known Platonic conception of unity.

In truth, Thomas is explicit (and correct) that he finds this distinction, and the reason for beginning from the divine as one and good, in Denys. Denys is explicit that he separates the consideration of the undifferentiated and the differentiated names into distinct treatises. He makes this distinction, and says that he wrote different treatises to embody the distinguished elements, and that he orders the movement outward from unity to division.

The Divine Names considers the names common to the divinity. Another treatise is said to have dealt with the names proper to the distinct persons. *The Divine Names* calls 'perfect' and 'one' the names 'most potent' because goodness and unity are the highest designations of God as cause. Thomas recognized that this argument gives goodness a priority. By the same reasoning, Thomas sees that 'unum habet rationem principii'.[116] So he imitates Denys almost exactly by beginning his own treatment of God's substance with perfection and goodness – which immediately follow simplicity – and ending it with a discussion of God's unity.

The same reasoning determines the priority of the *De deo uno* over the *De deo trino*. This tradition for structuring theology is very fruitful in the Middle Ages. A line connects Denys, Eriugena, Alan of Lille, Honorius Augustodunensis, Alexander of Hales, Bonaventure, Albert the Great,

Ulrich of Strasbourg and perhaps Richard of St Victor. On the other hand, Augustinians, like Abelard and Peter Lombard, eschew such speculative radicalism and, like their master, treat the one and the three together. As for the propriety of the logic of the One in Christian theology, Thomas thinks his beginning is only possible because of the divine revelation.

It is the privilege of sacred doctrine, because of its foundation in God's self-revelation to faith in Scripture, to begin with God. The other theology which is part of philosophy is, for Thomas, incapable of such a beginning. This is not to reduce God to a comprehensible concept. There can be no adequate representation in creatures of the divine simplicity (or, for that matter, of the divine Trinity). Thomas finds in Denys that neither the unity nor the trinity of God is adequately known from creatures.

Here we meet with the Neoplatonic elevation of the One as an object beyond science. Revelation is, for Denys and Thomas, a self-manifestation by the unknown God whose substance remains unknown. Sacred doctrine does not begin properly in philosophical reasonings. They are necessary to it but they do not provide its appropriate basis or origins. Its foundation is the unknown one as principle disclosing itself. No reduction of the full concrete life of God to an abstract category known to natural reason is implied. The opposition set up here is false, for no Neoplatonist, pagan or Christian, thought the principle conceptually knowable. When Christians unite the primal unity and *nous*, in order to think the Trinity, the priority of the simple mysterious beginning does not disappear. In this Professor Marion's *théo-onto-logie* is well founded. But this philosophy understands. The pagan thinkers, along with Boethius, Denys and Thomas, begin from the *occulta*. The common aim of their works is that which Thomas ascribes to the *De trinitate* of Boethius: 'finis uero huius operis est, ut occulta fidei manifestentur, quantum in uia possibile est.'[117]

Thomas is not, despite this, a Dionysian rather than an Augustinian in his trinitarian theology nor in his treatment of the divine being. Indeed, it is his understanding of how God is *esse* which gives a unified logic to his *De deo* and herein Dr Milbank shall also have his due.

BEING AS A NAME OF GOD

Professor Beierwaltes writes:

> Dionysius increases the absolute otherness of the divine One through the lavish use of the basically negative prefix 'super'. . . . *At the same time* . . . the implications of the '*being*-One' are valid for God or the Divine Unity in just the *same* intensity. This is so since He who Is . . . as unchangeable *Being himself* . . . is abiding identity in himself, and yet also is difference in the sense of constituting

being and giving share of his absolute goodness: He is the Cause of All; despite all the difference from thought in the realm of plurality: He is absolute Self-thinking, a thinking which embraces the ideas. The divine ideas constitute an intelligible framework of the world, *before* the world, unitary and unifying in divine thought.[118]

When this is seen as the development of a possibility within Neoplatonic thinking, one prefigured by Porphyry, the drawing together of Augustine's thought about the God Who Is and Denys's more negative theology by Aquinas and other medieval builders of summas, so as to name God *esse* in the identity of essence and existence, becomes intelligible.[119] For here belongs the logic by which God is called being itself in Denys, while, at the same time, this name is denied of the first. Being is both subordinated to the name Good and God is above being, superbeing.[120] God in Denys is called self-diffusive good, or ecstatic love, before he is named being. In the Dionysian hierarchical thinking, order is everything.

Aquinas understands what is happening to theology in Denys. He writes in his *Exposition of the Divine Names*:[121]

> The Platonists whom in this book Denys imitates much . . . posited separated realities existing *per se*. . . . Indeed, these separated principles they laid down as mutually distinct in respect to the First Principle which they called the *per se* good, and the *per se* one. Denys agrees with them in one way, and disagrees in another. He agrees in that he too posits life existing separately *per se*, and likewise wisdom, and being, and other things of this kind. He dissents from them, however, in this; he does not say that these separated principles are diverse entities [*esse diversa*], but that they are in fact one principle, which is God.

Thereby, Thomas locates Denys midway between himself and the Platonists.

Thomas has a good sense for the Procline developments reaching from Denys, that is from Greek Christianity, on the one hand, and from the *Liber de causis*, that is from Arabic Islam, on the other. His knowledge of these developments became more and more exact as his life went on and the texts available to him increased. He recognizes that these Platonists name God being, not absolutely, but in respect to creation, insofar as the first and most proper effect of God in things is their substantial *esse*. By this, God gives created things a participation in Himself. They imitate God in having an existence of their own.

Aquinas knows that for Denys, God is more properly called good. He also recognizes Denys's reason for this and gives place in his own system for such a view. Albert, Bonaventure and other Latin theologians do the same. He writes: 'In causation, then, the good precedes the existent as end precedes form; and for this reason, in any list of names designating divine causality, good will precedes existent.'[122] Nonetheless, for Aquinas, God is most properly designated as *ipsum esse subsistens*. He gives the side of division, that is Aristotelian self-knowing *nous*, self-reflexive form, reflexive being, thought and will, and, ultimately, the Trinity of Persons, more weight in his transforming acceptance of the Neoplatonic amalgam than Denys does in his. This also enables and requires Thomas to join the treatment of the divine being, God's operations, the divine Trinity and the act of creation in one continuous step by step argument beginning from the divine simplicity.[123]

In differing from Denys, Aquinas recognized how much he owed him. If Rudi te Velde's treatment of the relations between Thomas and Denys is correct, the key to how Thomas will relate participation and substantiality may well have come to him from Denys.[124]

> Aquinas will take the notions of participation which he received and forge of them a tool to explicate how God in one single act creates things 'according to their kinds', not only presupposing nothing but bestowing the richest diversity through that very ordering act.[125]

This understanding of Thomas's teaching on the creative act differs explicitly from that in the existential Thomism of Gilson and Fabro. John Milbank writes comparably to te Velde:

> God's *essential* Being, the *esse ipsum*, or the coincidence of Being with essence in God, is conceived as the full *giving* of Being as an infinitely determined essence, whereby, alone, there is 'to be'.

Milbank judges that in such a view there could be 'a stronger link between the theological account of *esse*, on the one hand, and trinitarian theology on the other'. But this is not 'beyond Aquinas'.[126]

There is a movement in and from Thomas's *De deo uno* in the *Summa theologiae*. This logical movement is essential to understanding how God is Creator. The development is from God's substantial names, which are dominated by being, understood through the notion of simplicity or absolute unity, to the names derived from God's activities or operations. The names derived from the operations of knowing, willing and power are dominated by the self-reflexive act of thought, so God is said to know. But this self-relation belongs already to the divine being which has *reditio completa* precisely because its simplicity requires the identity within it of essence and existence. The *reditio completa* of the divine *ipsum esse subsistens* is what unifies the treatises *De deo uno*, *De deo trino* and *De deo creante*.

In Thomas' treatment of the divine intelligence, God is called truth. God is named truth because of an act of comparison or self-reflection. God compares the divine ideas with creatures totally existing by a caused imitation of the divine being as idea.[127] God is the truth of things so far as their substantial being in its particular grade and character is a participation in divine being, not absolutely, but as thus imitable and imitated.

When Thomas understands causation in this way, he is both following Denys and pushing the Christian Neoplatonism of the Areopagite further. What distinguishes Christian from pagan Neoplatonism is the willingness of Christians to bring division into God:

> the divine essence is the idea of all things, not however as it is in identity with itself (*ut essentia*), but as known (*ut intellecta*), that is to say, as articulated and differentiated in God's knowledge according to the particular aspects under which this universal essence can be imitated by another being.[128]

In consequence,

> the effect proceeds from the cause in virtue of an active self-distinction on the part of the cause. . . . So the negation in the effect of the identity of essence and *esse* in God is included in the likeness each creature has of God.[129]

Underlying is the Iamblichan–Procline notion that, between the participated and the participating, a middle must occur. This becomes, for Denys in this context, the idea that creatures cannot participate in the divine being directly, but instead participate in its likeness. In Thomas a divine self-reflexive activity is involved to a degree Denys would have found difficult and a pagan Platonist impossible. Thus, Thomas can far more resolutely predicate being of God than Denys or Porphyry can.

These are quantum steps in a continuum. By locating our thinkers on a continuum in a tradition of interpretation and transformation, we shall understand them best. For there are differences in principle between these systems, and yet these very differences are best understood as moments in a continuous tradition.

CONCLUSION

I have been concerned with the contradictory and changing relations which our anti- and postmodern purposes and perspectives have imposed on Denys and Aquinas. The anti-modern Leonine revival of Thomism set them against each other for the sake of an Aristotelian Thomas. With better results, postmodern theologians have tended to judge Thomas from the perspective of Denys. I have tried to show that some of the twists and turns in the opposed evaluations stem from a theological antagonism to autonomous philosophy. This arises from antipathy to modernity common to both. Theological antipathy to modernity has the effect of separating us from our premodern past – just as we are also drawn to that past in search of things which all acknowledge modernity has forgotten. The result of this double-minded relation to our history is a grave difficulty in reading premodern texts. Trying to read them against both the content and character of our developed Western way of reading, trying to read them against our own traditions of reading, our interpretations become arbitrary.

I have suggested a solution in respect to Denys and Aquinas. I propose that we try to recuperate them as moments in a continuous Neoplatonic tradition beginning among the pagans. Denys's thinking is a transforming moment in the great change from pagan to Christian. Christianizing that theology requires transformations of it. These Denys begins, Aquinas pushes them further. Apart from looking at Denys within a Neoplatonic continuum, we cannot even understand what he did. Seeing him relative to Aquinas shows what further steps might be taken. These judgements we can make in virtue of some common criteria of understanding.

Aquinas gives the side of division, self-knowing *nous*, self-reflexive form, being which has *reditio completa*[130] and is therefore thought and will, and the distinct being of the Three Persons, more weight in his transforming acceptance of the Neoplatonic amalgam than Denys does in his. As a result, unlike Denys, he is able to draw the *De deo uno*, the *De deo trino*, and the *De deo creante* into one continuous argument and to unite a philosophical ascending logic with the descending logic of *sacra doctrina*. Doubtless such a synthesis causes problems which Denys does not have.[131] Equally, Aquinas detects and corrects incoherences in the Dionysian thinking. There is not a final systematic solution. But we shall follow neither of them if we attempt to separate ourselves from the systematic unification of philosophy and theology and of their elements which is both theirs and their Platonic predecessors.[132]

NOTES

1 See W. J. Hankey, 'Pope Leo's Purposes and St. Thomas' Platonism', in A. Piolanti (ed.), *S. Tommaso nella storia del pensiero, Atti dell'VIII Congresso Tomistico Internazionale*, Studi Tomistici 17, Vatican City, Libreria Editrice Vaticana, 1982, vol. 8, pp. 39–52; idem, 'Making Theology Practical: Thomas Aquinas and the Nineteenth Century Religious Revival', *Dionysius* 9 (1985), pp. 85–127; idem, 'The Bible in a Post-Critical Age', in W. Oddie (ed.), *After the Deluge: Essays Towards the Desecularization of the Church*, London, SPCK, 1987, pp. 41–92; idem, ' "Dionysius dixit, Lex divinitatis est ultima per media reducere": Aquinas, Hierocracy and the 'augustinisme politique" ', in I. Tolomio (ed.), *Tommaso D'Aquino: Proposte nuove di letture. Festscrift Antonio*

Tognolo, Medioevo. Rivista di Storia della Filosofia Medievale 18, Padua, Editrice Antenore, 1992, pp. 119–50.

2 For philosophy see F. L. Jackson, 'The Revolutionary Origins of Contemporary Philosophy', *Dionysius* 9 (1985), pp. 155ff.

3 Graham Ward, 'Introducing Jean-Luc Marion', *New Blackfriars* 76 (1995), p. 323.

4 See the third essay, sections 24–6, one of his many negative reflections on scientific history.

5 L. K. Shook, *Étienne Gilson*, The Étienne Gilson Series 6, Toronto, Pontifical Institute of Mediaeval Studies, 1984, p. 150, quotes Gilson on what he found at Harvard: 'As for the history of philosophy, they don't see any use for it. Perry is quite upset. He thinks that too much studying of the systems of others prevents young people from finding one of their own.'

6 See L.-J. Bataillon, 'Le edizioni di *Opera Omnia* degli scholastici e l'Edizione Leonina', in R. Imbach and A. Maierù (eds), *Gli studi di filosofia medievale fra otto e novecento: Contributo a un bilanico storiografico. Atti del convegno internazıonale Roma, 21–23 settembre 1989*, Rome, Edizioni di Storia e Letteratura, 1991, pp. 141–54; idem, 'La commission léonine pour l'édition des oeuvres de s. Thomas d'Aquin', *Analecta sacri Ordinis Fratrum Praedicatorum*, fasc. 1 (1983), pp. 72–83; idem, 'L'édition léonine des oeuvres de Saint Thomas et les études médievales', *Atti dell'VIII Congresso Tomistico Internazionale*, Studi Tomistici 10, Vatican City, Libreria Editrice Vaticana, 1981, pp. 452–64.

7 Aquinas draws both on the pseudo-Dionysius and the *Elements* of Proclus, just translated from the Greek, in his late (after 1268) *Super librum de causis expositio*, H.-D. Saffrey (ed.), Textus Philosophici Friburgenes 4/5, Louvain, Éditions E. Nauwelaerts, 1954, see St Thomas Aquinas, *Commentary on the Book of Causes*, tr. Vincent A. Guagliardo *et al.*, Washington, DC, Catholic University of America Press, 1996; C. D'Ancona-Costa, *Tommaso D'Aquino: Commento al 'Libro delle cause'*, Milan, Rusconi, 1986; W. J. Hankey, *God In Himself: Aquinas' Doctrine of God as Expounded in the Summa Theologiae*, Oxford, Clarendon Press, 1987, pp. 46–7; and Edward Booth, *Aristotelian Aporetic Ontology in Islamic and Christian Thinkers*, Cambridge Studies in Medieval Life and Thought III/20, Cambridge, Cambridge University Press, 1983.

8 H.-D. Saffrey and L.G. Westerink (ed. and tr.), *Théologie platonicienne*, 5 vols, Paris, Les Belles Lettres, 1968–87.

9 E. R. Dodds (ed. and tr.), *Proclus: The Elements of Theology*, Oxford, Clarendon Press, 1933.

10 The last of a series of articles is 'Nouveau liens objectifs entre le pseudo-Denys et Proclus', *RPT* 63 (1979), pp. 3–16; his conclusions about Denys are summarized in 'Les débuts de la théologie comme science (IIIe–VIe)', *RPT* 80 (1996), pp. 201–20.

11 See E. Lucchesi and H.-D. Saffrey (eds), *Memorial Andre-Jean Festugière: Antiquité païenne et chretiénne*, Cahiers d'Orientalisme 10, Geneva, P. Cramer, 1984, which contains a bibliography.

12 David T. Runia, 'Festugière Revisited: Aristotle in the Greek Patres', *Vigiliae Christianae* 43 (1989), pp. 1–2 and 26.

13 4 vols, Paris, Lecoffee, 1944–54.

14 Paris, Les Belles Lettres; for an incomplete bibliography of des Places see his festschrift *Études platoniciennes, 1929–1979*, Leiden, Brill, 1981.

15 For an incomplete bibliography, see *Néoplatonisme mélanges offerts à Jean Trouillard*, Les Cahiers de Fontenay 19–22, Fontenay-aux-Roses, 1981.

16 Stanislas Breton, *De Rome à Paris: Itinéraire philosophique*, Paris, Desclée de Brouwer, 1992, p. 31. For further relevant bibliographical indications to the work of Trouillard, Dumèry, Breton and critics like Y. Labbé, see Hankey, *God in Himself*, pp. 13–14.

17 Breton, *De Rome*, pp. 152–3.

18 Breton, *De Rome*, p. 154, see also, particularly, p. 164.

19 See Hankey, 'Pope Leo's Purposes'; idem, 'Making Theology Practical'; G. A. McCool, *Nineteenth-Century Scholasticism: The Search for a Unitary Method*, New York, Fordham University Press, 1989; idem, *From Unity to Pluralism: The Internal Evolution of Thomism*, New York: Fordham University Press, 1989. On the anti-idealist biases of the Thomist revival, see P. Poupard, *Un essai de philosophie chrétienne au xixe siècle: L'Abbé Louis Bautain*, Bibliothèque de théologie série 4, Histoire de la Théologie 4, Paris, Desclée & Cie, 1961; T. F. O'Meara, *Romantic Idealism and Roman Catholicism: Schelling and the Theologians*, Notre Dame, IN, University of Notre Dame Press, 1982; idem, *Church and Culture: German Catholic Theology, 1860–1914*, Notre Dame, IN, University of Notre Dame Press, 1991.

20 John Milbank, 'Only Theology Overcomes Metaphysics', *New Blackfriars* 76 (1995), p. 331; idem, 'Can a Gift be Given? Prolegomena to a Future Trinitarian Metaphysic', *Modern Theology* 11 (1995), p. 140; on the rationalism of Neoscholasticism, see Hankey, 'Making Theology Practical', pp. 91–2.

21 Hankey, 'Dionysius dixit', p. 131 and Breton, *De Rome*, pp. 78ff.: 'Idéalisme et thomisme'.

22 Hankey, 'Making Theology Practical', pp. 92ff.

23 On the question of Thomas's Aristotelianism, see Mark D. Jordan, *The Alleged Aristotelianism of Thomas Aquinas*, The Etienne Gilson Series 15, Toronto, Pontifical Institute of Medieval Studies, 1992; and idem, 'Aquinas in Aristotle's *Ethics*', in Mark D. Jordan and Kent Emery (eds), *Ad Litteram: Authoritative Texts and their Medieval Readers*, Notre Dame Conferences in Medieval Studies 3, Notre Dame, IN, Notre Dame University Press, 1992, pp. 242–5. On the character of and reasons for this 'philosophie aristotélico-thomiste', see Breton, *De Rome*, pp. 55ff., 'II. Rome. Apprentissage romain'.

24 M. B. Ewbank, 'Remarks on Being in St. Thomas Aquinas' *Expositio de divinis nominibus*', *AHDLMA* 56 (1989), p. 123.

25 T.-D. Humbrecht, 'La théologie négative chez saint Thomas d' Aquin', *Revue Thomiste*, 93 (1993), pp. 541 and 542ff.

26 See E. Booth, 'St Augustine's "notitia sui" related to Aristotle and the early neo-Platonists', *Augustiniana* 27 (1977), pp. 70–132 and 364–401, 28 (1978), pp. 183–221, 29 (1979), pp. 97–124; idem, 'St. Augustine's *de Trinitate* and Aristotelian and neo-Platonist Noetic', *SP* 16/2 (1985), pp. 487–90; idem, *Aristotelian Aporetic*; idem, *Saint Augustine and the Western Tradition of Self-Knowing*, The Saint Augustine Lecture 1986, Villanova, PA, Villanova University Press, 1989; also François-Xavier Putallaz, *Le sens de la réflexion chez Thomas d'Aquin*, Études de philosophie médiévale 66, Paris, Vrin, 1991, pp. 11–15.

27 The early Aquinas thinks that 'Dionysius almost always follows Aristotle', *Scriptum super Sententiis*, II, dist. 14, 1, 2, (Moos, p. 350); the most complete consideration of the reason in and for this apparently strange association is Booth, *Aristotelian Aporetic*. On his assimilation of Denys and Aristotle, see also W. J. Hankey, '*Magis . . . Pro Nostra Sententia*': John Wyclif, his 'Mediaeval Predecessors and Reformed Successors, and a Pseudo-Augustinian Eucharistic Decretal', *Augustiniana* 45 (1995), pp. 237–9; and idem, 'Dionysian Hierarchy

in St. Thomas Aquinas: Tradition and Transformation', in Ysabel de Andia (ed.), *Denys l'Aréopagite et sa postérité en Orient et en Occident*, série Antiquité 151, Paris, Études Augustiniennes, 1997, pp. 422ff.

28 Hankey, 'Making Theology Practical', pp. 101–21 and Putallaz, *Le sens de la réflexion*, pp. 221–6, 291–304, treat Rahner's understanding of the common *reditio* of being and intellect. François-Xavier Putallaz, *La connaissance de soi au xiiie siècle: De Matthieu d'Aquasparta à Thierry de Freiberg*, Études de philosophie médiévale 67, Paris, Vrin, 1991, pp. 386–403; Ruedi Imbach, 'Prétendue primauté de l'être sur le connaître: Perspectives cavalières sur Thomas d'Aquin et l'école dominicaine allemande', in J. Jolivet *et al.* (eds), *Lectionum Varietates: Hommage à Paul Vignaux (1904–1987)*, Études de philosophie médiévale 65, Paris, Vrin, 1991, pp. 122, 125–8; É.-H. Wéber, *La personne humaine au xiiie siècle: L'avènement chez les maîtres parisiens de l'acception moderne de l'homme*, Bibliothèque thomiste 46, Paris, Vrin, 1991, and A. de Libera, 'Une anthropologie de la grâce: Sur *La personne humaine au xiiie siècle* d'É.-H. Wéber', *RPT* 77 (1993), pp. 241–54 will provide access to the French scholarship showing the common logic of being and spirit in the medieval texts. There are recent treatments by J. M. McDermott, 'The Analogy of Knowing in Karl Rahner', *IPQ* 36 (1996), pp. 201–16; idem, 'The Analogy of Human Knowing in the *Prima Pars*', *Gregorianum* 77 (1996), which at pp. 261–86 and 501–25 is modestly critical of Putallaz (especially pp. 280, n. 19, 512–13, nn. 10–11). It is appreciative of P. Rousselot, s.j., whom a more complete history than the one attempted here would have to include.

29 'Is St. Thomas' "Science of God" Still Relevant Today?', *IPQ* 14 (1974), p. 453. See Luis Cortest, 'Was St. Thomas Aquinas a Platonist?', *The Thomist* 52 (1988), pp. 209–19. See also the references to R. L. Hurd in note 47 below.

30 See McCool, 'Is St. Thomas', and McDermott, 'The Analogy of Human Knowing', p. 520, n. 17 with its reference to E. Brito, s.j. on Aquinas and Hegel.

31 See Hankey, 'Making Theology Practical', pp. 93ff.; in contrast, M. B. Ewbank, 'Doctrinal Precisions in Aquinas's *Super Librum de Causis*', *AHDLMA* 61 (1994), pp. 7–29; idem, 'Diverse Orderings of Dionysius' *Triplex Via* by St. Thomas Aquinas', *Mediaeval Studies* 52 (1990), pp. 82–109, and idem, 'Remarks on Being', pp. 123–49 look at Gilson's conclusions in the light of the old and new evidence about the influence of Denys and Proclus on Thomas's doctrine of being and endeavour to rehabilitate Gilson's Christian metaphysic of *esse*.

32 See, for example, Jean-Luc Marion, *Sur la théologie blanche de Descartes: Analogie création des vérités éternelles et fondement*, Paris, Quadrige/Presses Universitaires de France, 1991, 2nd edn, and idem, *Sur le prisme métaphysique de Descartes: Constitution et limites de l'onto-théo-logie dans la pensée cartésienne*, Épiméthée, Paris, Presses Universitaires de France, 1986, and Ward, 'Introducing Jean-Luc Marion', pp. 318–21. This analysis is also picked up by Milbank, 'Only Theology Overcomes Metaphysics', p. 330.

33 For his view of what is common between Thomas and Heidegger, see, for example: É. Gilson, *Les tribulations de Sophie*, Paris, Vrin, 1967, pp. 69–72; idem, 'Sur les vicissitudes des principes', *Mélanges offerts à M.-D. Chenu, maître en théologie*, Bibliothéque thomiste 37, Paris, Vrin, 1967, pp. 281–4. On his relation to Heidegger, see Shook, *Étienne Gilson*, pp. 227–8, 334–5, 359–60. In North America this optimism was found in J. D. Caputo, 'The Problem of Being in Heidegger and the Scholastics', *The Thomist* 41 (1977), pp. 62–91, especially 84 and 88. Caputo's optimism corresponds to that of 'Document: M.

Heidegger, "Le retour au fondement de la métaphysique" ', *RPT* 43 (1959), pp. 401–33 and Georges Kalinowski, *L' impossible métaphysique: En annexe trois lettres inédites de Étienne Gilson*, Bibliothéque des Archives de Philosophie, nouvelle série 33, Paris, Beauchesne, 1981, pp. 136, 243. The problems are brought out by Hankey, 'Making Theology Practical', pp. 94–100; P. Aubenque, J. Beaufret, J.-L. Marion and J.-F. Courtine in Monique Couratier (ed.), *Étienne Gilson et nous: La philosophie et son histoire*, Paris, Vrin, 1980; J. Beaufret, 'ENERGEIA et actus', *Dialogue avec Heidegger, I. Philosophie grecque*, 'Arguments' 56, Paris, Minuit, 1974, especially pp. 109–12, 130, 141–4; idem, 'La philosophie chrétienne', *Dialogue avec Heidegger, 2. Philosophie moderne*, 'Arguments' 58, Paris, Minuit, 1973, pp. 9–27, 123; G. Prouvost, 'Postface'; Étienne Gilson and Jacques Maritain, *Deux approches de l'être: Correspondance, 1923–1971*, ed. G. Prouvost, Paris, Vrin, 1991, pp. 292–5. See note 47 below.

34 On Thomas's positive relation to Denys, see Paul Rorem, *Biblical and Liturgical Symbols within the Pseudo-Dionysian Synthesis*, Toronto, Pontifical Institute of Mediaeval Studies, 1984, pp. 149–50; idem, *Pseudo-Dionysius: A Commentary on the Texts and an Introduction to their Influence*, New York and Oxford, Oxford University Press, 1993, pp. 169–74; idem, ' "Procession and Return" in Thomas Aquinas and his Predecessors', *The Princeton Seminary Review* 13 (1992), pp. 147–63; Fran O'Rourke, *Pseudo-Dionysius and the Metaphysics of Aquinas*, Studien und Texte zur Geistesgeschichte des Mittelalters 32, Leiden, Brill, 1992; idem, '*Virtus essendi*: Intensive Being in Pseudo-Dionysius and Aquinas', *Dionysius* 15 (1991), pp. 31–80; Hankey, 'Dionysius dixit'; idem, 'Dionysian Hierarchy'; idem, 'Aquinas, Pseudo-Denys, Proclus and Isaiah VI.6', *AHDLMA* 64 (1997), pp. 59–93.

35 See on Thomas's Neoplatonism: W.J. Hankey, 'Aquinas' First Principle, Being or Unity?', *Dionysius* 4 (1980), pp. 133–72; idem, *God in Himself*, pp. 2–13; Eileen C. Sweeney, 'Thomas Aquinas' Double Metaphysics of Simplicity and Infinity', *IPQ* 33 (1993), pp. 297–317; Rudi A. te Velde, *Participation and Substantiality in Thomas Aquinas*, Studien und Texte zur Geistesgeschichte des Mittelalters 46, Leiden, Brill, 1995; Vivian Boland, *Ideas in God According to Saint Thomas Aquinas: Sources and Synthesis*, Studies in the History of Christian Thought 69, Leiden, Brill, 1996 and Patrick Quinn, 'Aquinas's Model of Mind', *New Blackfriars* 77 (1996), p. 223; idem, *Aquinas, Platonism and the Knowledge of God*, Aldershot, Avebury, 1996.

36 There is no place here to detail the criticism of Gilson's understanding of the character and influence of Neoplatonism in medieval philosophy, but some of the English language beginnings and its present state can be indicated. W. Norris Clarke, 'The Limitation of Act by Potency: Aristotelianism or Neoplatonism?', *New Scholasticism* 26 (1952), pp. 167–94 was ground breaking. After showing that 'existential Thomism' was the inappropriate standard of judgement in Gilson's *Jean Duns Scot*, George Lindbeck demonstrated that Thomas's philosophy of being was better viewed as participationist than as existential. See his 'Participation and Existence in the Interpretation of St. Thomas Aquinas', *Franciscan Studies* 17 (1957), pp. 1–22 and 107–25. From Augustinian Villanova came J. M. Quinn, *The Thomism of Étienne Gilson: A Critical Study*, Villanova, PA, Villanova University Press, 1971. T. C. O'Brien published a series of articles in *The Thomist*, collected as *Metaphysics and the Existence of God*, Texts and Studies 1, Washington, DC, Thomist Press, 1960. At present Lawrence Dewan, o.p., carries the torch against the errors of Gilsonian existential Thomism and the defence of it by Joseph Owen, c.s.b. See, for example, 'St. Thomas and the Causality of God's Goodness', *Laval*

Théologique et Philosophique 34 (1978), pp. 291–304; idem, 'St. Thomas and the Divine Names', *Science et Esprit* 32 (1980), pp. 19–33; idem, '*Objectum*: Notes on the Invention of a Word', *AHDLMA* 48 (1981), pp. 37–96; idem, 'St. Thomas, Metaphysical Procedure, and the Formal Cause', *New Scholasticism* 63 (1989), pp. 173–82; idem, 'St. Thomas, Aristotle, and Creation', *Dionysius* 15 (1991), pp. 81–90, which defends St Thomas's own understanding of Aristotle against that of Gilson and Owens. M. F. Johnson, 'Did St. Thomas Attribute a Doctrine of Creation to Aristotle?', *New Scholasticism* 63 (1989), pp. 129–55 supports Dewan against Gilson.

37 The French scholarship on the problems with a Gilsonian opposition between Neoplatonism and Thomas's metaphysic of being is now massive and elaborated. These collections will provide indications including references to essential work by P. Hadot and É. Zum Brunn: *Dieu et l'être: Exégèses d'Exode 3,13 et de Coran 20,11–24*, ed. Membres du centre d'études des religions du livre, CNRS, Paris, Études augustiniennes, 1978, especially the essays by Hadot, Zum Brunn and P. Vignaux; *Étienne Gilson et nous*, especially the essays by Hadot, P. Aubenque and J.-F. Courtine; Dominique Bourg, 'Epilogue: La critique de la "Métaphysique de l'Exode" par Heidegger et l'exégèse Moderne', *L'être et dieu*, Publication du Centre d'études et de recherches interdisciplinaires en théologie 13, Paris, Cerf, Cognitio fidei, 1986, pp. 215–44, especially 217–24; A. de Libera and E. Zum Brunn (eds), '*Celui qui est: Interprétations juives et chrétiennes d'Exode 314*', Centre d'études des religions du livre, CNRS, Paris, Cerf, 1986, especially the essays by Vignaux, de Libera, Courtine and É.-H. Wéber.

38 On his endeavour in the 1961 preparatory commissions of Vatican II to have 'idealismus' condemned see Breton, *De Rome*, pp. 86–93. His *God in Exile: Modern Atheism. A Study of the Internal Dynamic of Modern Atheism, from its Roots in the Cartesian Cogito to the Present Day*, tr. A. Gibson, Westminster, PA, Newman Press, 1968, displays the reasons for that attempt. Idealism from Neoplatonism through Descartes to Hegel is at the origin of atheism; Aquinas is the best defence against both.

39 Fabro's position is set out in O'Rourke, *Pseudo-Dionysius*, pp. 155–85; idem, '*Virtus essendi*'. O'Rourke carries over from Fabro the criticism of Gilson.

40 Velde, *Participation*, pp. 184–6, 221–6, 252.

41 Works of Fabro which establish his position on Thomas's relation to Denys, Platonism and Heidegger and which take into critical account the views of Gilson include 'The Problem of Being and the Destiny of Man', *IPQ* 1 (1961), pp. 407–36; idem, 'The Transcendentality of *Ens–Esse* and the Ground of Metaphysics', *IPQ* 6 (1966), pp. 389–427; idem, 'Platonism, Neoplatonism and Thomism: Convergencies and Divergencies', *New Scholasticism* 44 (1970), pp. 69–100; idem, 'The Intensive Hermeneutics of Thomistic Philosophy: The Notion of Participation', *Review of Metaphysics* 27 (1974), pp. 449–91 [as 'Platonism, Neoplatonism and Thomism', but more extensive, includes agreement with Lindbeck and works out his strong difference from Transcendental Thomism]; idem, 'Il nuovo problema dell'essere e la fondazione della metafisica', in A. A. Maurer (ed.), *St. Thomas Aquinas, 1274–1974: Commemorative Studies*, 2 vols, Toronto, Pontifical Institute of Mediaeval Studies, 1974, vol. 2, pp. 423–57; idem, 'L'interpretazione dell'atto in S. Tommaso e Heidegger', in A. Piolanti (ed.), *Atti del Congresso Internazionale Tommaso d'Aquino nel suo settimo centenario*, 9 vols, Studi Tomistici 1, Naples, Edizioni Domenicane Italiane, 1975, vol. 1, pp. 119–28.

42 Characteristic of their combination of a sophisticated understanding of the present problems for Thomism in France post Heidegger with an endeavour to save the Thomist tradition and kataphatic theology is the issue of the *Revue Thomiste* devoted to 'Saint Thomas et l'onto-théologie', 95 (1995), which contains articles by Bonino and Humbrecht. Bonino's 'Le concept d'étant et la connaissance de Dieu après Jean Cabrol' admits that the Thomist tradition has amalgamated heterogeneous elements but defends it against Gilson nonetheless (p. 136). See also his 'Influence du Pseudo-Denys sur la conception thomiste de l'*esse*', *Bulletin de Litterature Ecclésiastique* 94 (1993), pp. 269–74; idem, 'Les voiles sacres: A propos d'une citation de Denys', in *Atti del IX Congresso Tomistico Internazionale*, Studi Tomistici 45, Città del Vaticano, Pontificia Accademia di S. Tommaso Aquinas, 1992, vol. 6, pp. 159–71; Y. Labbé, 'La théologie négative dans la théologie trinitaire', *Revue des Sciences Religieuses* 67 (1993), pp. 69–86 and Humbrecht in 'La théologie négative'. See notes 16 and 25 above.

43 Gilles Emery, *La trinité créatrice: Trinité et création dans les commentaires aux sentences de Thomas d'Aquin et de ses précurseurs Albert le Grand et Bonaventure*, Bibliothèque Thomiste 47, Paris, Vrin, 1995.

44 For an example of Wéber's historical work as part of this community with its characteristic philosophical and theological questions see É. Zum Brunn *et al.*, *Maître Eckhart à Paris: Une critique médiévale de l'ontothéologie. Les* Questions parisiennes *no. 1 et no. 2 d'Eckhart. Études, textes et traductions*, Bibliothèque de L'École des Hautes Études, Section des Sciences Religieuses 86, Paris, Presses Universitaires de France, 1984, and notes 28 and 37 above.

45 Jean Duns Scot, *Sur la connaissance de Dieu et l'univocité de étant*, ed. Olivier Boulnois, Épiméthée, Paris, Presses Universitaires de France, 1988, and his 'Quand commence l'ontothéologie? Aristote, Thomas d' Aquin et Duns Scot', *Revue Thomiste* 95 (1995) pp. 85–108.

46 For a critical assessment of his position, see David Piché's review article '*Penser au Moyen Âge* d'Alain de Libera: Une perspective novatrice sur la condamnation parisienne de 1277', *Laval Théologique et Philosophique*, 52 (1996), p. 206.

47 A fraction of the possible examples are J. D. Jones, 'The Ontological Difference for St. Thomas and Pseudo-Dionysius', *Dionysius* 4 (1980), pp. 133–72; idem, 'A Non-Entitative Understanding of Be-ing and Unity: Heidegger and Neoplatonism', *Dionysius* 6 (1982), pp. 94–110; J. D. Caputo, *Heidegger and Aquinas: An Essay in Overcoming Metaphysics*, New York, Fordham, 1982. There are those who concede the content of metaphysics to the Heideggerian critique and attempt a Transcendental retrieval of theology, e.g. R. L. Hurd, 'Heidegger and Aquinas: A Rahnerian Bridge', *Philosophy Today* 28 (1984) pp. 105–37; idem, 'Being is Being-Present-to-Self: Rahner's key to Aquinas' Metaphysics', *The Thomist* 52 (1988), pp. 63–78. For more and my own judgement on the success of this effort see Hankey, 'Making Theology Practical', pp. 100–114. There is also a thoughtful reaction, e.g. O. Blanchette, 'Are There Two Questions of Being?', *Review of Metaphysics*, 45 (1992), pp. 259–87. See notes 29 and 33 above.

48 Foreword to Jean-Luc Marion, *God without Being: Hors-texte*, tr. Thomas A. Carlson, Chicago, IL, University of Chicago Press, 1991, p. x. Milbank judges one side of Marion's position to be still correlational, see 'Only Theology Overcomes Metaphysics', p. 325.

49 For references to relevant works see Hankey, *God in Himself*, p. 14, n. 47.

50 See Milbank, 'Only Theology Overcomes Metaphysics', p. 325.

51 For a sketch see Ward, 'Introducing Jean-Luc Marion'.

52 É. Gilson, *Le philosophe et la théologie*, Paris, Fayard, 1960, pp. 61, 94–5, 142–3, 191ff. The plurality of Christian philosophies identified by Gilson makes a choice by authority necessary.

53 J.-L. Marion, *L'idole et la distance: Cinq études*, Paris, Grasset et Fasquelle, 1977, pp. 177–243; idem, *Dieu sans l'être*, Paris, Quadrige & PUF, 1991 [1st edn 1982], pp. 111–22; Louis Bouyer, *Mysterion: Du mystère à la mystique*, Paris, OEIL, 1986, pp. 230ff.

54 Hankey, 'Dionysian Hierarchy'.

55 'Saint Thomas d'Aquin et l'onto-théo-logie', *Revue Thomiste* 95 (1995), pp. 31–66; the *retractio* is on pp. 33 and 65. In it Marion notes that he was already moving in this direction in the 1991 'Preface to the English Edition' of his *Dieu sans l'être*.

56 Milbank, 'Only Theology Overcomes Metaphysics', p. 328.

57 Milbank is trying to overcome an immanantizing reason which might be founded therein rather than the false transcendence Heidegger exposed, and judges Marion both to mistake the problem and to stay with a foundational subjectivity; see 'Only Theology Overcomes Metaphysics', pp. 329–41; idem, 'Can a Gift be Given?', pp. 132ff.

58 As for example with Nietzsche. John Milbank (*Theology as Social Theory: Beyond Secular Reason*, Oxford, Basil Blackwell, 1990) traces 'the genesis of the main forms of secular reason, in such a fashion as to unearth the arbitrary moments in the construction of their logic' (p. 3). Milbank's ultimate criticism of Marion in 'Can a Gift be Given?' is that his account of will is mistaken – taking love as will.

59 For what he did and did not find, see Marion, *Sur le prisme métaphysique de Descartes*, pp. 138–41, 147, 231–3; idem, *Sur la théologie blanche de Descartes*, p. 384.

60 See Hankey, 'Dionysius dixit', pp. 137–50 and 'Dionysian Hierarchy', pp. 435–8.

61 See Hankey, 'The Bible in a Post-Critical Age', pp. 49ff.

62 Milbank, *Theology as Social Theory*, p. 296. For a history of Neoplatonic Christianity, see 'Only Theology Overcomes Metaphysics', pp. 320–32, which is not far in its representation from that in Marion, 'Saint Thomas d'Aquin et l'onto-théo-logie'.

63 Milbank, *Theology as Social Theory*, p. 2.

64 John Milbank, 'Theology without Substance: Christianity, Signs, Origins', *Literature and Theology* 2 (1988), p. 2.

65 Marion, *L'idole et la distance*. My account of Marion's position owes very much to a paper by Michael Harrington for my Seminar on Neoplatonism at Dalhousie University in 1996. Ward, 'Introducing Jean-Luc Marion', p. 322 and Milbank, 'Can a Gift be Given?', pp. 137–8 treat the relation of Marion's argument to his dialogue with Heidegger and Levinas.

66 See W. J. Hankey, 'Augustinian Immediacy and Dionysian Mediation in John Colet, Edmund Spenser, Richard Hooker and the Cardinal Bérulle', for the Kolloquium 'Augustinus in der Neuzeit: Von Petrarca zum 18. Jahrhundert', Wolfenbüttel, October, 1996, forthcoming in the Acts of the Kolloquium, ed. Kurt Flasch and Dominique de Courcelle, Editions Brepols-Turnhout, 1997.

67 Milbank, 'Can a Gift be Given?', p. 137, see p. 152.

68 On this see Hankey, 'Dionysius dixit', 'Aquinas, Pseudo-Denys, Proclus and Isaiah VI.6' and 'Dionysian Hierarchy' with the references therein to the work of David E. Luscombe and O'Rourke, *Pseudo-Dionysius*, p. 263ff.

69 See T. C. O'Brien, 'The Dionysian Corpus', Appendix 3, in St. Thomas Aquinas, *Summa theologiae*, vol. 14, London and New York, Blackfriars, 1975, pp. 182–93. A doctrine of the *Liber de causis*, like that of Denys, that the being of intelligent souls is given by God but their intellectual activity by the intelligences (angels), Thomas found most objectionable; *Commentary on the Book of Causes*, xxvii and n. 65.

70 On the Donatist-like teaching of Dionysius, see Jaroslav Pelikan's introduction to C. Luibheid and P. Rorem (trs), *Pseudo-Dionysius: The Complete Works*, The Classics of Western Spirituality, New York, Paulist Press, 1987, pp. 17–19.

71 See Hankey, 'Dionysius dixit', pp. 143–50.

72 Milbank, 'Can a Gift be Given?', pp. 152 and 137 with 132.

73 See Booth, *Aristotelian Aporetic*, p. 218: 'Thomas's Aristotelian ontology is a prolongation and development of Pseudo-Dionysius's Aristotelianisation of Proclus's ontology', and pp. 76–80 and 217–252; Hankey, *God in Himself*, pp. 165–6; O'Rourke, *Pseudo-Dionysius*, pp. 118ff.; Velde, *Participation*, pp. 257–65.

74 Forthcoming SP; published in French as 'Les débuts de la théologie comme science (IIIe–VIe)', *RPT* 80 (1996), pp. 201–20.

75 See Milbank, 'Can a Gift be Given?' p. 143 and n. 64.

76 For an account of the argument and why Heidegger got it wrong, see Milbank, 'Only Theology Overcomes Metaphysics', pp. 329–35.

77 Milbank, *Theology as Social Theory*, p. 296.

78 Milbank, 'Only Theology Overcomes Metaphysics', pp. 340–41.

79 Marion, 'Saint Thomas d'Aquin et l'onto-théo-logie', pp. 37ff.; Milbank, 'Only Theology Overcomes Metaphysics', p. 334.

80 Milbank, 'Can a Gift be Given?', p. 152; see also his remark on Plato in 'Only Theology Overcomes Metaphysics', p. 341.

81 Saffrey, 'Les débuts de la théologie', p. 218.

82 *Summa theologiae* I.1.1 obj. 2 and ad 2.

83 See W. J. Hankey, 'The *De Trinitate* of St. Boethius and the Structure of St. Thomas' *Summa Theologiae*', in L. Obertello (ed.), *Atti del Congresso Internazionale di Studi Boeziani*, Rome, Herder, 1981, pp. 367–75; idem, 'Theology as System and as Science: Proclus and Aquinas', *Dionysius* 6 (1982), pp. 83–93; idem, *God in Himself*, pp. 24–71.

84 'Eadem via ascensus et discensus', *Summa contra Gentiles* IV.1. See Hankey, *God in Himself*, chapter 2 and *Super Boetium de trinitate*, cura et studio Fratrum Praedicatorum, *Opera Omnia* 50, Rome and Paris, Leonina and Cerf, 1992, QQ. I, II, VI.

85 See Henry Chadwick, *Boethius: The Consolations of Music, Logic, Theology, and Philosophy*, Oxford, Clarendon Press, 1981, pp. 225–9, and Ralph McInerny, *Boethius and Aquinas*, Washington, DC, Catholic University of America Press, 1990, pp. 6–8. On the divisions of philosophy, see *Super de trinitate*, V.1; on how *sacra doctrina* unites the practical and the theoretical, *Summa theologiae* I.1.4.

86 *Consolatio philosophiae*, I.1.

87 Compare conversion of the prisoner in *Consolatio* I–III and *Republic* 517b6–518d7. See W. J. Hankey, ' "Ad intellectum ratiocinatio": Three Procline Logics, *The Divine Names* of Pseudo-Dionysius, Eriugena's *Periphyseon* and Boethius' *Consolatio philosophiae*', *SP* 29 (1996), pp. 244–51 for this and for my understanding of the *Consolatio* generally.

88 For a list of parallels between the Bible and the *Consolatio*, see Edward A. Synan, 'Boethius, Valla and Gibbon', *The Modern Schoolman* 69 (1992), pp. 489–91.

89 *Consolatio* III.8.99; see John Magee, *Boethius on Signification and Method*, Philosophia Antiqua 52, Leiden, Brill, 1989, pp. 141–9.

90 *Consolatio* I; on the philosophical character of the poetry, see G. J. P. O'Daly, *The Poetry of Boethius*, London, Duckworth, 1991, pp. 60–69; *Republic* 376e–403c, 595a–608b. For a discussion of the issues for contemporary theology raised by Plato's use of myth see Lewis Ayres, 'Representation, Theology and Faith', *Modern Theology* 11 (1995), pp. 23–46.

91 O'Daly, *The Poetry*, p. 25 (accepting the conclusions of H. Chadwick). On the demand for logic and rational certainty, not scriptural authority, the reach of philosophy in Boethius, and on his influence in this regard, see Aquinas, *Super de trinitate*, Prologus 76, lines 97–114 and q. VI, and Boèce, *Courts traités de théologie: Opuscula sacra*, ed. and tr. Hélène Merle, Paris, Cerf, 1991, pp. 21–2, 87–124, 143, n. 33.

92 See Volker Schmidt-Kohl, *Die Neuplatonishe Seelenlehre in der Consolatio Philosophiae des Boethius*, Beiträge zur Klassischen Philologie 16, Meisenheim am Glan, 1965; Luca Obertello, *Severino Boezio*, 2 vols, Accademia Ligure di Scienze e Lettere, Collana di monografie 1, Genoa, 1974, vol. 1, part four, esp. pp. 571–6; Chadwick, *Boethius*, p. 20; Booth, *Aristotelian Aporetic*, pp. 66–75; O'Daly, *The Poetry*, p. 66; S. Gersh, *Middle Platonism and the Latin Tradition*, 2 vols, Notre Dame, IN, Notre Dame University Press, 1986, vol. 2, pp. 699–705, is rigorously sceptical on the Procline influence, but allows that Boethius at least knew the *De providentia*. Merle, *Courts traités*, p. 33, n. 14, compares Proclus and Boethius on the reading of Scripture.

93 On the relation of *The Divine Names* to the rest of the *corpus*, see P. Rorem, 'The Place of the Mystical Theology in the Pseudo-Dionysian Corpus', *Dionysius* 4 (1980), pp. 87–98; idem, *Pseudo-Dionysius*, pp. 29, 194–205.

94 See, on the Scriptural aspect, Rorem, *Pseudo-Dionysius*, pp. 134–7, on the relation to Proclus who is reaching back to the *Parmenides* of Plato; see Saffrey and Westerink, *Théologie platonicienne*, vol. 1, pp. lxiii, cxci–cxcii; Saffrey, 'Les débuts de la théologie', pp. 215–19; Salvatore Lilla, 'Denys l'Aréopagite', in R. Goulet (ed.), *Dictionnaire des philosophes antiques*, Paris, CNRS, 1994, vol. 2, pp. 735–6; Hankey, *God in Himself*, pp. 7–13.

95 So, at least, in the Arab and Latin hermeneutic of which Aquinas is heir; see Booth, *Aristotelian Aporetic*, pp. 76–152 and 217–52; Hankey, *God in Himself*, pp. 165–6; Velde, *Participation*, pp. 166–70, 257–79, *Commentary on the Book of Causes*, p. xxx.

96 Hankey, *God In Himself*, p. 122, n. 18 quoting S. Gersh, *KINHSIS AKINATOS*: 'love manifests itself in two forms: (i) as the complete cycle of remaining, procession and reversion . . . '

97 See Hankey, 'Aquinas, Pseudo-Denys, Proclus and Isaiah VI.6'; idem, 'Augustinian Immediacy and Dionysian Mediation'.

98 Gregory Shaw, 'Theurgy as Demiurgy: Iamblichus' Solution to the Problem of Embodiment', *Dionysius* 12 (1988), pp. 39–40. See also his 'Theurgy: Rituals of Unification in the Neoplatonism of Iamblichus', *Traditio* 41 (1985), pp. 1–28.

99 *De divina predestinatione* I (PL 122 357–8). On Porphyry see the conclusion of Andrew Smith, *Porphyry's Place in the Neoplatonic Tradition: A Study in Post-Plotinian Neoplatonism*, The Hague, Nijhoff, 1974. On the contrast between the two Neoplatonic traditions, see Hankey, 'Ad intellectum ratiocinatio', 248.

100 On their 'crossing' see W. J. Hankey, 'The Place of the Proof for God's Existence in the *Summa Theologiae* of St. Thomas Aquinas', *The Thomist* 46 (1982), pp. 379–82; idem, 'Dionysius dixit', pp. 130–34; idem, '*Magis . . . Pro Nostra Sententia*', pp. 235–9; idem, 'Dionysius Becomes an Augustinian: Bonaventure's *Itinerarium* vi', *SP* 29 (1996), pp. 252–9; idem, 'Augustinian Immediacy and Dionysian Mediation' and the pregnant remark of Milbank, 'Theology without Substance', pp. 11–12.

101 *In quatuor libros sententiarum*, vol. 1, *Opera omnia*, ed. R. Busa, Stuttgardt and Bad Cannstatt, Frommann and Holzboog, 1980, pt. 2, ds. 10, qu. 1, ar. 2, corpus, p. 152, *Summa theologiae*, I.112.2, resp.

102 See Hankey, 'Dionysian Hierarchy', pp. 414–22; idem, 'Aquinas, Pseudo-Denys, Proclus and Isaiah VI.6', and 'Augustinian Immediacy and Dionysian Mediation'.

103 *Mystical Theology* (= MT), I.1, PG 997B, Luibheid translation in *Pseudo-Dionysius: The Complete Works*, p. 135.

104 On these lost or unwritten treatises see *Divine Names* (= DN), I.1; I.4; I.6; II.1; XIII.4 and MT III. On their relations see Rorem, *Pseudo-Dionysius*, pp. 194–205.

105 Salvatore Lilla, 'Denys l'Aréopagite', p. 730; for Lilla the description of Hierotheus is an analogue of that of Proclus in the *Vita Proclus* of Marianus.

106 DN, XIII, PG 977B, Luibheid, p. 139. Beginnings from unity other than that in DN I are DN II, which insists on *The Divine Names* as a treatment of what refers 'indivisibly, absolutely, unreservedly and totally to God in his entirety', and DN 3, which is of the Good.

107 DN I.4, PG 589D, Luibheid, p. 51.

108 W. Beierwaltes, 'Unity and Trinity in Dionysius and Eriugena', *Hermathena* 157 (1994), p. 5.

109 On the developments in Porphyrian trinitarian theology see Salvatore Lilla, 'Un dubbio di S. Agostino su Porfirio', *Nuovi Annali della Facoltà di Magistero dell'Università di Messiana* 5 (1987), pp. 319–31; idem, 'Pseudo-Denys l'Aréopagite, Porphyre et Damasius', in Ysabel de Andia (ed.), *Actes du Colloque sur Aréopagite et sa postérité en Orient et en Occident*, série Antiquité 151, Paris, Études Augustiniennes, 1997, pp. 117–52; idem, 'Neoplatonic Hypostases and the Christian Trinity (from Clement of Alexandria to Pseudo-Dionysius)', in M. Joyal (ed.), *Studies in Plato and the Platonic Tradition: Essays Presented to John Whittaker*, Aldershot, Avebury, 1997, in press; Werner Beierwaltes, 'Unity and Trinity in East and West', in B. McGinn and W. Otten (eds), *Eriugena: East and West. Papers of the Eighth International Colloquium of the Society for the Promotion of Eriugenian Studies, Chicago and Notre Dame, 18–20 October 1991*, Notre Dame Conferences in Medieval Studies 5, Notre Dame, IN, University of Notre Dame Press, 1994, pp. 209–31; idem, 'Unity and Trinity in Dionysius and Eriugena', n. 10 and pp. 13–14. These studies rely upon the earlier work of Pierre Hadot and others.

110 On the errors involved in opposing the Dionysian and Augustinian approaches to the Trinity see Hankey, 'The De Trinitate of St. Boethius' and articles of Beierwaltes cited.

111 Beierwaltes, 'Unity and Trinity in Dionysius and Eriugena', p. 6.

112 Beierwaltes, 'Unity and Trinity in Dionysius and Eriugena', p. 5.

113 DN II.4 (PG 641A*), Luibheid, p. 61.

114 Beierwaltes, 'Unity and Trinity in Dionysius and Eriugena', p. 7.

115 Beierwaltes, 'Unity and Trinity in Dionysius and Eriugena', p. 6.

116 *In librum beati Dionysii de divinibus nominibus*, ed. C. Pera, Rome, Marrietti, 1950, II.2.143.

117 *Super de trinitate*, prologus, 76, lines 114–15. For the argument of this section see Hankey, 'The De Trinitate of St. Boethius'; idem, *God in Himself*, pp. 12, 129–35; Rorem, ' "Procession and Return" in Thomas Aquinas'; idem, *Pseudo-Dionysius*, pp. 169–74. McInerny, *Boethius and Aquinas*, pp. 11–14 sets out positively Thomas's argument for finding a similar Neoplatonic *exitus-Peditus* pattern in the theological treatises of Boethius. Merle, *Courts traités*, outlines the pattern, pp. 26–7.

118 Beierwaltes, 'Unity and Trinity in Dionysius and Eriugena', pp. 6–7.

119 See Hankey, *God in Himself*, pp. 4–6; idem, 'Aquinas' First Principle', pp. 139–43, and Milbank, 'Can a Gift be Given?', p. 143.

120 For Denys, in contrast to Aquinas, being is properly and affirmatively predicated of creatures not God, see O'Rourke, *Pseudo-Dionysius,* pp. 123 and 275 and *Commentary on the Book of Causes*, xxviii, n. 61.

121 *In de divinibus nominibus*, V.1.634. For discussions see Booth, *Aristotelian Aporetic*, p. 77 and Milbank, 'Can a Gift be Given?', p. 143 with notes.

122 *Summa theologiae* I.5.1 ad 1. See Hankey, 'Aquinas' First Principle', esp. pp. 145–54; idem, *God in Himself*, pp. 72–4; idem, 'Dionysius Becomes an Augustinian'; Milbank, 'Can a Gift be Given?', p. 143. Jan A. Aertsen, 'Ontology and Henology in Medieval Philosophy (Thomas Aquinas, Master Eckhart and Berthold of Moosburg)', in E. P. Bos and P. A. Meijer (eds), *On Proclus and his Influence in Medieval Philosophy*, Philosophia Antiqua 53, Leiden, Brill, 1992, pp. 121–3 puts the other side against Hankey.

123 This is the overall argument of my *God in Himself*.

124 Velde, *Participation*, pp. 93ff. and pp. 254–79.

125 David Burrell in a review of Velde in *IPQ* 37 (1997), p. 102.

126 Milbank, 'Can a Gift be Given?', pp. 153–4.

127 Hankey, *God in Himself*, pp. 74–6 and 98–103.

128 Velde, *Participation*, p. 115.

129 Velde, *Participation*, p. 116. See Burrell (n. 124 above), pp. 102–3. This approach is agreeable with that in Hankey, *God in Himself* and in McDermott, 'The Analogy of Human Knowing', at pp. 284–5, and n. 26, and in Boland, *Ideas in God*, pp. 297–332.

130 See Hankey, *God in Himself*, p. 55, chapter 5, and pp. 141–2, and Velde, *Participation*, pp. 278–9.

131 Hankey, *God in Himself*, pp. 147ff.

132 This chapter was originally delivered as a lecture for the School of Hebrew, Biblical and Theological Studies, Trinity College, Dublin on 10 May 1996. I am grateful to Dr Lewis Ayres for the invitation, and to Trinity College, Dr Fran O'Rourke, Fr Vivian Boland, o.p., and the Dominicans of Tallaght for generous hospitality. I thank David Burrell, Paul A. Fletcher, Michael L. Harrington, D. Gregory MacIsaac, J. M. McDermott, Robert C. Miner and Ian G. Stewart for their help. They have changed it for the better.

9

ASCENDING NUMBERS

Augustine's *De musica* and the Western tradition

Catherine Pickstock

The following chapter examines the metaphysical category of 'music' in the Western tradition with special reference to Augustine's *De musica* (composed in AD 391). In his treatise on 'the science of proper modulations', Augustine codified what Boethius was later to call the *quadrivium*, the 'fourfold path', according to which mathematics was subdivided into arithmetic, geometry, music and astronomy.[1] This curricular articulation was therefore centred upon sciences of measurement: geometry measured inert, inorganic, sublunary spaces; music measured the relationship between the soul and the body (i.e. the proportions between the psychic and the organic), and also proportions within the soul itself; astronomy measured the time and movements of the heavenly bodies (often regarded as moved by the World Soul); and arithmetic, the most abstract, was the science of numbers in themselves. Thus, the order of these disciplines – the higher liberal arts – ascended through increasing degrees of abstraction from material to incorporeal contemplation, encouraging the knower towards the vision of God.[2] However, in the tripartition of music itself, the first category, the *musica mundana*, overlapped in its concerns with astronomy, as the heavenly spheres were thought to compose through their movements and ratios a music unhearable by us.[3] Moreover, as we shall see, because musical measurement is applied by Augustine even to God, on account of the relationality between the persons of the Trinity, the supremacy of arithmetic as *transcending* measure is implicitly surpassed. In this way, music becomes the science that most leads towards theology, and it is not accidental, perhaps, that Augustine's only lengthy treatise on a single liberal art concerns music.

After the *musica mundana*, the other parts of music, according to the Boethian classification which was adopted in the Middle Ages, and which blended with Augustine's analysis, were *musica humana*, which concerned the harmonies between the body and the soul as well as the musical relationships within both the body and the soul, and *musica instrumentalis*, which concerned aspects of audible music governed either by a tension upon a string, by breath, by water or by percussion.[4] This latter category underlines the societal nature of music as envisaged by Augustine. In keeping with this tripartition, in this chapter I will treat music in three sections: the cosmic, the psychic and the ethical. However, it is necessary to modify the rigidity of these categories to the extent that, as we shall see, the very idea of music as a science of measurements (*modulatio*) displaces the isolation of these realms as discrete edifices in favour of relationality itself.[5]

In my consideration of the *De musica*, I will suggest a three-fold contrast between the Augustinian (and Boethian) tradition which was influential for Western thinking up until the Renaissance and (1) the non-Western Indian tradition; (2) the disintegration of the Western tradition after Descartes; and (3) postmodern musical theory as exemplified by Philippe Lacoue-Labarthe and Jacques Attali, which I will suggest reinvokes certain aspects of that tradition, but in nihilistic cast. I will argue that this nihilism, despite its exhaustive claims as to the universality of the flux, is an arbitrary phenomenology, and that the Augustinian tradition can once again become available as a key to ontology, psychology and to the political order. However, for this to become a coherent possibility, it is necessary that music be understood as more than merely human.

COSMIC MUSIC

A comparative examination of Indian thinking about music and the Western tradition reveals two strikingly different ontological conceptions of music. The Indian paradigm for sound is a distinctively Dionysian, exclusively time-bound flow of a continuous, fluidic stream or vital, inner substance along the channels of the human body, or emergence from a tube.[6] These images combine to form the idea of *nada* which, via the atavistic roles of gesture and respiration, construes musical sound as a recreation of ancient sacrificial ritual. But it remains a wholly immanent conception of music, making use of the human voice as its primary model, a medium which evolves a continuous drone as a symbolic representation of unceasing world process, and which is characterized by a nasal timbre which draws attention to the resonance of the facial cavities. This configuration of emission and bodily expulsion, articulated through serial and organic forms, is paradoxi-cally at once both 'humanist' and 'nihilistic' since on the one hand the aim is to rid the self of phenomenal reality by attaining a powerful indifference to, and control over, suffering emotions, and on the other hand, the ultimate transit of the soul and the perfect degree of power is an obliteration of any separate identity.

The ideal attainment of such a state of Nirvana, embodied in the flat-tening-out of hierarchies into a flow of extended phrases which are neither differentiated from, nor subordinated to, the complete musical composition, contrasts with the Greek and medieval European paradigm for music for which the dominant metaphor was the tensed bow string, ready for the impact of plucking.[7] This paradigm gave rise to various consequences for the development of later musical style in the West, namely a preference for distinct, impacted sounds and structural clarity, the principle of tension and release, of numerical proportions, the caesura, and a hierarchical and syntactical articulation of form. The metaphysical principle which undergirds this inclination towards an ordering of the whole, and most differentiates the Eastern from the Western conception of music, is the doctrine of harmony. For whilst, in effect, the Indian ultimacy of *nada* aims to displace the cosmos in favour of a uniting of the self with an undifferentiated continuum, harmony (the science of proportioned sounds) was a symbol of universal order, uniting all levels of the cosmos – the four basic elements (earth, water, fire, air), human beings, angelic persons and the heavenly bodies into a numerically proportioned whole. Even though, for the early Greeks, there was no concept of concordant tones being sounded simultaneously, the harmonic notion of simultaneity was none the less presupposed in several ways. First, Western harmony extends from the antique paradigm of the unification of opposites (linked to the paradigm of the tensed bow string)[8] as a kind of redeemed binarity. Indeed, the Greek interest in mathematical proportions in music presupposes the bringing together of successive notes into a psychically spatial ratio, in a way that seems to anticipate harmonic relations in actual sound. Secondly, despite the absence of harmony in music, it was present in their metaphysics: for the notion of the cosmos itself as a balance of four elements, and of the paths of the celestial bodies, involved the simultaneity and interdependence of none the less distinct continua.[9] Their revolving paths suggested a harmony which, whilst mobile, was not subject to decay or any dissolute successiveness. Thirdly, harmony was something that existed in the mind. For whilst notes could only be sounded successively by a singer, the harmonious relationship between, say, the consecutive sounding of a tonic and its dominant would have been apparent to a hearer.[10] It should be noted that this notion of a psychically apprehended harmony depends first upon the invocation of memory, and secondly, on the segmentation of a musical line into distinct units. By contrast, the continuous flow of Eastern music is more allied to the inducing of a trance-like state which is inherently amnesiac, conserving the essence of what has passed only in its dissolution into something else. In this conception, both music and selfhood are approximated to impersonal, unconscious organic processes of flow and development.[11]

In spite of the association of Western harmony with the plucking of the Apollonian lyre, one should not follow Nietzsche in interpreting Greek culture in terms of an opposition between the Dionysian spirit of music and the Apollonian spirit of the visual arts, or of music rationalized.[12] In fact, the notion of musical harmony amongst the Greeks holds in tension the Dionysian temporal and the Apollonian spatial, as can be deduced from the fact that they did not conceive of harmony as arising from a statically spatial simultaneity, but from the coincidence of distinct and dynamic cosmic paths or else from the synthesis performed by the temporal recall in the soul.

This same balance was preserved in the later development of Western music, the audible realization of this harmonic synthesis of the spatial and the temporal with the rise of polyphony. Whilst, formerly, liturgical plain-chant obeyed the ineluctable structures of divine revelation, dictated to St Gregory,[13] polyphony, which arose from around the tenth century, was an apparently more 'rationalized' musical form. In Notre Dame, Magister Leoninus composed a collection of two-voice polyphonic settings (ca. 1182) where a deceleration of liturgical melodies was sustained by the *tenores*, beneath the melodic arc of the *vox organica* whose line was governed by a creation of strictly ordered numerical proportions and rhythmic modes which were defined into *ordines* by the articulation of pauses or rests.[14] However, this polyphonic expression of human reason, although opposed by those who thought that music should be monodic so that its words might speak more directly to the soul unencumbered by complex musical arti-fices,[15] was not an *unambiguous* expression of the triumph of human reason. For despite its numerical structures, there is a sense in which polyphonic music, when it is *sounded*, lies always beyond our grasp; our assertion of human reason is a deliberate, humble, doxological abasement of the same, in honour of the superlative Reason. In fact, composers of polyphonic music made explicit appeal to the (unhearable) harmonies of the cosmos in order to counter monodistic oppositions. Their arguments were anticipated in the ninth century by Johannes Scotus Eriugena who defended complex music on the grounds that the harmonies and rhythms of humanly produced music and its internal mathematical relationships could be equated with the invis-ible musical and mathematical relationships of the cosmos. He argued that if cosmic order is itself complex and multidimensional, those terrestrial sounds embodying numerical principles proportionate to those of the cosmos could be complex and multidimensional in comparable ways.[16] This spatial assim-ilation of timelessness is not an idolatrous spatialization, because the unhearable simultaneity never remains still, even for a fraction of a second.[17] The interweaving melodic lines ensure that the vertical is always equally balanced with the horizontal, while the hierarchical character of the vertical itself ensures that the horizontal points beyond itself rather than inculcating a flattened-out spatial immanence.

According to William Waite, there is a strong possibility that these architects of polyphony were influenced by Augustine's *De musica*, since we know that many theologians of the time drew upon his definition of music as 'the science of proper modulation'.[18] Indeed, there is an almost perfect correspondence between the modal systems of the Notre Dame composers and the doctrines of rhythm enunciated by Augustine, in particular his equal stress upon the measurement of the *absence* of sound (in rests) as its presence.[19]

Whatever the case for influence may be, the same co-articulation of time and space in order to achieve the best possible representation of (and offering to) eternity is apparent in Augustine's treatise, as it was in the composers of this complex music.

In the *De musica*, musical rhythm, which Augustine takes as applying, as much or more to poetry as to what we would describe as music, is characterized, first, by the classification of rhythmic patterns in proportions which remain the same regardless of length of sounding,[20] and second, by a stress on the importance of intervals as elements which can themselves form part of a rhythmic structure, but which also serve to divide up musical sequences. This dual stress on relative proportion in abstraction from isolated units, and on unhearable intervals, is reflected by Augustine in his treatment of cosmic music, or of music as an ontological category.

Any rhythmic proportion is given by Augustine the name of 'number'. Created reality itself consists, for his adapted Pythagorean view, of nothing but numbers. This is equivalent to saying that it consists in nothing but relations ordered in certain regular and analogical proportions. This is so much the case that for Augustine the entire cosmos itself is not a total 'thing' to which one could accord a size, even a maximum size. On the contrary, it is rather an assemblage of all the relations that it encompasses, in such a way that since there is nothing else with which it can be compared or is related to, it cannot in itself be accorded a size, measure or rhythmic modulation. One might say that the totality of reality is not one big note, but instead, as Augustine says, a poem or song (*carmen*), and so, in other words, the total series of numerical interactions.[21]

If musical rhythm is exemplified, for Augustine, on a cosmic scale, so also is the musical interlude or rest, which, as we have seen, is crucial to the entire character and development of Western music as based upon articulated phrases.[22] The alternation of sound and silence in music is seen by Augustine as a manifestation of the alternation of coming into being and non-being which must characterize a universe created out of nothing. Augustine thus Christianizes the Pythagorean view and is able to give a serious ontological role to 'nothing', in contrast to a Platonic scheme which would envisage numbers as imposing merely a *degree* of order upon chaos. To the contrary, for Augustine, creation exhibits a *perfect* order or beauty, albeit in its own restricted degree, and the nothingness intrinsic to creation on its own is a necessary part of this order.[23] Indeed, it is when human creatures fail to confess this nothingness, when their life in time is without pauses, that this order is denied and a greater nothingness of disharmony ensues.[24] Furthermore, the 'nothings' do not for Augustine merely segment rhythmic phrases into regular metric units, they also enter into the constitution of the rhythmic units themselves. This is because, as he puts it, a line is a proportion between an unextended point and its own length; thus it is a mysterious finite measure of an infinite distance. The same structure is repeated in the case of a two-dimensional surface which measures the distance from a line without breadth, and for a three-dimensional figure, which measures the distance from a two-dimensional one without depth.[25] Augustine suggests, on this basis, that all spatial reality is continuously generated from something without extension by a power essentially alien to this spatial reality. He pursues this contention with examples of both artificial and natural processes. In the first place, he argues that the process of human artistic creation precedes the substantiality of its product. And in the second place, he argues that the time-spans of a tree precede its space-spans because a tree gradually emerges from a seed.[26] In this way, substantiality is perpetually crossed out by temporal emergence, or creation. In the case of human artistic endeavours, Augustine notably omits here the traditional view that the completed work exists primarily as a kind of 'given' in the mind of the artist. On the contrary, he appears at the end of the *De musica* to recognize that human art can truly create something new and, indeed, it is just this circumstance which suggests to Augustine that this is possible because human beings are situated within a universe which springs from nothing. The fact that things are continuously *coming to be* and continuously emerging from points which are nothing implies, for Augustine, that it is most rational to see finite reality as having emerged in its entirety from nothing.[27] One should note that the nothingness of the 'point' indicates for Augustine at once the abyss of finitude and a participation in the plenitude of the infinite. Thus he evacuates reality in a way that seems to include a nihilistic moment, only to affirm all the more an absolutely infinite order which nonetheless finitude can never fully grasp.[28]

It is this suspension of the created order between nothingness and the infinite which demands that its order be a temporal, audible sequence, rather than a spatial, visible one. This might seem a paradox in that it makes time, which does not stand still, closer to eternity than space, whose permanence might more easily seem to mimic it.[29] However, the whole point is that such mimicry risks a substitution for eternity which I dub 'spatialization'. Whereas by contrast the passage of time continuously acknowledges the nothingness of realized being, and can become the vehicle of a desire for a genuine infinite permanence. Moreover, since this genuine permanence, as infinite, is not circumscribed, the non-closure of time is in fact the best finite image of this.[30] It is just for this reason that Augustine regards only infinity, which is without measure, as the one true equal measure. It is to be noted that this claim radically redefines order as not opposed to freedom, and as no longer to be associated with fixed boundaries and unrevisable rules.[31] By comparison with eternity, created realities are, for Augustine, only imperfectly equal and only imperfectly harmonic. This is because no finite position (point, line, surface, body) is ever perfectly instantiated, since every finite point already has some extension. Thus nothing finite is ever equal to itself,[32] nothing finite is ever perfectly one, nothing finite is ever perfectly exact or measured. And yet, for Augustine, the true unity, the infinite One, is not itself a true (univocal) unity, but on the contrary, coincides with the perfect harmonic relation in such a way that the divine Father *is* the communication of His unity to the perfect measure of His Son.[33]

The nearest approximation to true infinite measure is therefore the temporal striving towards greater and greater exactitude.[34] For Augustine, this is not just something which conscious, rational human beings do, but in fact is what sustains every creature in being.[35] Every creature is perpetually seeking to be 'like itself' or to occupy more precisely its proper position in time and space. Every creature is a specific rhythm. However, despite this necessary primacy of time over space, Augustine also exhibits an equivalence of the balancing of time and space which we saw in the case of polyphonic music.[36] Were it the case that space were merely hierarchically subordinate, then the supreme ideal would be something like the pure flow of the Eastern paradigm, which seeks the dissolution and forgetting of every spatial articulation. As we have seen, such a privileging of Dionysian flow has acosmic, 'nihilistic' connotations. However, just as important as the priority of time, for Augustine, is the insistence on articulation into distinct musical units or phrases, the very move which allows a stress upon the simultaneity of harmony, whether in memory or in the actuality of performed polyphony. What mediates and allows this double stress is precisely the centrality of the silent caesura, for, first, this suggests how music constantly emerges in time from nothing, and secondly, it divides each musical phrase from every other, and in reality this means every creature from every creature. This division by the point or the 'nothing' can be seen as the transcendental precondition for the possibility not of spatial totalization, but of spatial relationship which is to a degree simultaneous. Thus music, although initiated by the flow, is not primarily a matter of flow 'over against' articulations. On the contrary, it is only constituted *as* flow by the series of articulations mediated by a silence which allows them also to sound together. It is on the basis of this conception that Augustine can make the astonishing assertion at the end of the *De musica* that the salvation of every creature consists in its being in its own proper place as well as time.[37] Both aspects are equally necessary if there is to be a cosmic poem. (This same integration of rhythmic and melodic flow with harmony implies also a possible integration of the audible and the visible in an 'operatic' unity.)

Augustine's synthesis of the spatial and the temporal, of articulation and flow, producing the best possible expression of the eternal music, is a distribution of the spiritual and the real which disallows any crude dualism, for his transcendent context, as we have seen, releases the ultimacy of such contraries by encompassing and redeeming them. However, if one examines post-Cartesian theories of music, one finds that Nietzsche's distinction between the Apollonian (spatial) and the Dionysian (temporal) now becomes relevant.

The theory of music expounded by Rameau (principally in *Génération harmonique* (1737), *Démonstration du principe de l'harmonie* (1750) and *Observations sur notre instinct pour la musique* (1754)) and the counter-theory presented by Rousseau (in his *Essai sur l'origine de langues où it est parlé de la méléodie et de l'imitation musicale* (1761) and throughout his fictional and non-fictional writings) seem to distort the chronotope of their Augustinian inheritance in opposing, but dialectically identical ways. For, as I shall show, Rameau stresses the exclusively spatial origins of all music, whilst Rousseau opposes this view by focusing on the nature of music as a derationalized flow of subjective expressiveness.[38]

For Rameau, the origin of music lies in the essentialized triadic chord always hearable in the sounds generated by the resonant objects of nature. He thus identified the unalterable physical laws of the *corps sonore*, that is, the fundamental tone sounding in simultaneity with its two harmonics, and argues from this triadic disposition of resonances for the priority of a fixed spatial harmony over the more temporal flow of melody: 'Music is ordinarily divided into Harmony and Melody, although the latter is only a part of the former.'[39] This primacy of harmony, because based upon a physical law, is unalterable in historical or cultural terms. In a gesture of universalization influenced by Descartes's 'Method',[40] Rameau sought to show that this single principle of the origins of music could be extended to become a *mathesis* for all the sciences, for

> it is in Music that nature appears to designate the Physical principle of those first and purely Mathematical notions on which all the Sciences are based; I mean, the Harmonic, Arithmetic, and Geometric proportions from which follow progressions of the same type and which are revealed at the first instant of the resonance of a *corps sonore*.[41]

Thus, whilst for Augustine the liberal arts ascended upward to a transcendent contemplation of divine ineffability, Rameau suggests that such an all-encompassing epistemological cyclopaedia can be derived from the result of a physical action upon resonant matter. The cosmic consummation of harmony is therefore immanentized to the level of air, 'stirred up by the impact of each particular *corps sonore*'.[42]

Rousseau, on the other hand, stresses that monodic music ('a simple unison') is more primary than the fundamental bass suggested by the *corps sonore*. He dismisses Rameau's theory, characterizing modern European (harmonic and chordal) music as a repressive distortion of an unblemished, original sonority found only in the music of oriental cultures,[43] which speaks directly to the heart.[44] In keeping with this Eastern preference, Rousseau argues that the paradigm for such music is *vocal*, thus stressing the constitutive ties between language, music and culture.

In the above analysis of Augustine's musical chronotope, space is represented by an implicit vertical axis by which a hierarchy of numbers links the
higher to the lower, although not in such a way as to cast the lower things as
quantitatively lesser counterparts of higher things. Rather, as we have seen,
Augustine suggests that the lower elements have their own irreplaceable
value – so much so, in fact, that it becomes possible to be *jealous* of lower
things.[45] The vertical axis of space, for Augustine, complements the horizontal axis of time which is seen to represent both process and development.
This model of time and space is exemplified by the structures of polyphony,
in whose interweaving lines the temporal, melodic component, despite its
successiveness, preserves an integrity and coherence, while the hierarchy of
its parts, despite its spatial distribution, must perpetually redefine its path.
In contrast to this model, the Rameau-esque chord, by essentializing a
static, vertical universal, paradoxically surrenders its hierarchical differentiation, because the value of each component, and historical instantiation of
this 'origin', are equalized as infinitely transferable, irrespective of circumstance. Furthermore, the chord is here regarded as a purely physical
phenomenon, bearing no relation to the hierarchy of soul and body. It no
longer points beyond itself to a transcendent consummation of harmony, but
rather, to further chordal progressions, or modulations into indifferently
varied inversions. Thus the spatial hierarchy is flattened into a linear succession of interchangeable variables. On this view, melody is reduced to a
regrettable necessity occasioned by our inability to apprehend everything at
once, as the only means by which harmony can be experienced in time. And
'ideal' music is implicitly represented as a spatially simultaneous universal
chord, in contrast to the Augustinian poem of the universe. This baroque or
classical spatialization of music is also exhibited in the drift towards music
as 'spectacle', all the way from the court masque through public opera to the
bourgeois concert.[46]

Whilst Rameau's insistence upon harmony seems to denude the spatial
axis of its hierarchical aspect, Rousseau's model of music as primarily
melodic and temporal seems paradoxically to spatialize time. For by
insisting on melody as a purely temporal duration of experienced process, he
reduces time to a formless flow without articulation or distinguishing parts.
Such a flow seems reducible to a spatial continuum. One could say, by
contrast, that, for Augustine, time makes space more properly space, and
space makes time more properly time.[47]

The inevitable consequences of no longer regarding time as a moving
image of eternity are exhibited in Kant's treatment of time in the First
Critique. For although Kant sees both time and space as *a priori* forms of
sensibility (in that neither objectively belongs to the world), he regards
them as separate: space is the form of outer sense, and time is the form of
inner sense. (Time is thought to be not something one can sense, but is that
which links sensations through memory.)[48] He then argues that if time is

the ground for comprehending both succession and simultaneity, then time as such does not change, but becomes itself the *substratum* of appearances (rather than things in themselves). As an epistemological version of substance, time is turned into the most stable (and therefore spatial) thing there is.

As we have seen, modern music theory, at least from the eighteenth century onwards, and (perhaps with some important exceptions) the Western tradition, broke with the synthesis of time and space that was secured by the idea that they both imaged eternity. Seemingly, so-called postmodern thought makes some attempt to overcome this modern separation and especially its spatializing of time and subordination of space to a mere linear punctual temporality (Rameau). Thus, in the case of Heidegger as compared with Kant, one finds a re-ontologization of time: time is no longer simply the form of appearances, but the inseparable mode of Being itself. Time, for Heidegger, has a certain priority over space and yet in our ontological fallenness we can never fully step outside the sense of a present 'now' and its spatial concomitants.

This dual stress upon a temporal flow which 'gives' Being and, at the same time, upon the occurrence of this flow only through temporal spacings (which must be at once both temporal and spatial intervals) is taken up by Jacques Derrida as a theory of transcendental differentiation and deferral governing both Being *and* knowledge. Derrida's disciple, Philippe Lacoue-Labarthe, explicitly recognizes that this constitutes a kind of musical ontology.[49] Thus it would seem that we have been returned to a Pythagorean/Augustinian perspective. Moreover, Lacoue-Labarthe places an especial stress upon the inescapability of the subjective or 'autobiographical' moment, the moment of 'making music' which would provide an equivalent to Augustine's granting privileged place to the *psyche* in this ontology.[50] For Lacoue-Labarthe, the indeterminacy of differentiation is the site of the opening-out of subjectivity, while the presence of a specific temporal-spatial ordering grants to the subject a specific rhythm, *typos*, or character.[51] It would seem that Lacoue-Labarthe is attempting to integrate the Dionysian and the Apollonian, since the continuous flux of music, its audibility and languishing/desiring agony, cannot occur without Apollonian mimesis, by which the subject composes itself in terms of repetition of other 'musical' instances which have preceded it.[52]

However, this postmodernism remains immanentist. Without Augustinian transcendence it is easy to demonstrate that it actually lapses back into modern (metaphysical) music, the very structure it apparently overcomes. First, since Heidegger does not regard time as a moving image of eternity, his diagnosis of the ecstatic character of time or the non-punctual inter-involvement of past, present and future at every moment must regress into a Kantian substantialization of time, albeit now in ontological and not epistemological terms. (Although it is possible to argue that Heidegger remains secretly a prisoner of epistemology, because he still thinks he can determine the ontological difference according to its appearance/non-appearance to the knowing subject).[53] According to this new substantialization, the aporias of ecstatic temporality do not point, as for Augustine, to the inherent non-being of time taken by itself,[54] but rather indicate directly a paradoxical 'essence' which is the constitution of all Being by nothing, which only *is* through this constitution. Thus nothing, the secret real, only asserts itself as Being which nonetheless immediately dissolves back into nothingness. This is a nihilistic version of Augustine's Christian Pythagorean dissolution of finite reality through his reflection upon numbers and music or, as Derrida might say, differentiation.

The same nihilism governs Lacoue-Labarthe's reflections. First, we find that there is here after all no easy co-existence of the Apollonian and the Dionysian. The mimetic and representational, although inevitable, is always contaminated for Lacoue-Labarthe by a metaphysical claim for essential identity. Thus his primary appeal is to audibility in order to sustain his dissolution of metaphysics.[55] Compared with Derrida, this does seem to constitute a new appeal to orality and, indeed, Lacoue-Labarthe does insist that deconstructive differentiation always and only occurs through subjective reflection (in a sense, for Lacoue-Labarthe, difference is subjectivity), and that this moment of subjective intervention will include a new instance of self-characterization which none the less will have to be immediately overcome in order to avoid a new lapse into the metaphysical.[56] This latter point shows that Lacoue-Labarthe is unable to use the notion of orality to fuse the integrity of the speaking body with the flux; it is therefore no accident that he sometimes wishes to characterize music rather as *writing* than as audibility. This shows that he is unable to resolve the modernist hesitation between the essence of music as being in the written work and, on the other hand, being in repeated performance (this dualism is another outcome of the breakdown of the Pythagorean inheritance – see below). In the end, he seems to opt for music as written, and therefore for the Dionysian as an unconscious process. The spatial is finally subordinated to that which has therefore become a new substantial 'essence', a new metaphysical substance, such that time is here spatialized – because it now has an essence which is an indefinite flux, a rhythm which mourns an origin that never was, and encourages a desire destined to frustration.[57] Since space is subordinate, there can be no notion here of finding one's proper place in time, thus salvation is precluded from the picture. It is notable that Lacoue-Labarthe claims that if one sees a configuration of dancing couples through a sound-proofed window, one will 'see' no rhythm; only the music will provide the key to their movements.[58] This seems quite arbitrarily to deny the traditional Pythagorean truth that rhythm can be incarnate as much in the visual as in the audible, two embodiments which are integrated in poetry, which for the tradition is perhaps even more musical than music itself. The paradox here is that rhythm is banished by Lacoue-Labarthe from the public spatial dance, and yet supremely located in intrinsically private spatial writing. This is because the true objective spatial substance is for Lacoue-Labarthe this impersonal flux of mutually cancelling absence and presence which is correctly and exactly measured by the arbitrary and open-ended indifference of the private subject. Thus the precise co-ordination of the isolated individual with an objectively measuring *mathesis* characteristic of modernity is hereby repeated in a nihilistic guise. Lacoue-Labarthe, like Rousseau, suppresses the spatial axis of harmony but no longer through expressive, Romantic melody: instead, through the dull beat of impersonal, 'pulsional' rhythm which imposes its violent writing regardless.

PSYCHIC MUSIC

Indian music is not concerned with the establishment of *typos* or character. On the contrary, it is concerned with a purging of emotions and sufferings according to a process of sacrificial offering which releases the self from *care*, not into a higher care, as for Augustine (see below), but from the burden of self altogether, that it may eventually merge with Nirvana. Similarly, on this view, there is no cosmos, since the world is not a site of order but ordering rather is a progressive dissolution of the world. So, likewise, there is no microcosmic order or *psyche*.

By contrast, in the West, there is *psyche*, and not only is music concerned with the imprinting of its *typos*, the *psyche* itself is a musical reality. It exists, as we have seen, in a musical proportion to the body and in turn to the whole cosmos. Thus music is at once a thing measured and the measure itself; it is for us supremely the measure of the psychic-corporeal relationship. It is this notion which always held together what we now think of as sciences and arts,[59] and ensured that the topics of the quadrivium always had a qualitative aesthetic dimension. To say that the essence of beauty is in number, as Augustine does,[60] and later Bonaventure and a host of medieval followers, sounds to us like an attempt to reduce aesthetics to science and formal rules. However, this would be to neglect the fact that for the tradition, number had a qualitative dimension and a mysterious, inexhaustible depth. The break up of this tradition in fact generated the duality of science and art, along with a series of other dualities in which the modern West remains trapped.

Augustine, as we have seen, reinvokes this Pythagorean tradition and adapts it to the outlook of his newly acquired Christian faith.[61] He regards both soul and body as numbers, and this ontology reveals a monism more fundamental than Augustinian dualism which commentators have more frequently insisted upon. For Augustine, in addition to the unconscious regulation of all bodily movements by the soul, the knowing and desiring of finite things is a matter of specific musical proportions. His treatment of musical sound in the *De musica* is just one exemplification of this relation. His account of how we sense musical sound is quite a complex one, for, on the one hand, he rejects the Neoplatonic view that the soul creates the body, since this is incompatible with the Christian view that all finite existences derive from a divine creator. And yet, like the Neoplatonists, he cannot accept that the soul as a more powerful number (a more intense harmony) can be causally influenced by the body.[62] In consequence, he will not allow, like Aristotle and later Aquinas, that the soul itself senses, since it is passively informed by corporeal stimuli. And yet his rejection of the Neoplatonic position means that he must allow for some passivity in sensation. He incorporates this by stressing, firstly, that one's body passively receives sensations from other bodies,[63] and, secondly, that this event of reception *occasions* an active production by the soul, not of the physical sound itself, but of an internal image of that sound.[64] In this 'act' of occasioning, it is as if the sensation does pass into the soul, but is received in an entirely active manner because the soul transfigures the sensation into a comprehensible reality according to its recollection of eternal harmony which includes all possible harmonies, corporeal and incorporeal. This, however, is not at all equivalent to a Kantian *a priori* since there are no harmonic categories latent in the soul. On the contrary, the memory which the sensation stimulates is truly of divine transcendence. This is not, of course, for Augustine, based upon the pre-existence of the soul. Accordingly, he resolves the aporia of learning, namely, the question of how it is that the soul can search for, and later reactivate, harmonies which it does not at present know, by appeal to the role of desire. Indeed, for Augustine, desire always accompanies judgement, in such a way that even a realized judgement is only *true* in terms of its desiring anticipation of the relation of a present harmony to other future things with which it could come to be in harmony.[65] This co-belonging of desire and judgement is summed up for Augustine in the image of reason become the burning fire of charity.[66]

According to this model of 'active reception', described above,[67] the numbers of sensation have priority, for Augustine, over the external sounding numbers.[68] After the numbers of sensation come the memorial numbers, which are in turn superior, because to sense any single harmony of two things one must already have brought together a merely remembered past sound with a sensed present sound. Above the memorial numbers come the numbers which judge spontaneously a sensory stimulus, and which allow the mind to create a sensory image on the occasion of a bodily stimulation.[69] However, above the initial number of judgement (*numeri sensuales*) comes a reflexive or recursive judgement (*numeri iudiciales*) which judges the first judgement, either accepting, rejecting or modifying an initial enthusiasm or distaste.[70]

This bare account of Augustine's classification, however, conceals certain nuances which are crucial for his musical psychology. First, although the sounding numbers (*numeri corporeales*) eventually drop out of consideration, Augustine never takes back his affirmation that one only becomes aware of one's sense of harmonic proportion from a particular instance of hearing an actual, physical harmony.[71] So, once again, one can see that possession of a faculty of judgement does not in his case amount to a possession of *a priori* Kantian-type rules (if one is thinking of the First Critique and not the Third).[72] Also, one can see how Augustine's Platonic theory of recollection actually fuses a 'memory' of the transcendent with a triggering-off of this memory by events in time which have to be empirically registered.[73]

The second nuance follows closely upon the first. It would be easy to imagine that Augustine's category of initial, spontaneous judgement is freer and more ineffable than a possibly colder, rational or more codifiable higher judgement. In fact, it is really not like this at all, because the recursive judgement is an open judgement, in principle never finished, and is therefore a non-codifiable judgement which always exceeds any given rules since these can always be subject to further judgement.[74] This higher judgement is an inherently incomplete judgement, but it is a *true* judgement precisely because incomplete, since, as we have seen, nothing finite is truly equal to itself. Just as there is only a measure of objective equality insofar as finite things participate in divine unity, so also there is only a measure of subjective equality insofar as our judgement participates in the divine infinite judgement.[75] As we have seen, our lack of perfect judgement has to be supplemented by an exercise of true desire if there is to be any participation in judgement whatsoever. Thus we can see that the higher judgement is the very opposite of a *mathesis*, and Augustine frequently inveighs against a mechanical following of empty rules,[76] just as he celebrates rhythmic proportions which remain analogously the same in very different embodiments.[77] Moreover, he associates this empty rule-following with a judgement that does not refer itself to the divine infinite judgement, or does not refer the *usus* of finite things to eternal fruition: for if one is left merely with *usus*, one is left also only with a utilitarian calculation of the predictable effects of sounds. Without the higher judgement, spontaneous judgements would have to remain fixed and unquestionable, and it would become possible to have a strict science of musical harmony which one could deploy to produce predictable effects in the social sphere.[78] The two possible tendencies of judgement are contrasted by Augustine in terms of opposite implications of the word *cura*. If we are merely *curious* about finite harmonies, then we will fall victim to the burdensome *care* of discovering and preserving them. If, on the other hand, one takes *care* to refer finite harmonies beyond themselves to eternity mediated by new relational arrivals in time, then one will discover that the yoke of this care is, after Christ's words cited by Augustine, easy, and its burden light.[79]

A third nuance must be mentioned. We have seen that, for Augustine, our judgement is inherently limited.[80] This circumstance should be connected with the non-dualism of his Pythagorean ontology, for according to this ontology, the contrast of objective unity with subjective judgement so far invoked must in fact be relativized. For an antique and medieval outlook, there was no such thing as our post-Cartesian contrast between the objective fact measured and the subjective measurer. On the contrary, the heavenly bodies, for example, constituted at once the supreme harmony and the supreme *measure* of that harmony; they were their own best perfect measure.[81] Inversely, precisely to the degree that we are judges or measurers, we are measurers mainly of ourselves, 'ourselves' being identical with the proper proportions in which we stand to everything else. Or to put this another way, we remain incorporated within the poem of the universe whose parts we seek to measure, and any true act of measuring can only mean our fulfilling our role within that poem. To measure music means no more than to sound our right note which no other can sound and which then forms part of the cosmic poem which is its own best measure.

This perspective, recalling Augustine's account of the originality of human art, allows him to attain to perspectives which to our ears sound 'post-Renaissance'. (The question of the degree to which such perspectives were in fact known about in the Middle Ages should perhaps remain open.) Thus Augustine can account for a certain relativity in aesthetic judgement, or the idea that there are certain things which one needs to be in the right position to appreciate, precisely because one is a constitutive part of that picture which one is appreciating. This perspective does not degenerate into relativism, because Augustine has faith that all these limited perspectives or instances are themselves beautifully integrated into the cosmic poem. Secondly, this same perspectivalism is applied by Augustine to time as well as to space and so to societies as well as to individuals, for he is able to recognize that judgement gives birth to contrasting customary norms which can themselves undergo change, and yet be integrated within an overall sense of rightly judged proportion.[82] For one can have a sense of different customs fitting different times and places. This socio-historical dimension is in accordance with Augustine's musical definition of salvation and one can relate it to remarks made elsewhere by Augustine, for example, regarding the appropriateness of the Old Testament Law for a particular time and place in human history.

Whilst, as we have seen, for Augustine and the tradition, music is the measure of the soul's relation to the body, in the post-Cartesian era the domain of music is split into two. For either, as in the case of Rameau's theory of music, it pertains to a physical principle which explains the passions as purely natural phenomena, or, as for Rousseau, music severs its link with measure of any kind, and becomes a pure expression of subjective communion in successive impressions. A crucial consequence of this bifurcation of harmony and melody seems, in the case of Rameau and Rousseau, to be a concomitant separation of reason and passion which, as we have seen above, were previously regarded as less obviously separable.

In recent twentieth-century musical theory, there is a debate between those who uphold a 'Platonic' theory of music, according to which music is an essentially mental phenomenon, and the 'real work' is something which exists outside its instantiation in performance (in parallel with the so-called Platonic view of mathematics according to which abstract numbers are realities), and others who take a nominalist approach. The former view was exemplified by Charles Ives, forerunner of musical modernism, who under the influence of American Transcendentalism saw performance as a lapse and at best a tiresome necessity: 'Why can't music go out in the same way it comes into a man,' he wrote, 'without having to crawl over a fence of sounds, thoraxes, catguts, wire, wood and brass.'[83] By contrast, earlier composers – one might think of Bach – remained essentially craftsmen for whom composition and performance were mutually informing activities. In the case of the alternative consequence of the collapse of this integral musical nominalism, a musical work is something continuously repeated as different, and has no essential identity whatsoever. This obviously tends towards a postmodern dissolution of the integrity of the 'work'.

However, this alternative, like the Rameau–Rousseau debate, can be seen as the result of the breakdown of the Pythagorean/Platonic/Christian traditions of reflection upon music. For so-called modern 'Platonism' mentioned above is only a pseudo-Platonism infected by modern *a priori*ism. According to a genuine Platonic view, ideal music is not something possessed by the mind, but, on the contrary, arrives from without and is fully instantiated only in a transcendent source. Hence, while this view would allow that every composed work was in excess of its performed incarnations, nonetheless, every new performance would constitute an indispensable means for recollecting aspects of that ideality of the original work which could not be known by us from the outset without its being instantiated in time. Hence, only the idea that there is an infinite eternal music holds in tension text and performance, and ensures that the ideality of a work is not something to do with the genius of the isolated individual composer (who, on the modern 'Platonic' view, constitutes an absolute origin), but with its participation in an unknown music, and thereby its co-ordination with all other true musical works, or human participations in eternal harmony. Normally one sees modernity as the great age of the subject, and postmodernity as the time of the dissolution of the subject. However, we have just seen that there really is no characterized subject in modernity. For the Rameau-esque post-Cartesian view, the subject is just a passive mirror of a series of objective natural proportions which instil passions in us. (Ultimately, for Descartes, these passions are linked to pragmatic purposes of self-preservation and procreation.)[84] Conversely, for the Rousseauian full admission of emotions to primary subjectivity, emotions have become merely subjective and political, without reference to an objective nature. Therefore the integrity of valid passions is already threatened. By contrast, Lacoue-Labarthe seems to be making an attempt to inscribe subjective indeterminacy and mimetic 'typing' into a fundamental ontology.[85] In a sense, he almost seeks, like Augustine, to link again *psyche* and *cosmos*, and yet without transcendence, this becomes impossible. Instead, he merely brings the *modern* obliteration of the subject to fruition. Thus, a Rousseauian expression of emotion has collapsed into arbitrary preference which merely manifests an ineluctable rhythm which we cannot in any sense control.[86] Unconscious rhythmic processes are in command, and therefore the highest 'numbers' are no longer, as for Augustine, those of judgement, but rather, the sounding numbers (*numeri corporeales*) which we cannot in any way influence. Thus, for Lacoue-Labarthe, there is no active reception of rhythm, but the subject is entirely at the mercy of an ineluctable process.[87] This is despite the fact that the reading of temporal flux in this anarchic way, rather than as participation in transcendence, is merely an act of subjective judgement. Lacoue-Labarthe conceals the moment of judgement in the affirmation that judgement has no purchase, no ontological reality beyond *illusion*.

For Lacoue-Labarthe, our being passively at the mercy of rhythm means that we are also always passively entangled with the other. Since we *are* first through imitation of rhythm, our identity is first of all that of an other (as for Lacan). Therefore, since this 'other' is always past, 'we' are always already dead, we are always haunted by our own (lack of) identity. And this is a ghost with which we must always struggle. The self we have lost is always a self we must overcome, since we can only establish our identity by being different from the other who alone gives us identity. (This is the Girardian double-bind which Lacoue-Labarthe takes over.)[88] This means that the true situation of the self is that it has always lost itself in the mourned other, and yet this other never was one's self in the first place: what is mourned never *was*. This anguish and agonism is, for Lacoue-Labarthe, precisely what constitutes the 'music' of our reality.[89] This reads theologically like a nihilistic satire of the Augustinian view that a self involved in patterns of attempted domination, usurpation and rivalry, since it fails to envisage the possibility of analogical repetition (everything continuously in its proper place and time through a musical integration of flow and articulation, ratio-nally ungraspable, and yet hearable as an echo of eternity), is indeed a self that has lost itself but not a self that never was; rather, a true self whose possibility is still contained in God. Furthermore, besides the aspect of orig-inal sin in the loss of self, there is also, for Augustine, an ontological aspect germane to creation as such. Just as one cannot rationally grasp the echo of eternity in music, so also one cannot grasp the coherence of the self which has only a musical expression or 'measure'. This musical measure is indeed caught up in both melancholia and longing. But these things, for Augustine, are not to be immanently ontologized as final realities. Rather, they are signs of the rooting of times in eternity. Just because we cannot grasp our self does not mean that there is no self. Rather, it indicates that the self exceeds itself precisely because there is only self through the participation of self in transcendent unlimited subjectivity.

POLITICAL MUSIC

In all traditions, it seems, music, religion and politics are intimately linked. They all pertain to the most secret and ineffable emotional forces which bind us together. However, the Indian paradigm of music goes as far as possible in the direction of constituting the political through its deconstitution. This is because at the top of the social scale exists the king-guru who is the most powerful man by virtue of being the most free from corporeal and social ties. The very aim of the rise in the social, personal, biographical or musical scale is to rid oneself of relations and emerge supreme and purged from this ladder of ascent.[90] Thus whereas in Greek culture the lone Pythagorean philosopher was a rebel, and Orphics were an exceptional 'cult', in India, the isolated guru constituted the ultimate social aim. This is why Louis Dumont realized that individualism was born in the East, albeit in an other-worldly form. This apolitical character of Indian music is all of a piece with its fusion with religious sacrifice. Music, on this view, is one mode of sacrificial offering which repeats and yet seeks to undo in reverse the original sacrificial constitution of the universe. For Hindu mythology, the universe came into being through the sacrificial sundering of an original primal man (Purusa) and this renders the whole of reality guilty. (Perhaps this is not so utterly unlike Heidegger's 'ontological guilt', attendant upon presence as such.) The point of our sacrifices is ceaselessly to atone for this guilt, and indeed, every expiration of breath can be integrated into this act of atonement. Through musical flowing-out of breath, the self is gradually freed from its contamination by the guilt of appearance.[91]

The Greek view of music and the social is radically otherwise. For Pythagoras and Plato, music is very close to law (*nomos*) and, indeed, for Plato, it is musical modes covering all matters of aesthetic style in the city which most require legislation since this will produce the best characters, and from thereon more precise matters of law can be left to their equitable judgement. The point of music, as of Greek religion, is not at all to escape from the human and the civic (not even for Socrates and Pythagoras who were dissidents in the existing *polis*), but rather to grant to gods and to different types of human beings what is properly due to them. Thus the purpose of Greek sacrifice is not primarily or usually to atone, but rather to express a manifest order of respective proportions.[92] Whereas for the Indian model, music and sacrifice flow away in offering without remainder, a 'remaining' portion of the Greek sacrificed animal, and of Greek music, persists to express the integrity of the city in harmonic proportions. This notion of a 'remainder' concords with the Western emphasis on harmony. Just as we have seen that in relation to music there is neither *cosmos* nor *psyche* in the East, so now we see also that there is no *polis* either.

Through the Augustinian refraction, all these three phenomena remain, although they are also challenged and reformed by Augustinian relationality which renders them part of one continuous reality. We have already begun to see this; now the analysis will be completed.

For Boethius, the Platonic tradition of regarding music as being of political significance is fully continued. This means that the rhetorical and instrumental aspects of music are just as crucial as the psychic aspect. Boethius discusses the way in which music wields a fundamental influence over peoples' mood, character and behaviour.[93] This same outlook tended, in the Middle Ages and Renaissance, to accord music a medical use. By hearing particular kinds of harmony, the soul was able to mend distortions of the humours which, although of physical origin, disturb the balance of the soul. For the same tradition, disordered music reflects imbalances in the political, psychic and even cosmic orders, while, inversely, good music can help re-order the *polis*, the soul and even the cosmos. The latter constitutes an aspect of the magical use of music, most encouraged by the Hermetic tradition, but not necessarily at variance with an orthodox Christian outlook.[94]

The twentieth-century composer Paul Hindemith, reacting against the attempt of the Nazis to censor music (an attempt which surely had little to do with a genuine Platonic view of musical politics), sought to draw a fundamental contrast between the Boethian rhetorical view of music and the Augustinian view of true music as internal and spiritual. He described the Boethian view as *ethical* since it seeks to influence public *ethos* through external music, and the Augustinian view as *moral*, since it seeks to rise above external music and attain to psychic music.[95] However, this contrast is entirely erroneous. It ignores the way in which, as already described, a Platonic transcendent view of music holds the psychic and rhetorical aspects in balance. Historically, it also ignores the fact that Augustine and Boethius share a common Christianized inheritance. Boethius by no means omits an interior psychic aspect, while Augustine is interested in external, relational aspects of music which involve the effect of voice and musical instrument upon the other. However, Augustine *does* contribute a modification of the antique 'ethical' view of music. This is because he makes a democratic distinction between the attempt to dominate others and genuine persuasion of others.[96] The domination of other people is an assertion of an absolute right of rule of one human soul over another. This rule, according to Augustine, is inherently unjust, because all human souls are on the same ontological level, and to assert psychic priority amounts to a reduction of the other person to a bodily instrument of one's soul.[97] For Augustine, the body is literally a musical instrument of the soul,[98] as such indispensable to the soul, and the very means by which the soul communicates itself to the *polis*, and so assumes ethical responsibilities. But the other person, however much one might make his body and voice part of a conducted choir, can never be reduced in his psychic aspect to a mere instrument. To do so would be to reduce the musical instrument to the merely instrumental, and such a move would mean that psychic numbers have been subordinated to bodily numbers, and the higher judgement to rule-bound spontaneous judgement. Domination of others through music can only be achieved through a distortion of musical harmonies in which psychic ends are manipulated towards false material goals of power for its own sake, knowledge for its own sake and attainment of desire for its own sake, which is possessiveness.[99] Hence Augustine first of all democratizes the notion of musical *ethos*,[100] and, secondly, insists that attempts to manipulate through propagandistic use of the arts inevitably involve a use of perverse and distorted musical modes. There is no possibility of using good music to a bad end.[101]

Inversely, good musical modes invoke, as part of their practice, a genuine persuasion of other people towards the good. This is because, for Augustine, the final human end of love of God includes love of one's neighbour, as he stresses in the *De musica*.[102] It is impossible to be in psychic harmony with God without simultaneously trying to communicate this harmony as love to one's neighbour. This, for Augustine, is an inseparable aspect of music as offering, music as worship.

Finally, Augustine provides a remarkable Christological integration of the theme of soul–body relation (*the topos* of music) with the question of the instrumental and political aspects of music. When discussing the seeming inappropriateness of the body influencing the soul, he allows, as we have seen, that this can occur by means of an 'active reception'. This is possible for Augustine because, although the beauty of the body is subordinate, nonetheless it has its own proper beauty which is qualitatively distinct, not merely a quantitatively lesser degree of psychic beauty.[103] Thus it is possible for the soul to be jealous of corporeal beauty.[104] The body has a beauty of its own which it can communicate to the soul, and provides an irreplaceable assistance to the soul in reminding it of the plenitude of eternal beauty.[105] In consequence, Augustine is able to link this place for the body and for instrumental music to the event of the incarnation, and the full manifestation of divine beauty in time in a human being possessing a body as well as a soul.[106] Christ can only accomplish our salvation, can only influence us, through corporeal means. Moreover, Augustine argues that one effect of the Fall is that the body often assumed a perverted command over the soul. Sin renders the soul passive, or apparently passive, setting up an ontological impossibility. Yet this circumstance prevents the soul from re-establishing the right order, since it is now weakened. Right order can only be re-established from the side of the body, and therefore, in a fallen world, corporeal and instrumental music acquires even more importance. Only God incarnate possesses the correct ordering of soul and body, and this can only be mediated to us by physical means. The restored order is therefore first seen, or glimpsed, in the external physical world. That which is beyond the world, the ultimate measure, nonetheless *contains* the world. As Christ's perfectly ordered body is inserted into a world of sin, this order is manifest as the suffering of Christ's body. This suffering is for us the first mode of access to a perfected music and beauty. Augustine says that 'neither its (the body's) wound nor its disease has deserved to be without the honour of some ornament'.[107] He then continues to the effect that 'the highest wisdom of God designed to assume this wound by means of a wonderful and ineffable sacrament when he took upon himself man without sin'.[108] For Augustine, therefore, the highest music in the fallen world, the redemptive music, is initially corporeal rather than psychic, although it is the *cure* of the soul. It is none other than the repeated sacrifice of Christ Himself which is the music of the forever repeated Eucharist. It follows, for Augustine, that even when the soul is suffering, since it is receiving something passively from the body (or at least appearing to do so, since actually what occurs is that on the occasion of a bodily suffering, the soul distorts its own harmony),[109] and so receiving a distorted music, nonetheless, by participation in Christ's sufferings, this discordance can be transfigured into a rightly ordered music. This redemptive process most of all fulfils Augustine's contention that nothing falls outside the harmony of the cosmic poem. Hence his Christian account of music introduces the new aesthetic idea that every apparent discord can in the course of musical time be granted its concordant place. Indeed, for Augustine, in a fallen world true harmony can only resound via this passage through discordant noise which nonetheless ceases in time to be mere noise. The ontological dialectic of being and non-being in creation, reflected in music as the alternation of caesura and sounding note, is redoubled by a salvific dialectic of discordance and concordance, which here constitutes the theme of sacrificial passion. Earlier we saw that for Augustine salvation means that everything is in its own proper time and place, that everything is separated by the appropriate intervals. Now we can add that in a post-fallen world, the proper time and place is always the place of the Cross, or rather, the temporal passage through the Cross. In this sense *only* is music, for Augustine, a sacrifice, a mourning and a Passion, not ontologically, but contingently and yet universally and inescapably, in a fallen order. This sacrifice and Passion is at once an undergoing of our sins and an offering to God and to others for their own healing. Later, it will be shown how this understanding of music as atoning is to be contrasted with the postmodern understanding of music as inherently sacrificial.

We have seen that, in the case of Augustine, a balance is maintained between internal and performed music, just as earlier we saw that he maintained a balance between the fluctional and the articulated, and between the psychic and the cosmic. In the latter two instances, we saw how post-Cartesian philosophy dissolved this balance. In the case of the political dimension of music, a parallel breakdown occurs. First, the Rameau-inspired reduction of melody to obeisance before a primary, natural harmony opens the way towards the idea of a manipulation of peoples' minds through their bodies, which is adverse to the traditional notion of a rhetorical effect of music upon the judgement of the soul. This can be seen to have encouraged the gradual commodification of music whereby it increasingly emanates from one centre, and is used to pacify, banalize and compensate a mass audience.[110] Increasingly there has arisen a mass music in this idiom which is neither elite nor ethnic (or 'folk') in character.

Again, Rousseau provides an example of an opposite arm of bifurcation. Whereas for Rameau music is entirely naturalized, opening a way to an objectified political use, for Rousseau music is, from the outset, political, and is natural only to a human social reality. This would seem to preclude the packaging and exploitation of music, but Rousseau is only able to construe the political character of music in formalistic terms. He reduces music to the event of association as such, without any hierarchical preference for certain modes over others. Music, therefore, seems to be a matter of allowing sympathy with the expression of other peoples' private emotions, or else with the expression of one particular ethos of one community. What is lacking here is the Augustinian notion that the subjectivity of measure is subordinate to the measured character of the measurer himself, his belonging within the scansions of the cosmic poem. For this allows that my recognition of the rhythm of the other (not just the *freedom* of the other, as for Hegel) is a necessary aspect of my own rhythm, in the same way that cultural expressions only have validity through the enterprise of harmonizing one culture with another, one age with another, without obliterating their differences.

The political function of music as holding people in thrall round one centre is fully acknowledged by postmodern theorists of music, especially Lacoue-Labarthe and Jacques Attali. They also recognize that this one centre is a sacrificial centre, as it was in different ways for ancient India, ancient Greece, St Augustine and the Christian Middle Ages (when cosmic music had become also music of the Passion). So, once again it might seem that we have a postmodern retrieval of aspects of a premodern understanding of music. However, the postmodern sacrifice invoked is, if anything, most like the Indian sacrificial paradigm, but rendered more explicitly nihilistic. We have already seen how, for Lacoue-Labarthe, music is a tragically and yet necessarily substitutional reality. It is mourning for what has never been; it is the attempt of every note or character-type agonistically to oust its predecessor. What we hear in music, therefore, is always the discordant clash of incompatibles which are never to be subject to dialectical resolution. The only joy to be gleaned from this music must be the song of selfish triumph over one's dead rival, which is commensurate with an evasion of one's own deadness.[111] There is here no resurrection of the other,[112] and therefore no resurrection of the self either. Although Lacoue-Labarthe rejects René Girard's notion of an original murderous rivalry for which sacrifice, language and music are relatively less violent, medicinal substitutes, this is only in order to advocate the view that such violent substitution for an imaginary naked original that never was, has been the order of things from the beginning.[113] For Lacoue-Labarthe, all music is literally 'rough' music, that music which in European folk tradition was deployed to terrify and expel the unwanted scapegoat.

The same perspective upon music in all essential respects is articulated by Attali. What is crucial to his philosophy of the history of music, which he takes to be a philosophy of history as such, is the view that noise has ontological priority over music.[114] Thus all music is but mitigated noise.[115] Such noise is seen as the precise point of intersection of real and symbolic violence, and, therefore, one might say, of redoubled violence. Noise is the most violent thing of all. Perhaps one could therefore argue for a structural similarity between such noise and the evil of phenomena in the Indian paradigm, which both music and sacrifice must atone for and ultimately expel. However, for Attali, no such ultimate expulsion is possible, and the only attainable Nirvana is a resignation to the flux of noise, and the chaos of music become merely private composition.[116] Attali takes this to be oppositional in relation to commodified identically repeated music. But it is surely only its collusive reverse face, since it fails to re-establish a community of participation and still leaves the public space open to musical manipulation. And indeed, it seems dishonest of Attali to proffer any positive musical politics since, if music is but mitigated noise, then, as he says, all music is, of its very essence, a domination, and there is no such thing as genuine persuasion. And the harmony of the cosmos is no more than a political ruse. Of course, it may often, or usually, have been such, but this should not hide from our view the truth that if there is no cosmic harmony, then there is no ontological possibility of a time and space for social harmony. A radical politics has to have faith and hope that there is a concealed cosmic harmony, otherwise there is only postmodern despair.

Since for Attali music is but mitigated noise, he argues that it has a function identical with that of Girard's sacrifice which substitutes for rivalrous violence.[117] Music is always a merely phenomenal and apparent harmony whose whole point is to exclude certain arbitrarily unwanted noises. This view, however, seems to assume the closure of the musical work which, as Attali points out, is only true of modern music. Every medieval composition was seen to run into every other, and to be open to future developments. The conception of music at this period was in fact strictly *liturgical*.

Nonetheless, Attali shares with Augustine the view that none of our harmonies are perfect harmonies. But two things differentiate their outlooks. First, there is a generosity in Augustine's invocation of the plenitude of

Being: that is to say, he recognizes that a lower and limited harmony can still possess a certain inimitable, although lowly, perfection, like that of the body. The second difference concerns Augustine's interpretation of the fact that finite harmony is never absolutely perfect, but must always strive for a greater perfection of equality. He does not read this as an attempt to suppress a preliminary chaos, which would render every harmony merely a lesser degree of chaos, but instead assumes that the imperfection of our harmonies is a sign that harmony is otherwise and elsewhere located, harmony is not our possession, but our borrowing from eternity. Thus, instead of mitigated noise, one has a sharing of rhythm to a degree. The mitigation of noise is only a response to the contingency of the interruption of harmony by sin. But because of the ontological priority of the participation model, noise itself can be perfectly integrated through the innocent suffering of Christ and its imitation in our passionate music, into a harmony uncontaminated by violence, either real or symbolic, that is to say, discordant 'noise'.

Thus it seems that the postmodern perspective on music is after all even more resolutely apolitical than the modern one, or rather, perhaps, realizes an apoliticism intrinsic to musical enlightenment. It is impossible, given Lacoue-Labarthe's and Attali's view of musical sacrifice, to have any hope for social harmony, since every harmony is merely an illusion, and expulsion of certain unwanted noises. To say, 'Let all noises flourish in confusion', is only to invoke the mythical Girardian original scene. What would bind together such a society? It could only be certain formalized rules of a musical *mathesis*, implying a public musical puritanism beyond anything imagined by Plato. Thus the only ethics which postmodernism can instil in the realm of 'music' would be a resigned acceptance of the impersonal flux, whose inevitable mediation via Apollonian appearances constituted, for Nietzsche, the endless sacrificial sundering of the Dionysian body of time. All postmodernism does is repeat over and over the Nietzschian identification of tragedy with Dionysian music, where a lurid beauty (sublimity) is what reconciles us to suffering, death and loss. It is a new variant of an old Stoic impersonal and politically quietist theodicy.

CONCLUSION

This chapter has been a brief appeal for a restoration of the integrity of the Western tradition concerning musical theory, which is an appeal for a restoration of the Western (Platonic/Christian) tradition as such. For against fashionable invocation of the non-Western, the pluralistic and the post-metaphysical, this chapter has sought to show, especially in the last section, exactly why only this Western musical succession foreshadows a possible future political 'equality' or harmony. At the same time, it has been shown how this same tradition can heal the rift between body and soul, arts and sciences, etc., which are not a legacy of the tradition from its beginning, but of its modern refraction. The non-dualism present in the notion of music as measure of the soul/body ratio has proved to be linked to a perspective for which reality itself is meaningful, and yet meaning itself is seen to be only available for a subjective judgement. For in music, uniquely, there is in a beautiful phrase at once an objectively expressible proportion, and subjective selection and appreciation of this proportion as beautiful. Meaning, therefore, is seen to be the *world's* meaning, and yet, at the same time, our *own* meaning.

Finally, we saw in the first section how music, for the traditional view, holds in balance time and space under transcendence. By contrast, after the rejection of transcendence, time and space become separate and distorted as 'opposites' of one another. This process, which is characteristic of modernity, has simply been fully realized as nihilism in so-called postmodernity. It is therefore no accident that the very thing which postmodernism *most* denies is music, for its core belief is that flux and articulation are both necessary to each other, and yet mutually cancelling. And yet in music we hear the flux only as articulated, and articulations only in the flux. It is impossible, rationally, to resolve the aporias of time. Neither a pure flow nor pure present moments make any coherent sense. And yet in music we *hear* this impossible reconciliation. To believe the evidence of our ears is therefore to deny nihilism. Moreover, it is to believe in transcendence. More, it is to believe in the healing of time, and, therefore, sacramentally to receive the incarnation of God in time, His Passion and resurrection. For theology, although it cannot provide a logos which once and for all resolves the aporias of time, can nonetheless develop another logos which indicates a positive reason why these aporias are irresolvable. That is to say, they are the mark of our created finitude. We are spared a denial of hearing harmony through our acknowledgement of the triune God. Furthermore, our hearing of the harmony despite and through undeniable worldly disharmonies can only be taken as more than a mere mitigation of noise if we take this harmony to be the echo of the re-beginning of human music in time by God Himself.[118]

NOTES

1 The concept, not original with Augustine, was first put forward in the fourth century BC by the Pythagorean Archytas, and Plato adopted a similar formula in his education of the Philosopher-Guardian in the *Republic*. See Jamie James, *The Music of the Spheres: Music, Science and the Natural Order of the Universe*, London, Abacus, 1993, p. 72.

2 See Bonaventure's summary of Augustine's numerological ascent, Ewert Cousins (tr.), *Bonaventure: The Soul's Journey into God et al.*, Classics of Western Spirituality, New York, Paulist Press, 1978, paragraph 10; see also Augustine, *De musica* VI.i.1 (I have used the text from BA 7).

3 *De musica* VI.xvii.58 (tr. in R. C. Taliaferro, *Augustine: The Immortality of the Soul et al.*, Fathers of the Church 4, Washington, DC, Catholic University of America Press, 1974, pp. 377–8): '(We) can only receive and hold local numbers seemingly in a state of rest if temporal numbers, in motion, precede within and in silence.'

4 Boethius, *Fundamentals of Music* I.2. Tr. Calvin M. Bower, New Haven, PA, Yale University Press, 1989.

5 See John Milbank, 'Sacred Triads: Augustine and the Indo-European Soul', *Modern Theology*, forthcoming.

6 Lewis Rowell, 'The Idea of Music in India and the Ancient West', in Veikko Rantala *et al.* (eds), *Essays on the Philosophy of Music*, Helsinki, The Philosophical Society of Finland, 1988, pp. 322–39; idem, *Music and Musical Thought in Early India*, Chicago, IL, Chicago University Pess, 1992.

7 Boethius, *Fundamentals*, I.3; Rowell, 'The Idea of Music', pp.332–3.

8 Rowell cites Theon of Smyrna: 'The Pythagoreans, whom Plato follows in many respects, call music the harmonization of opposites, the unification of disparate things, and the conciliation of warring elements', 'The Idea of Music', p. 340, n. 13.

9 *De musica* VI.xi. 29.

10 The story of Pythagoras and the anvils suggests that concordant tones were being produced in unison, as does Plato's account of the Sirens in the Myth of Er. See James, *The Music of the Spheres*, p. 79.

11 Rowell, 'The Idea of Music', pp. 329–39 and *passim*.

12 Friedrich Nietzsche, *The Birth of Tragedy*, tr. Francis Golffing, New York, Doubleday, 1956, pp. 1–146.

13 Nino Perrotta, *Music and Culture in Italy from the Middle Ages to the Baroque*, Cambridge, MA, Harvard University Press, 1984, pp. 15–18.

14 Perrotta, *Music and Culture*, pp. 15–17, 369–70, n. 14; William G. Waite, *The Rhythm of Twelfth-Century Polyphony: Its Theory and Practice*, New Haven, PA, Yale University Press, 1954, pp. 112–13.

15 See James, *The Music of the Spheres*, pp. 95–100 on Galilei's opposition to polyphony.

16 Lydia Goehr, *The Imaginary Museum of Musical Works: An Essay in the Philosophy of Music*, Oxford, Clarendon Press, 1992, p. 132.

17 At VI.iv.6, the Master argues that sounds which last longer are not to be compared in ratio with shorter sounds as eternity is compared with time. From this notion that longevity is no closer to eternity, we can infer that, for Augustine, eternity is qualitative, and that enforced persistence in time is an idolatrous pseudo-eternity. Indeed, throughout the *De musica*, it is clear that the temporal is to be regarded as closer in likeness to eternity than the reified or the spatial. See, for example, VI.iv.7, where the Master explains that the solid insensitivity of certain inert phenomena is not to be substituted or mistaken for the quality of peace, not least because, despite appearances, no finite thing is ever equal to itself. It seems that such stable substances as hair and nails can mislead the soul into such an idolatrous substitution. We later learn that it is the quality of open-endedness which most images eternity: VI.v.15, Vl.viii.22, VI.xvii.58.

18 Waite, *The Rhythms of Twelfth-Century Polyphony*, pp. 36–7.

19 Waite, *The Rhythms of Twelfth-Century Polyphony*, pp. 36–9.

20 The ratios persist regardless of their actual longevity of duration: VI.ii.3, VI.vii.17–18, VI.xii.35.

21 *De musica* VI.xi.29: Ita coelestibus terrena subjecta, orbcs temporum suorum numcrosa successione quasi carmini universitatis associant. Cf. VI.vii.19.

22 *De musica* VI.x.27: Cur in silentiorum intervalis nulla fraude sensus offenditur, nisi quia eidem juri aequalitatis, etiamsi non sono, spatio tamen temporis quod debetur, exsolvitur?

23 *De musica* VI.x.28: et tamen in quantum imitantur, pulchra esse in suo genere et ordine suo, negare non possumus. Cf. VI.iv.7, VI.xiv.46, VI.xvii.56.

24 Emilie Zum Brunn (tr.), *St. Augustine: Being and Nothingness*, New York, Paragon House, 1988, ch. 3.

25 *De musica* VI.xvii.57.

26 *De musica* VI.xvii.57.

27 *De musica* VI.xvii.57: Unde, quaeso, ista, nisi ab illo summo atque aeterno principatu numerorum et similitudinis et aequalitatis et ordinis veniunt? Atqui naec si terrae ademeris, nihil erit. Quocirca omnipotens Deum terram fecit, et de nihilo terra facta est. Cf. *De libero arbitrio* II.xvii.45–7.

28 Whilst for Augustine the 'rest' constitutes rhythm, for Jacques Derrida and Philippe Lacoue-Labarthe the 'hiatus' is primarily deconstitutive. See Derrida's introduction, 'Desistance', to Lacoue-Labarthe's *Typography: Mimesis, Philosophy, Politics*, ed. Christopher Fynsk, Cambridge MA, Harvard University Press, 1989, pp. 1–42, 35. It seems, therefore, that Derrida *et al.* have not offered an exhaustive phenomenology of the 'nothing'. Its presiding status could equally be used to prove the createdness of phenomenal reality.

29 See n. 17 above.

30 *De musica* VI.viii.21–2, VI.xvii.58–9. See John Milbank, 'Sacred Triads'.

31 *De musica* VI.xi.29: the only true measure is in eternity. There is a dialectical irony here, for while Augustine stresses that enforced limitation is to be seen as inimical to any attempted 'imaging' of eternity, yet it is precisely our own remaining-within-limitation (spatial and temporal) which provides us with the only route by which to attain the infinite, albeit ony partially. VI.xi.30: Quoniam si quis, verbi gratia, in amplissimarum pulcherrimarumque aedium uno aliquo angulo tanquam statua collocetur pulchritudinem illius fabricae sentire non poterit, cujus et ipse pars erit.

32 *De musica* VI.xi.29.

33 *De musica* VI.xvii.56. See *De beata uita* 34, where Christ is described as the 'summum modum'.

34 *De musica* VI.xvii.56: Quamobrem quisquis fatetur nullam esse naturam, quae non ut sit quidquid est, appetat unitatem, suique similis in quantum potest essse conetur . . . See also VI.x.26.

35 *De musica* VI.xvii.56.

36 *De musica* VI.xi.29, VI.xi.30, VI.xiv.46.

37 Every created thing which strives for the ultimate unity, VI.xvii.56: atque ordinem proprium vel locis vel temporibus, vel in corpore quodam libramento salutem suam teneat. This is a musical model of redemption. One's uniquely right position is nonetheless harmonious with the whole. Thus redemption is at once aesthetic and ethical.

38 Downing A. Thomas, *Music and the Origins of Language: Theories from the French Enlightenment*, Cambridge, Cambridge University Press, 1995, pp. 82–142.

39 *Traité de l'harmonie*, cited by Thomas, *Music and the Origins of Language*, p. 92.

40 Thomas, *Music and the Origins of Language*, p. 91.

41 Thomas, *Music and the Origins of Language*, p. 93.

42 Thomas, *Music and the Origins of Language*, p. 91.

43 Thomas, *Music and the Origins of Language*, p. 137.

44 Thomas, *Music and the Origins of Language*, p. 139.

45 *De musica* VI.xi.29.

46 Jacques Attali, *Noise: The Political Economy of Music*, tr. Brian Massumi, Minneapolis, MN, University of Minnesota Press, 1985, ch. 3.

47 Suzanne Langer uses a similar argument to criticize Henri Bergson's attempt to resist any symbolization of duration, in *Feeling and Form: A Theory of Art Developed from Philosophy in a New Key*, London, Routledge, 1953, pp. 110–16.

48 *Critique of Pure Reason*, tr. Norman Kemp Smith, London, Macmillan, 1978, p. 213.

49 P. Lacoue-Labarthe, 'The Echo of the Subject', in *Typography*, pp. 139–217, 149, 165–74, 195. 'We ("we") are rhythmed', in *Typography*, p. 202.

50 Lacoue-Labarthe, 'The Echo of the Subject', pp. 140–6.

51 Lacoue-Labarthe, 'The Echo of the Subject', pp. 196–203.

52 Lacoue-Labarthe, 'The Echo of the Subject', pp. 187–8.

53 Catherine Pickstock, 'Necrophilia: The Middle of Modernity', *Modern Theology* 12 (1996), pp. 405–33.

54 Augustine, *Confessiones* XI.12 to end.

55 Lacoue-Labarthe, 'The Echo of the Subject', p. 195: 'Rhythm, then, is heard. It is not seen – (it) is prior to the figure or to the visible schema whose appearance it conditions.' See also p. 145.

56 Lacoue-Labarthe, 'The Echo of the Subject', pp. 161, 173, 184 and *passim*.

57 Lacoue-Labarthe, 'The Echo of the Subject', pp. 174–9.

58 Lacoue-Labarthe, 'The Echo of the Subject', pp. 193–5.

59 *De musica* VI.xii.24.

60 *De musica* VI.iv.7, VI.v.8.

61 See Robert J. O'Connell, *Art and the Christian Intelligence in St. Augustine*, Oxford, Blackwells, 1978, pp. 10–27.

62 *De musica* VI.iv.7, VI.v.8.

63 *De musica* VI v.9.

64 *De musica* VI.iv.7.

65 (a) *De musica* VI.xii.3. We could not begin to activate our desire for perfect equality unless it were already known somewhere. Thus, desire is already a kind of knowledge – or, could one say, desire is the way things are? – desire is what is known? (b) Whilst it might seem to us natural to link 'curiosity' with the discovery of truth and therefore with knowledge, for Augustine it is precisely that which leads us away from the truth. He argues that *curiositas* is a quality concerned only with the discernment of proportionality for its own sake – i.e. not in relation to other things. It does not, therefore, lead to genuine knowledge. This implies a second aporia, which is that one can only 'know' something *in relation to* everything else, which means that we must know the known in relation to the unknowable. This is because we only occupy a limited corner of the poem of the universe, as Augustine constantly reminds us. Thus the only hope for knowledge lies in desire: *De musica* VI.xiii.39.

66 *De musica* VI.xvii.59: Hi enim non scintillantibus humanis ratiocinationibus, sed validissimo et flagrantissimo charitatis igne purgantur. In this passage, Augustine contrasts the *scintilla* of human reason to the infinitely more valid and most flagrant 'fire of charity'. The metaphor of increasing intensities of light stresses that reason and love are not opposed (as for a post-Enlightenment view), and that love is an immeasurably more powerful enlightenment. Further, the metaphor implies that genuine knowledge and purification (or purging by flames) are commensurate. By progressing from light to fire, Augustine's metaphor accomplishes a subtle overtone. First, the progression

temporalizes the visual. And second, the flames of charity are the 'site' of a transition from the *visible* to the *temporal* and the *audible*, a transition which does not leave one stage in order to arrive at the next, but combines each stage in a synthesis.

67 *De musica* VI.v.9–10; see Milbank, 'Sacred Triads'.

68 *De musica* VI iv.5.

69 *De musica* VI i.1–VI.i.5.

70 *De musica* VI.ix.23–4. This higher judgement (*diligentior judicatio*) judges the 'delight' of the first, spontaneous judgement. It is a meta-judgement which Augustine sees as consisting in 'more powerful numbers which judge our initial judgement'. His ascription of both kinds of judgement, the affective and the reflective, to an ascending scale of numbers, suggests that there is something more fundamental than any opposition between affections and reason included here. Further, the reflective 'delay' of the higher judgement suggests that the possibility of further alteration of judgement is never fore-closed, that 'reason' is recursive and closely linked with desire and hope. See Augustine's own summary of the scale of numbers at *De musica* VI.x.25.

71 *De musica* VI.ii.3.

72 *De musica* VI.xii.36.

73 See Jean-Louis Chretien, *L'inoubliable et l'inespéré*, Paris, Desclee, 1991.

74 See n. 70 above.

75 *De musica* VI.xiii.38. For Augustine, beauty itself is a relation between things seen and our seeing of them, in a synthesis of the objective and subjective. Thus everything becomes relative, but without disintegrating into mere 'taste'. The Master explains to the Disciple that although there are harmonies which lie *beyond* our recognition, this does not mean that things are *only* beautiful for our own point of view. Rather, our 'point of view' is itself another aspect of the work of art which composes the universe.

76 *De musica* VI.xi.32, VI.xi.36. VI.xiii.39: the Master argues that one should not become fixed by the numbers of (spontaneous) judgement, which contain the *regulae* of an art, like the purely immanent music he imagines at *De musica* VI.xiii.40. At the end of his treatise, Augustine notes that the promises of reason and false judgement (*rationis et scientiae fallici*) are to be avoided because they lack the higher (recursive) judgement.

77 *De musica* VI.vii.17.

78 *De musica* VI.xiii.42.

79 *De musica* VI.xiii.39: et ex his curiositas nascitur ipso curae nomine inimica securitati, et vanitatis impos veritatis. See also *De musica* VI.v.14.

80 *De musica* VI.vii.19, VI.viii.21.

81 *De musica* VI.x.25: *bona modulatio* is defined as (a) a certain *motu libero*, free movement; (b) a movement ordained to an end which requires the beauty of that end. Certain implications arise from this definition. (a) The 'end' is the beauty of the free movement itself, which means that the beauty is not 'beyond' the movement. (b) The act of measuring is not only beautiful, but free; it is not 'over against' that which is measured. It is more an ontological than an epistemological category. (c) Its freeness also suggests that there is no given or static measurement. The act of measuring is a creative gesture (related to the way in which Augustine discerns a culturally specific aspect to the inter-vals which, paradoxically, *also* exceed particular instantiations). The aim of measurement is not domination of the measured, but the beauty of the move-ment, a dynamic teleological aesthetic which seeks 'incorporation within'

rather than 'dominion over' the measured phenomena. See the discussion of the word *modulatio* at BA 7, p. 417, n. 1.

82 *De musica* VI.ii.3, VI.vii.19–20.

83 Cited by Goehr, *The Imaginary Museum of Musical Works*, p. 229.

84 See Descartes, *Meditations on First Philosophy*, in John Cottingham *et al* (trs), *The Philosophical Writings*, Cambridge, Cambridge University Press, 1984, vol. 2.

85 Lacoue-Labarthe, 'The Echo of the Subject', pp. 196–203.

86 Lacoue-Labarthe, 'The Echo of the Subject', pp. 175–9. See also Derrida, 'Desistance', p. 2.

87 Derrida thus ingenuously invokes the category of the middle voice in his introduction, p. 5.

88 Lacoue-Labarthe, 'The Echo of the Subject', pp. 153–8 and *passim*. See also John Milbank, 'Stories of Sacrifice: From Wellhausen to Girard', *Theory, Culture and Society* 12 (1995), pp. 15–46.

89 Lacoue-Labarthe, 'The Echo of the Subject', pp. 174–9.

90 Louis Dumont, *Homo hierarchicus*: Chicago, Chicago University Press, 1980; Jean-Pierre Vernant, 'The Individual Within the City-State', in *Mortals and Immortals: Collected Essays*, Princeton, NJ, Princeton University Press, 1991, pp. 318–34; John Milbank, 'The End of Dialogue', in Gavin D'Costa (ed.), *Christian Uniqueness Reconsidered: The Myth of a Pluralistic Theology of Religions*, New York, Orbis Books, 1990, pp. 174–9; I. C. Sharma, *Ethical Philosophies of India*, London, G. Allen & Unwin, 1965; idem, *Presuppositions of India's Philosophies*, Westport, CT, Greenwood Press, 1963.

91 Rowell, 'Ideas of Music'; Milbank, 'Stories of Sacrifice'.

92 Vernant, 'The Individual Within the City-State'; Milbank, 'The End of Dialogue'.

93 Boethius, *Fundamentals of Music*, p. 10.

94 This falls within the scope of benign, natural magic, whereas some Renaissance attempts to effect even the supra-mundane angelic level seem to relate to a post-Christian magical hubris which challenges the sovereignty of the divine Creator.

95 Paul Hindemith, *A Composer's World: Horizons and Limitations*, Cambridge, MA, Harvard University Press, 1952, pp. 5–7, 13–17.

96 *De musica* VI.xiii.41–xiv.46.

97 *De musica* VI.xiii.42.

98 *De musica* VI.v.15: cum igitur ipsum sentire movere sit corpus adversus illum motum qui in eo factus est . . .

99 *De musica* VI.xiii.42, VI.xiii.41.

100 The good use of numbers involves directing the hierarchical control of one's body towards developing equal relations with other people: *De musica* VI.xiv.45.

101 The progressing numbers and reacting numbers, insofar as they are applied to other people, should be directed towards uplifting and developing them, rather than dominating them: *De musica* VI.xiv.45.

102 Loving one's neighbour is part of 'keeping musical order': *De musica* VI.xiv.46.

103 *De musica* VI.iv.7.

104 *De musica* VI.xi.29.

105 *De musica* VI.ii.3.

106 *De musica* VI.iv.7.

107 *De musica* VI.iv.7: quod tamen habet sui generis pulchritudinem, et eo ipso dignitatem animae satis commendat, cujus nec plaga, nec morbus sine honore alicujus decoris meruit esse.

108 *De musica* VI.iv.7.

109 *De musica* VI.iv.7, VI.v.9.

110 Attali, *Noise*, ch. 3.

111 (a) 'This is why the music laments – music in general laments, be it "joyous", "light", "pleasant" (inverting the lamentation into an exaltation of my immortality . . .). What touches or moves me in music, then, is my own mourning', Lacoue-Labarthe, 'The Echo', pp. 192–3; (b) 'The death of the other (the hero, the rival) is always at bottom my own death,' Lacoue-Labarthe, 'The Echo', p. 192.

112 Lacoue-Labarthe is only able to construe resurrection as one's own triumph over the rival, which is always perforce illusory: 'The Echo', p. 154.

113 Lacoue-Labarthe, 'The Echo', p. 204.

114 Attali, *Noise*, p. 3 and *passim*.

115 Attali, *Noise*, pp. 20–25.

116 Attali, *Noise*, final chapter, 'Composition'. See also Douglas Collins, 'Ritual Sacrifice: The Political Economy of Music', in J. Rahne (ed.), *Perspectives on Musical Aesthetics*, New York, W. W. Norton, 1994, pp. 9–20, esp. p. 20.

117 Attali, *Noise*, p. 30.

118 I am grateful to Dr John Milbank for discussions concerning the issues raised in this chapter, and, more generally, to Rupert Jeffcoat for all his musical inspiration.

INDEX